EXPOSED

EXPOSED

THE DARK SIDE OF THE AMERICA'S CUP

ALAN SEFTON AND LARRY KEATING

ADLARD COLES NAUTICAL

BLOOMSBURY

LONDON · OXFORD · NEW YORK · NEW DELHI · SYDNEY

Adlard Coles Nautical
An imprint of **Bloomsbury Publishing Plc**

50 Bedford Square
London
WC1B 3DP
UK

1385 Broadway
New York
NY 10018
USA

www.bloomsbury.com
www.adlardcoles.com

ADLARD COLES, ADLARD COLES NAUTICAL and the Buoy logo
are trademarks of Bloomsbury Publishing Plc

First published 2017

© Alan Sefton and Larry Keating, 2017

British Library Cataloguing-in-Publication Data
A catalogue record for this book is available from the British Library.

Library of Congress Cataloguing-in-Publication data has been applied for.

ISBN: HB: 978-1-4729-4289-0
Trade PB: 978-1-4729-4662-1
ePDF: 978-1-4729-4291-3
ePub: 978-1-4729-4290-6

2 4 6 8 10 9 7 5 3 1

Typeset in Haarlemmer MT by Deanta Global Publishing Services, Chennai, India
Printed and bound in Great Britain by CPI Group (UK) Ltd, Croydon CR0 4YY

CONTENTS

01

ENDLESS INTRIGUE AND CONTROVERSY

The 166-year history of the America's Cup – the oldest trophy in sport – is a tale of seemingly endless intrigue and controversy peopled by some of the most powerful men of their times – the JP Morgans, the Vanderbilts, the Liptons, the Sopwiths, the Packers, the Bonds, the Fays, the Turners, the Ellisons, et al.

Some have been attracted to the fray by the sporting challenge alone – the ultimate test at the highest level of a sport that has long been the domain of the wealthy. Others have used the Cup to circumvent social barriers and societal constraints. Then there are those who have sought to use the Cup for political and/or business gain.

Whatever their objectives or agendas, they have been drawn almost inexorably to the contest and have brought with them all the drive and determination to succeed that made them so successful in everyday life, sometimes no matter the cost (figuratively and literally).

And thus they became acquainted with a little item called the (America's Cup) Deed of Gift, a brief and deceptively straightforward document that was drafted by the owners of the schooner *America* when they donated to the New York Yacht Club (NYYC) the trophy they'd won in a race around the Isle of Wight, in southern England, in 1851. What became the America's Cup (named after the yacht that won it) was presented to the NYYC 'as a perpetual challenge cup for friendly competition between foreign countries', and the transaction was formalised with a Deed of Gift that was vested in the New York Supreme Court. Known simply as 'The Deed', it laid out the terms and conditions that had to be met in order to challenge and race for the trophy. Those terms and conditions were first drafted in May 1852 by George L Schuyler (one of *America*'s six owners) and have, with little amendment, prevailed through all manner of tests and challenges, ancient and modern, in the century and a half of continuous competition that has since occurred.

Some of the ensuing 35 matches for the Cup have been in keeping with the donors' intent to foster 'friendly competition between foreign countries'. Others, though, have been blatantly hostile, even opportunistic, and controversy has never been far away. Some would lay the blame at the door of the Deed, and it's true that the Cup's reputation for intrigue and dissension was engendered by the New York Yacht Club's high-handed conduct when it was dealing with initial challenges in the late 1800s. The response of the challengers, particularly of two high-profile gentlemen from Britain, was on occasion so hostile that the NYYC twice called in George Schuyler to clarify the intentions of the donors. The Deed's author made it clear that he was not happy with the way the club was conducting its Cup affairs. Once Schuyler had finished redrafting what became the October 1887 edition of the Deed, however, the fundamental elements of a competition that would become unique in sport were set in stone and, largely, would serve the Cup well.

There are those today who would assert that Schuyler's covenant is way past its use-by date and has little or no relevance in the modern world of professional sport. More often than not, though, those taking such a position have agendas and choose to use and/or interpret the Deed in ways that suit their schemes. In modern times, this has led to two long-running and exceedingly contentious court cases that made the full legal journey from New York's lower court in Manhattan, through that court's

Appellate Division and finally on to the Court of Appeals in Albany, New York, and, in the process, held the event prisoner for years at a time.

The first of those, in 1987–1988, involved San Diego real-estate developer Malin Burnham and legendary Cup skipper Dennis Conner. Through their Sail America Foundation for International Understanding (SAF), they influenced the San Diego Yacht Club (SDYC) to ignore what would prove to be a perfectly legitimate challenge from New Zealand merchant banker Michael Fay (in the name of the Mercury Bay Boating Club), in 90ft waterline monohulls (the biggest sloop-rigged yachts allowed by the Deed). The New York Supreme Court ordered San Diego Yacht Club to defend or forfeit, as was required by the Deed, and this in turn led to San Diego's infamous 1988 defence in a wing-sail catamaran (against Mercury Bay's nominated 90ft waterline sloop) after telling the New York court that multihulls racing against monohulls was normal in sailing competition. It also led to one of the august panel at the Court of Appeals asking where in the Deed of Gift it said that the America's Cup had to be fair – despite it being carefully laid out for the court that Schuyler's 'cardinal principle' for a match was 'one party contending with another party on equal terms as regards the task or feat to be accomplished'.

The second dispute, in 2007–2010, saw Swiss biotech billionaire Ernesto Bertarelli and the Société Nautique de Genève (the defender) and San Francisco software tycoon Larry Ellison and the Golden Gate Yacht Club (the would-be challenger) make the same journey through the New York courts to Albany, when the Swiss engineered a challenge from a newly formed yachting organisation – Club Náutico Español de Vela (CNEV) – in order to facilitate an event in which all rights and powers were vested in the defender, which was clearly not what was envisioned by the donors. The Court of Appeals ruled Société Nautique de Genève's challenger invalid and instructed the Swiss to defend against the next challenger in line, Golden Gate Yacht Club, which it finally did in 2010 in a match that featured giant and outrageously hi-tech (and expensive) multihulls.

Both of these prominent legal spats entailed close scrutiny of, and comprehensive legal argument about, the wording and meaning of Schuyler's Deed. One of the only upsides of the arguments was that most of the potentially contentious elements of the Deed were interpreted by the ultimate authority, whose various rulings were now the precedents for any future attempts to circumvent the donors' terms and conditions.

Just as importantly, though, the Deed was shown to be as relevant as it always had been – a wonderful anachronism that sought to cherish and preserve attributes of sportsmanship and fair play from another age.

The two individuals primarily responsible for the content of the Deed of Gift were the founder (and then commodore) of the New York Yacht Club, John Cox Stevens, and his good friend and contemporary George L Schuyler. The original document, drafted by Schuyler, amounted to all of 374 words and was more a brief letter outlining what the donors had in mind for the trophy. By the time it had been exposed to the heat of several confrontational challenges, though, that letter had morphed into what became known as the 'Third Deed of Gift' – a 1,256-word document, again drafted by Schuyler but this time with input from NYYC, which was full of legalese and contractual language that (supposedly) made the donors' intentions abundantly clear.

To anyone who doesn't have ulterior motives, Schuyler's Third Deed is straightforward enough. If you are a bona fide yacht club (not an individual) with the appropriate credentials, you can challenge for the Cup in a yacht or vessel that meets certain guidelines as to size and rig. You must give 10 months' notice of challenge and can negotiate with the defender the details of the 'match' to be sailed. If you can't agree on those details, the Deed lays down a three-race formula for getting the job done. Oh, and racing will be 'on ocean courses, free from headlands'.

It's as uncomplicated as that but, as they say, the devil is in the detail – and in the interpretation – and the last 30-odd years of Cup competition in particular have shown that when you turn loose a bevy of highly qualified lawyers and judges and task them with interpreting what was intended by the principals of a trust established more than a century earlier, in different times and reflecting different social standards, there is nothing straightforward or uncomplicated about the process. Particularly when it takes place under the blowtorch of professionalism in modern sport and at the behest of very wealthy and ambitious individuals used to having their own way.

Away from the legalese and arguments about meanings and intentions is the race itself, wherein lie the scintillating legends of the 'Auld Mug' and the powerful men, and clubs, who have competed for it. One of these clubs was the original trustee of the Cup, the NYYC, which went to great lengths to ensure that the trophy remained bolted down in its West 44th

Street premises, turning defences of the Cup into an art form of resource and people management that doomed challenger after challenger to failure, even before they started building their boats.

The New York Yacht Club started to develop the technique of defending the Cup in the early matches of the 19th century and then refined the process in the event's modern era (post World War II) of racing in 12-Metres. That refinement began with the successful defence in 1958 by Briggs Cunningham in *Columbia*, and then in 1962 by Bus Mosbacher in *Weatherly*. Mosbacher was a great sailor, strategist and leader and with his help, and that of the commodores, the club developed its strategy on how to keep that Cup. They ran summer-long trials with the best boats and skippers vying for the right to be the defender, and these trials invariably were more difficult to win than the America's Cup match itself. They knew how to get America's finest sailing talent together, how to raise the money, who to go to for the right boat design – the total package – and because of that the NYYC controlled the game.

A lot has been said and written on the subject and, at times, it has been inferred that the NYYC ignored the rules. That, however, was almost certainly not the case. What the club did do was ensure that it knew how to play the game better than anyone else and it wasn't until 1970, when the rest of the world finally began to work things out and run eliminations between multiple challengers, that the gap started to close.

The New York Yacht Club was tough but it was fair, and it relished the Corinthian way of doing things. It may have pushed the rules but it would have played within them, even if close to the edge at times. Moreover, all the controversies that seemed to inevitably arise became an integral part of the fabric of the Cup.

New Zealander Michael Fay (now Sir Michael), who challenged three times for the Cup in six years and fought the oh-so-influential Deed of Gift court case against San Diego Yacht Club and the Sail America Foundation in 1988–1989, termed the Cup: 'The hardest deal in town' – a view that was shared by the late Warren Jones, the man credited with masterminding Alan Bond's *Australia II* to her historic Cup victory in 1983. Fay explained:

'When we [New Zealand] challenged for the 1987 Cup, we knew it had to be hard because no one had beaten the New York Yacht Club for 132 years.

So, it wasn't going be a walk through Central Park and down to the yacht club for lunch and say, "Thank you, we'll take the trophy". It was only with hindsight, though, that I was able to appreciate just how hard a deal it was – that and Warren Jones telling me once that the real test was that for the three years before the event, you had to make every decision right – no room for error, every decision right for three years. That's a stern test and that degree of difficulty appealed to me enormously. There's no tougher forum than the heat of battle, if you will, in the middle of an America's Cup campaign and, in that sense, for me it was much better than doing an MBA at Harvard or similar.'[1]

And, of the Cup's proclivity for the controversial:

'The Cup has never been without controversy. People complain about it, that it's contentious, but the event seems to thrive on that controversy.'[2]

If that in fact is the case, then the America's Cup should be in good heart today because the 2017 edition (the 35th) in Bermuda broke new ground on all fronts when it came to not honouring the spirit and intent of Schuyler's Deed of Gift, let alone the specific requirements of that document.

First up, on 30 September 2013, just five days after they had successfully defended the Cup with a come-from-behind 9–8 victory over Emirates Team New Zealand on San Francisco Bay, GGYC/Oracle announced that the Hamilton Island Yacht Club (HIYC), located on the edge of the Great Barrier Reef in Queensland, Australia, had been accepted as the challenger of record (COR) for the 35th America's Cup and a new protocol for the event was already a priority.

There was nothing wrong with that except that on 19 July 2014, the Aussies folded their tent and withdrew from the event, with billionaire wine baron Bob Oatley, the owner of Hamilton Island and its yacht club, conceding that mounting costs had forced them to pull out. Oatley, best known for his Sydney–Hobart race triumphs in a succession of maxi ocean racers named *Wild Oats*, was reported that same day by the Australian Associated Press (AAP) as saying:

'The challenge was initiated with a view to negotiating a format for the 35th America's Cup that was affordable and put the emphasis back on

sailing skills. Ultimately our estimate of the costs of competing were well beyond our initial expectation and our ability to make the formula of our investment and other commercial support add up. We are bitterly disappointed that this emerging team of fine young Australian sailors will not be able to compete at the next America's Cup under our banner.'[3]

From here on, Cup affairs only got murkier.

For reasons that appeared to be driven by the need to preserve voting numbers and protect various items in an increasingly worrying protocol, GGYC/Oracle declined to introduce a replacement COR (which should have been the next challenger in line, the far more independent Circolo della Vela Sicilia, represented by Prada boss Patrizio Bertelli's Luna Rossa syndicate).

They got murkier still when it became clear that GGYC/Oracle or, more precisely, Sir Russell Coutts, now the CEO of the America's Cup Event Authority (ACEA), in addition to being the CEO of the defending syndicate, Oracle Team USA, was in advanced negotiations to make Bermuda the next venue for the Cup, even though the Deed of Gift very clearly anticipates that the yacht club holding the trophy will defend in its home waters. Bermuda was/is a British Overseas Territory in the North Atlantic Ocean comprised of 181 islands (mostly rocky islets) with a total land mass area of 53.4 square kilometres (20.6 square miles) and a population of just 64,237 souls.

On 2 December 2014, fiction became fact when Bermuda was announced as the 'Home of the 35th America's Cup'. There were already five challengers: Artemis Racing – representing Kungliga Svenska Segel Sällskapet (KSSS) – the Royal Swedish Yacht Club; BAR (Ben Ainslie Racing) – representing Britain's Royal Yacht Squadron; Emirates Team New Zealand (ETNZ) – representing the Royal New Zealand Yacht Squadron; Luna Rossa – representing Circolo della Vela Sicilia from Italy; and Team France – representing Le Yacht Club de France. Japan was touted as another entry, representing the Kansai Yacht Club.

Racing would be on a 'stadium course' on Bermuda's Great Sound in the already-announced new class of 62ft high-speed foiling catamarans that would replace the troubled 72-footers used in San Francisco for the 34th defence in 2013. It was quickly obvious that while the setting was idyllic, it would be a tight area of water on which to race the speedy new Cup class of 62ft catamarans. Hold on though – help was on its way!

On 2 April 2015, some 10 months after the new class had been announced and by which time ETNZ had confirmed its participation, it was revealed that, by a majority vote of defender and challengers, the intended new 62-footer was to be dumped and replaced by a 48ft version of the wing-sailed flyers, even though syndicates such as Italy's Luna Rossa had already spent millions on 62-footer design and research.

This dramatic change was almost leaked to the sailing world, prompting columnist Matthew Sheahan, in the April 2015 edition of *Yachting World* magazine, to observe that, in contrast to 'the usual razzamataz of a busy press conference' hosted in the next Cup location, the announcement of the new class for the next America's Cup had been a quiet online affair, even though it represented a huge alteration of plans.

Sheahan commented:

> *'While the change required a majority vote and, as yet, no team has said it is pulling out, not everyone is entirely happy. Since the vote, no one has heard from Luna Rossa, and the Kiwis – while they have accepted the new design – are [also] believed to be less than happy…'*[4]

The reaction was swift coming. That very same day, *Reuters* reported that Luna Rossa had 'angrily pulled out of the 35th America's Cup … in protest at a vote to reduce the size of the catamarans to be raced in the 2017 event.'[5]

The Italian racing team had issued a statement saying: 'Following a careful evaluation of the serious implications of this unprecedented initiative, Team Luna Rossa confirms that it will withdraw from the 35th America's Cup.'[6]

The *Reuters* piece went on to say that Emirates Team New Zealand had joined with Luna Rossa in protesting the decision (to reduce the size of the boats) without unanimous agreement, the Italian challenger warning it would have to withdraw if the change was made – which it was by four votes to two. The Italian syndicate considered the procedure adopted to be: 'illegitimate … and founded on an evident abuse of process … this is an attempt to introduce boats that are substantially monotypes [one-designs] and in total contrast with the ultra-centennial tradition of the America's Cup,' adding that the change, at this juncture, was a 'waste of important resources already invested based on the rules that were sanctioned last June'.[7]

While organisers said the new catamarans would be more manoeuvrable than before and cost savings could also be made, Luna Rossa countered with: 'The claim to reduce costs reveals itself as a pure pretext aimed to annihilate research and development achievements of some teams and to favour instead preconceived technical and sporting positions.'

Team principal Patrizio Bertelli said painful decisions sometimes had to be made: 'In sports, as in life, one cannot always go for compromise after compromise after compromise.'[8]

This chain of events rocked the America's Cup community, especially given that the America's Cup had already lost its most prestigious sponsor, upmarket French luggage company Louis Vuitton, which had walked away from the event before the 33rd defence in Valencia, taking with it a raft of its other top brands, including the inimitable Moët & Chandon. This had occurred as the result of an acrimonious dispute with the 2007 America's Cup Management (ACM), in which Louis Vuitton argued that the America's Cup, now ruled by Alinghi supremo Ernesto Bertarelli, was heading in a direction that was out of step with the quality objectives of Louis Vuitton and its associated brands. Following an earlier argument involving non-performance issues and many millions of dollars of withheld progress sponsorship payments, this became a last straw. And now, less than eight years later, another of the world's great luxury brands, Prada, had turned its back on the Auld Mug, albeit for different reasons.

Common sense dictated that something needed to be done to halt and reverse the attrition rate. There were, after all, very few other luxury brands in the world that were prepared to invest as heavily in the Cup as Louis Vuitton and Prada had done. The 2017 Cup was to have been the Prada-sponsored Luna Rossa's fifth involvement while Louis Vuitton had been the sponsor of the challenger eliminations on nine occasions since the introduction of the Louis Vuitton Cup in 1983.

Of equal concern, though, should have been the way in which Oracle, through the America's Cup Events Authority (ACEA), appeared to be using the majority control it had achieved in the competitors' forum, which had assumed the decision-making role of the Challenger of

Record, to railroad through other protocol changes. The original group of three challengers (from Britain, France and Sweden) was soon bolstered by a fourth – Softbank Team Japan, representing the Kansai Yacht Club – that enjoyed an unprecedented relationship with the defender. This saw them share design and construction R&D and work-up together, all now allowed by continuous changes to the protocol.

So, the defender had the voting numbers to assume complete dominance of the event and Coutts was viewed as using this to completely isolate and derail the one remaining independent challenger, Emirates Team New Zealand. Moreover, to make sure the Kiwis could not kick up too much of a fuss, yet another new protocol item had been introduced – nicknamed 'The Dalton Clause' – that banned any criticism of what the defender and its group of challengers were doing.

ETNZ's cause wasn't helped by another low blow when ACEA reneged on a signed deal to stage one of its series of build-up regattas in Auckland. That regatta was an essential element in an arrangement for more New Zealand government financial support that ETNZ boss (and major fundraiser) Grant Dalton was working on, and what was now a survival task only got tougher when the loss of the build-up event put an end to any chance of more government money coming their way.

ETNZ thus went to the event's independent Arbitration Panel seeking significant compensation to make up for funds lost due to the withdrawal of the regatta. Because of 'the Dalton Clause', nobody would confirm or deny the outcome but the rumour mill reported that the panel ruled in favour of ETNZ and ordered compensation to the tune of $US7 million.

Then, Bernie Wilson, of Associated Press, on 25 August 2016 wrote:

> *'Harvey Schiller, a former executive director of the U.S. Olympic Committee, is stepping down as commercial commissioner of the America's Cup. Will Chignell, the chief marketing and communications officer with the America's Cup Event Authority, said Monday that it was Schiller's decision to leave. Schiller has held the position for two years. He did not immediately respond to calls or an email from The Associated Press seeking comment Monday.'*[9]

The well-informed Wilson said that it was not known if Schiller's departure was related to the case brought by Emirates Team New

Zealand, and that ACEA boss Russell Coutts didn't immediately respond to an email seeking comment. He added:

> *'It's believed that the arbitration panel recently heard the case brought by the Kiwis after the ACEA pulled a qualifying regatta that had been planned for Auckland next year. In March 2015, Schiller notified Team New Zealand that it was losing the qualifier in part because it had supported another syndicate in a dispute over Coutts' plan to downsize the boats that will be used in the 2017 America's Cup in Bermuda.'*[10]

The isolating of ETNZ was carried to a disturbing climax when, on 25 January 2017, Oracle and its 'club' of four challengers announced a plan that, they proclaimed, was 'a vision for the future of the America's Cup … that would see long-sought stability and continuity in the competition.'[11]

During a press conference at The House of Garrard in London, where the Cup was crafted in 1848, skippers and team leaders of Oracle Team USA, Artemis Racing, Groupama Team France, Landrover Ben Ainslie Racing and Softbank Team Japan revealed a Framework Agreement that would cover the next two editions (the 36th and 37th) of the America's Cup, that they had arbitrarily scheduled to take place in 2019 and 2021. The new Cup cycle would kick in after the 35th America's Cup in Bermuda.

The agreement and attendant protocol bound the signatories to deliver the 36th America's Cup (AC36) and the 37th America's Cup (AC37) under the following terms:

- The America's Cup would be on a two-yearly cycle for AC36 (2019) and AC37 (2021);
- The America's Cup World Series (ACWS) would start as soon as the autumn of 2017. Venues, sponsors and media partners would be approached over the following six months to secure up to 12 international events over the next two years;
- The first year of the America's Cup World Series (ACWS) would be raced in AC45 foiling catamarans – the same boats used in America's Cup World Series (ACWS) in the 35th America's Cup;
- The second year would see a transition to the America's Cup Class (ACC) boats to be raced in Bermuda in 2017 (with a slight rule

modification to extend their wind range to 4–26 knots). After this transition, the AC45s would be retired from the America's Cup competition;

- The America's Cup World Series (ACWS) would culminate with a final event at the venue for the next America's Cup and the final standings from the America's Cup World Series (ACWS) will be used to qualify teams for the America's Cup Challenger Playoffs;
- The America's Cup Challenger Finals and America's Cup Match would be held in 2019 in a venue selected by the winner of the 35th America's Cup;
- This above will repeat for AC37, with the exception that all racing will take place in America's Cup Class (ACC) boats.

In a press conference release, posted that same day on the AC 2017 website, www.americascup.com, Oracle Team USA skipper Jimmy Spithill was quoted saying: 'This announcement will go down as one of the defining moments in America's Cup history. It's great for fans, athletes, and commercially – a win win for everyone. This is a huge step forward, with the sky the limit.'[12]

Spithill's boss Larry Ellison was reported as stating:

'It is a very modern sport, it's a very extreme sport, it's a team sport and it's country v country so I am very optimistic that we can make this sport very attractive to the next generation of athletes. The kids love it, and this will also help make it attractive to people who don't go out and sail every day, but love watching the competition on TV.'[13]

The release made a point of explaining that: 'Emirates Team New Zealand is not here today, but they have been kept updated on all developments throughout the creation of the Framework Agreement [and] we remain optimistic that they will come on board in the future…'[14]

However, it failed to contemplate that the Framework Agreement would not be worth the paper it was written on if the one challenger that wasn't party to the deal – Emirates Team New Zealand – won the match and took the America's Cup back to Auckland.

ETNZ simply turned its back on the Framework Agreement and on further tampering with the protocol, and used its time and resources more constructively back in New Zealand.

Others, however, had woken up to what was going down. One such was *New Zealand Herald* sports columnist Paul Lewis who, under a heading that read 'The Coutts Club' in the 26 March edition of New Zealand's largest-circulation newspaper, observed:

> 'Oracle Team USA have altered the rules so much, the challengers are barely worthy of the name. Whatever this regatta to be held in Bermuda is, it doesn't feel much like the America's Cup … The latest reworking of the rules to suit Oracle Team USA and its cosy little band of challengers underlines the point. OTUSA have so comprehensively de-knackered the challengers, they seem barely worthy of the name so far.
>
> Things will liven up a bit when the racing starts – though the latest, retrospective changes allowing challengers (and Oracle) to test their boats together before racing may also reduce the anticipation and mystery of the first days of the regatta, when eager eyes strain to identify the fastest boat. These days the America's Cup, once a fascinating zoo of antipathy and rivalry, is a chummy cabal of OTUSA and challengers Land Rover BAR (skippered by Sir Ben Ainslie), Artemis, Softbank Team Japan and Groupama Team France – toy poodles dancing on their hind legs when Oracle commands.
>
> Emirates Team New Zealand sits quietly off to one side, like the disgraced handbag dog who crapped in the handbag. Has there ever been an America's Cup with one challenger so clearly ostracised by the others as well as the defender?
>
> … [ETNZ] are thought to have won a victory in the arbitration room after Oracle's unhelpful – and some say punitive – decision to deny them a home regatta in the build-up series, thereby costing ETNZ government funding and time on the water. Rumour has it they have won $NZ15 million in damages – maybe too late to be worth anything in Cup-winning terms. But the gag order means ETNZ can't talk about it; members of the team look like they might pitch themselves off the end of the jetty if you mention it…
>
> So it remains to be seen if OTUSA and their acolytes succeed, whether the Cup (like the once prestigious One Ton Cup and Admiral's Cup) fades

*into obscurity if its traditions and history are submerged. Will Coutts'
attempt to shift it into a new future succeed or, as Dalton put it, will it
become "just another dirty little regatta?"*[15]

These were the darkest of days for ETNZ. While the other challengers
(the French excepted) all looked to be well funded and had set up shop
early in Bermuda to maximise time on the Great Sound race course,
ETNZ remained at home, battling to raise the money it needed to make
its challenge a reality. Big-ticket items, such as building its boat and wing
sail, were all delayed until the absolute last minute, as was the team's
departure for Bermuda.

Dalton, however, had two invaluable supporters on his board of
directors in the team's patron, Swiss-Italian businessman Matteo de
Nora, and Kiwi business success story (and philanthropist) Sir Stephen
Tindall, both of whom put their own money into the campaign when
times were really difficult. In addition, there were to be some silver
linings to the seemingly endless travails.

The rumoured $US7 million compensation order by the Arbitration
Panel, if it was fact, would have come as a welcome injection of much-
needed cash, but it was the inspired work that was going on behind
closed doors at the team's waterfront base near downtown Auckland
that would bear even sweeter fruit.

ETNZ had been, very wisely, pushing the envelope and working
tirelessly and innovatively on its conceptual processes and on the design
and engineering of its new boat. In this process, it employed to the full
a super-smart simulator with very advanced programming that enabled
it to pre-evaluate new design features with uncanny accuracy and also to
engage in simulated America's Cup races on the Bermuda course, with
all sorts of sailing challenges and opposition dialled in. The outcome
was a boat bristling with renowned Kiwi ingenuity at a new level of
excellence.

Immediately evident when the boat was finally unveiled, on 16
February 2017, were the four 'cyclor' positions running forward from
the helm and wing trim positions at the rear end of both hulls. ETNZ had
decided early on that legs were far more efficient than arms when it came
to generating the hydraulic 'oil' pressure that would power the wing
sail and daggerboard trim systems. So, traditional arm-powered coffee

grinders made way for the four 'cyclor' positions through which ETNZ was able to generate a significant one-third more 'oil' for its helmsman and trimmers to work with.

Other innovations were not so obvious but they were all over and through the boat, ranging from skipper Glenn Ashby's X-Box-like remote control for trimming the wing sail to dramatically different hydrofoil shapes that covered a wider wind range than those of their rivals. The original thinking was everywhere and, as the new breed of young Kiwi 'sailors' got to grips with the total speed package that had been delivered to them by the team's designers and engineers, they became a force on the water – quicker and higher upwind, faster and lower downwind, and blisteringly fast on the reaches.

To the keen-eyed on Auckland's waterfront, the indicators were there early that ETNZ had come up with something special and very quickly comparisons were being made with the original Team New Zealand campaign in 1995 when NZL32 (*Black Magic*) swept all before her to win the Cup off Dennis Conner and the San Diego Yacht Club.

ETNZ's *Aotearoa* and her crew enjoyed 21 days of almost uninterrupted sailing on a summery Hauraki Gulf with the wing-sail catamaran looking fast and stable on its foils as 26-year-old helmsman Peter Burling put her through her paces. Much of this build-up was done as far out of sight of prying eyes as possible but, soon enough, reports emerged that *Aotearoa* was racing solo around full-length America's Cup courses without letting down off her foils – a significant accomplishment in a skittery cat that would make you pay a heavy performance price if you dipped her hulls in the water.

It was the same when the team finally got to Bermuda. 'Pistol Pete' Burling had his moments on the start line in the early skirmishes of the challenger qualifiers, particularly against the defender Oracle Team USA and nemesis helmsman Jimmy Spithill. However, one by one he despatched the opposition until, come the America's Cup match showdown itself, he was almost completely dominant.

The upshot was that ETNZ won eight of the nine races sailed in the Cup match. It had to give Oracle Team USA a one-point start because of controversial rules that allowed the defender to race in the challenger eliminations and carry a bonus point into the finals, so ETNZ's final winning margin was 7–1.

While Spithill had earned the wrath of many New Zealanders for his brash media conference performances in San Francisco, on this occasion he and his crew earned only admiration and praise for their graciousness in defeat, with bonus points for joining the New Zealand dock celebration afterwards.

It was now that the inanity of the competitors' Framework Agreement was brought into proper perspective.

Because of the terms and conditions laid down in Schuyler's venerable Deed of Gift, all of the signatories to that agreement, including Oracle Team USA and its boss Russell Coutts, were now completely disenfranchised. As intended by Schuyler, all the power and control in terms of the next America's Cup were vested in the new trustee/ defender, the Royal New Zealand Yacht Squadron, and its challenger of record, the Circolo della Vela Sicilia.

That irony was not lost on the traditionalists who had been less than impressed by the previous trustee, its representatives and their agendas.

Former Cup helmsman and Louis Vuitton media guru Bruno Troublé, interviewed on Television New Zealand's current affairs programme *Seven Sharp* on 1 July 2017, said:

> 'Coutts and company – they were great sailors, they are great sailors, he is the best sailor in the AC history maybe. But he's not a very good organiser. He's been trying over the last years to change the America's Cup to a Formula One circus. I think what's really wrong with Russell Coutts is he tried at all costs to keep the Cup. I think New Zealand should organise a nice event, very international with a lot of countries, fair and simple, and then think about how they could keep the Cup.'[16]

In New Zealand for the welcome-home parade in Auckland on 6 July 2017, Troublé expanded on his thoughts (in interview with Larry Keating for *Exposed*):

> 'We must return to the roots of the Cup, and I feel sure New Zealand will do that.
>
> The foiling catamarans that we saw in Bermuda have clearly brought something to sailing but the only conversation was about foils and, for me,

that is not the America's Cup. With their padded suits, crash helmets and oxygen bottles, the sailors resembled Robocop.

It [the regatta] had no elegance and that is a problem for the luxury brands that have been the usual sponsors of the Cup – your Louis Vuittons and Pradas. For the sailors, there was no time to think about tactics – it was all reflex – and, so, it was no surprise when the youngest skippers – Peter Burling (21) and Nathan Outteridge (31) came out on top in the challenger eliminations. Reactivity took precedence over reflection.

If we were to continue in those boats, the future winners would be hyperactive kids of 20 – champions in the video games. In my view, the Cup should not be taken hostage to arrive at that. We could very well have continued in monohulls.

I know there are those who think that going back to monohulls would be a retrograde step but monohulls have also made tremendous performance gains, and if as much energy went into designing modern, fast foiling monohulls as has gone into these flying catamarans, we would see dramatic results.

I am also in favour of a return to nationality rules, to return to the intent that the Cup should be "friendly competition between foreign countries" as prescribed in the Deed of Gift. Today, the event is largely peopled by mercenaries who are mainly attracted by money.

Ernesto Bertarelli, of Alinghi, wants to return to the Cup but he also wants a rule of nationality. He says that in Switzerland, there is enough talent to create a team almost 100 per cent Swiss. Just like Patrizio Bertelli, of Luna Rossa, he's addicted to the Cup. Nationality requirements would also help the French who would have no problem meeting any such constraints.

The Cup must also be defended in a club's home waters, again as required by the Deed. The Americans made a huge mistake when they left San Francisco to go to Bermuda, an island that offered a lot of money to host the event but where, in the end, there were not many people.

And then, I did not like the regatta format in Bermuda. Eliminating a team after only ten races in eight days, as happened to the French, was not good considering the money and the time and energy spent.

In the Louis Vuitton Cup challenger eliminations of old, you could not be eliminated for at least a month of racing so the teams had time to improve and provide media exposure for their sponsors.

Today, the defender participates in the challenger eliminations qualifying and then ducks out with a point that he takes into the match itself – the final. That is scandalous.'[17]

Interviewed by Rachel Smalley on the Newstalk ZB radio network in New Zealand, Dennis Conner said: 'I like what I'm hearing about the possibility of going back to a monohull and not making it the same circus that we have [in Bermuda]. The America's Cup used to be something special and they've turned this into a completely different event.'[18]

Conner believed that Oracle Team USA's move to take the Cup to Bermuda had had a detrimental effect:

'[People] don't like it. There's not many big boats in Bermuda, the hotels are empty, the TV ratings are bad and the whole thing, I think, will be an economic disaster [for the island nation].

People want to go back to what they saw in Auckland [in 2000 and 2003] with a downtown event the centre of the America's Cup, everybody having a great time, lots of people, lots of boats, lots of spectators – and I see nothing but good to come out of it."[19]

Veteran Cup aficionado Angus Phillips, who covered numerous America's Cups in his 30 years as outdoors editor of the *Washington Post*, wrote in the *Weekly Standard* magazine on 17 July 2017:

'Well, that was quick! The 35th America's Cup was over in a heartbeat. It took barely a month for Emirates Team New Zealand to buzzsaw through a fleet of four challengers before shellacking the U.S. defender, Oracle Team USA, 7–1, to snatch yachting's oldest prize. This was not your father's America's Cup – the boats were 50-foot dragonflies skeeting across the water on hydrofoils at nearly 50 mph and the sailors wore armour, not Izod Lacoste. Now what? I say let's make the America's Cup great again.

As a reporter for the Washington Post, I covered every Cup from Dennis Conner's successful defence in Newport, R.I. in 1980, to Larry Ellison's weird win in Valencia, Spain, in 2010. I watched the America's Cup sail off to Australia in 1983, come back in 1987, then go away again [to New Zealand] in 1995. I even sailed in some Cup trials, on Team New Zealand in 1995 and Ellison's Oracle in 2000, as nonparticipating 17th man. The most exciting events I saw were in 1983, when *Australia II*, the wing-keeled wonder from Down Under, beat Conner's *Liberty*, 4–3, to end the New York Yacht Club's 132-year stranglehold on the Cup, and 1987, when Conner went to West Australia in *Stars & Stripes* and won the "Auld Mug" back from a fleet of 16 other entrants in the wild winds and churning seas off beautiful, breezy Fremantle. Those were drama-filled events that dragged on and on in grand, slow boats. The Cup summer of 1983 began in June and ended in September, and the Australian spectacle four years later started in October and ended in February. It meant months of intrigue, drama, and champagne-soaked social events that ink-stained wretches like newspaper reporters could only dream about the rest of their lives. What glamour!

The little whiz-bang Cup final in Bermuda in June lasted only 10 days and was laughable by comparison. The races were 20 minutes, so they could cram TV commercials in, and most of the time the boats were so far apart they couldn't fit in the same frame. Was it cool to watch a sailboat go 45 miles an hour? Sure, for a little while – and if you call a 50-foot, hydrofoiling catamaran a sailboat. I watched the first race of the 2017 America's Cup at the Oar on Block Island, a sailor's bar if ever there was one, where you can get a shower and a Narragansett draught for $5, all up. Patrons at the Oar can tie a bowline behind their backs. It was opening weekend of Block Island Race Week, and the place was jammed with yachties. But almost nobody was watching the sport's premier event on the television, and the few that were had the same take: "I hope New Zealand wins."

Well, the Kiwis did, emphatically. Now the hope is they will do the right thing and turn the Cup back into a sailing event instead of a crude reality-TV show. I'll risk sounding like a fuddy-duddy: Bring back monohulls, and sailors in shorts and polo shirts. I know scores of great sailors but I don't know any that wear flak vests and helmets when they race, and none of them trims wings and underwater appendages with an X-Box. They don't pedal a stationary bike to build hydraulic pressure when they go sailing or wear oxygen bottles on their back in case the rig comes down in a catastrophic crash.

The reason people love the America's Cup, or used to, is that it embodies grace and style and glamour. It is wretched excess at its glorious best. The truest explanation of the Cup's appeal was the following comment from

Annapolis-based yacht designer Bruce Farr, who drew the lines for several Cup entries: "The America's Cup isn't about making money; it's about spending money."

That's the charm. That's what brought bigger-than-life figures like Harold S. Vanderbilt, Sir Thomas Lipton, Baron Marcel Bich, T.O.M. Sopwith, Bill Koch, and their pals to the game, along with the world-class sailors they hired, like Buddy Melges and Charlie Barr, Lowell North and Dennis Conner.

Why do people love Wimbledon, the Kentucky Derby, the World Series, the Olympics? Tradition. The grass courts were the same for Margaret Court, Martina Navratilova, and Serena Williams. The rackets are a little better, the costumes slicker, the athletes fitter, but the game is the same; the rules are the same. The 1500-meter Olympic final doesn't get shortened to fit into a broadcast schedule, and a baseball game can still go on all night if nobody scores the winning run. A soccer field is 22 guys and a ball. Maybe some broadcast genius thinks it would be better if everybody could use their hands, or if the goalie could use a big fishing net. But they can't.

The America's Cup has painted itself into a silly little corner, playing to the fantasy that by abandoning the audience it built over 175 years, it can attract a new audience of couch-slouch thrill-seekers who get their kicks watching high-speed crashes on TV. But the cup is in Kiwi-land now, the land of the long, white cloud, tucked away in Auckland, a seaside town that calls itself the "City of Sails". These folks know what a sailboat looks like. Will they do the right thing? One can only hope.'[20]

Well, New Zealand and the Italians took their first steps towards helping Angus and his mates at the Oar bar on Block Island sleep better at night when, in September 2017, they released their protocol for America's Cup 36.

The deceptively succinct document would do much to encourage those who wanted to see restored the history, tradition and prestige that had made the Auld Mug one of the most sought-after trophies in sport (see chapter 13 – Back to the Future).

02

DOWN-UNDER PLUNDER

Australia II's drama-filled victory in the 1983 America's Cup match is part of sporting folklore. Alan Bond's wonder boat from Down Under didn't just end the longest winning streak in sport – 132 years – beating 'Mr America's Cup', Dennis Conner, and *Liberty* 4–3 in the fabled Cup waters off Newport, Rhode Island, but in order to do so, she had to recover from 1–3 down in a cliffhanger best-of-seven match and produce more of the impossible by coming from nearly a minute behind at the penultimate turning mark in an extraordinary last race.

Moreover, even to get to the match at all, the Aussies had to fight off a determined, summer-long campaign by the powerful New York Yacht Club (NYYC) that sought to have *Australia II* banned and her designer, Ben Lexcen, branded a cheat – a battle that the media dubbed 'Keelgate'.

The growing rumour around the docks in Newport in that Cup summer of '83 was that Bond's new challenger had wings on a very unusual keel. Nobody knew what the set-up looked like – the boat's underbody was shrouded in all-encompassing skirts whenever she came out of the water – but the Aussies were smart enough to know that, in an environment like Cup-mad Newport, in the midst of a Cup summer, they would not keep their secrets for long.

So, instead of getting paranoid, they decided to have some fun. Warren Jones, Bond's right-hand man and campaign manager, explained:

> 'The interest in our boat and what was below the waterline became intense as the New York Yacht Club pulled out all the stops to pin down what we had.
>
> That could have destroyed us, so we turned it into a positive and reduced the pressure by playing games with the NYYC (they really were quite a mess, psychologically). We hid the keel so that Australia II arrived in Newport, Rhode Island, with her nether regions completely covered by a "modesty skirt", and that's like taking a Christmas present home, stashing it somewhere in the house and saying to your kid: "I've got you a Christmas present but you mustn't look for it." He'll tear the house apart to see what it is.
>
> They [the NYYC and its defence favourite Dennis Conner] didn't like it at all and they started to knee-jerk, doing dumb things like adding wings to their existing keels without doing us the credit of acknowledging that, whatever it was that we had down there, it would have been a lot more sophisticated than the tack-on wings that they began experimenting with.'[1]

The Aussies knew what incredible psychological weapons the keel and the skirts were and Jones was adept at milking the situation, as he remembered fondly:

> 'Benny [Ben Lexcen] was an unusual man – a very talented, unusual man. One day he walked into my office, waving a smallish drawing of the keel, and said, "Warren, we've got to plant this." I reply, "OK, let's go over to Newport Offshore, photocopy it and leave the original in the machine."
>
> So that's what we did and, an hour later, we went racing back to Newport Offshore and said that we'd left a document in the photocopier and needed it back, urgently. They replied, all innocent-like: "This one?" I grabbed it and off we went. The next day, the drawing was in

the Providence Journal *newspaper and a short time later they were fastening a set of wooden wings on the bottom of the keel of Dennis Conner's* Freedom *[the 1980 defender and 1983 trial horse]. We couldn't believe what we were seeing. A 22-ton yacht would have torn them to bits in minutes. Benny was having a great old time. He knew all of Dennis's guys well and could walk into their compound unchallenged. They would say, "We're only doing what we're told," but we knew they were foxing too.'[2]*

Bill Trenkle, one of Conner's key men, confirmed what the Americans were up to:

'While we were fitting a wing to the bottom of the keel of Freedom, to see if there was anything to the idea of having a wing on the bottom of the keel acting as an end plate, Ben Lexcen came over and was watching us, with a big smile on his face. Someone asked him what he thought of our wing, and he said "Looks to me like more wetted surface area on which to grow barnacles," and walked away, laughing his head off. He was right – the wing was very slow and we took it off after one day of testing.'[3]

Warren Jones continued:

'By this stage we had very heavy security on our boat and we got to be very good at drawing those skirts closed when the boat came out of the water at night. We also painted the keel like it was conventional, with the extremities a different colour that made it very difficult to identify from the air. Lots tried but, as far we knew, nobody got more than a tantalising glimpse of what we had.'[4]

The revolutionary keel on *Australia II*, of course, had not been created overnight and nor was it the result of someone doodling with design ideas on a scratch pad. There was a lot of cutting-edge technology involved and the origins of that technology would become one of the longest-running disputes in sport.

The Australians had, for some time, been working to persuade the New York Yacht Club to relax the rules around the use of towing tanks to test large-scale models of new 12-Metre designs. Those rules were silent on the subject but the NYYC's view was that it was covered by the all-embracing requirement that yachts contesting the America's Cup had to be designed and constructed in the country of origin of the campaign. And the NYYC's interpretation was that 'constructed' meant 'designed and built', and designed in a country meant that 'the designers of the yacht's hull, rig and sails shall be nationals of that country'.

The NYYC was, however, conscious of the fact that few nations in the world possessed towing tanks of any size. They were a facility usually linked with the testing of large-scale models of commercial shipping and/or warships and only a relatively few nations had cause to be involved in such activity or, in turn, to build such expensive research amenities. By the time Bond and Jones made their move in terms of tank-testing *Australia II*, the NYYC was prepared to deal, on a case-by-case basis, with any applications to use testing facilities (towing tanks or wind tunnels) in another country if there were no such facilities in the country making the application.

Surreptitiously, Bond and Jones wanted to pursue an approach they had received from the Maritime Research Institute Netherlands (MARIN), in Wageningen, 69 kilometres (43 miles) south-east of Amsterdam. Peter van Oossanen, head of the Design Research Department at MARIN, was seeking an opportunity to get involved in the America's Cup and, in 1979, wrote to Bond offering the facilities and expertise of the Dutch towing tank and its technicians.

Peter van Oossanen: 'I was working with what, in those days, was called the Netherlands Ship Model Basin (NSMB). We'd followed Alan Bond's Cup endeavours with great interest and thought we could help improve his designs and certainly his model testing.'[5]

Bond responded expeditiously, asking van Oossanen to come to Australia to explore further and, two weeks later, the Western Australian entrepreneur was explaining that, while there was a budget for further boat development for the 1980 America's Cup, time was rather short. Van Oossanen explained:

'I flew to Sydney where I met twice with just Alan at the Sebel Town House. He wasn't sure that we were going to be able to do anything for him for that particular event [the 1980 Cup] but he asked me to meet with Ben

Lexcen. So, Ben was there for our third meeting, following which I spent a long weekend with Ben discussing yacht design and many other things. I then returned to Holland, expecting something of a reply like "Thanks and yes we might use your facilities soon". But I didn't hear a thing from them until January of '81, when Ben was in Amsterdam and wanted to see the test tank and talk further about things that, perhaps, we could be doing for the 1983 America's Cup.'[6]

To the surprise of many, the NYYC had given its approval for the Australians to use the Dutch facilities, on the grounds that there are no such amenities in Australia. A deal was agreed between the Aussies and the Dutch, and Lexcen headed to Wageningen to oversee tank tests of a model of Bond's 1980 challenger, the Lexcen-designed *Australia*, and of some new keel shapes. He was also preparing drawings for Lloyd's' approval of the construction of the 1983 boat.

According to Jones:

'After a few weeks had gone by, I got a call from the Netherlands. It's Benny, who blurts out: "Hey, Warren, I'm doing some really strange things over here."

Sometime later, I got another Benny call. It is very early in the morning in Perth, which means it's very late at night in Holland. Without much ado, Benny says: "Hey, I've done it!" I asked what he meant and he said: "I've designed a boat that will beat any America's Cup yacht around the course by 20 minutes." I asked what he'd been drinking because, I mean, that's impossible. He replied: "Honestly – come over and see for yourself."

We were all at Cowes, in England, for the 1981 Admiral's Cup (with Bond's Apollo V). So off we went to Holland – Alan Bond, John Bertrand [skipper] and myself. It was really the first time that we had physically seen what he [Benny] was doing over there and it was quite staggering. The keel was upside down and it had wings.

We all got very excited because we were looking for something that was different – an edge. But I have to say there was also a degree of skepticism and a lot of debate. In the end, Alan Bond – it was going to be his money – said: "Build it." That was the strength of Alan Bond. If there was a decision to be made, he would make it.'[7]

In the coming months, with nobody paying much attention to what was happening in Australia, the Bond group launched its new boat with its revolutionary keel, and set about getting to grips with her idiosyncrasies and handling differences. They soon realised that *Australia II*, with its winged appendage, represented a winning difference. The all-concealing secrecy skirts were quickly introduced and the psychological warfare began.

The rumours of a revolutionary new keel development caused great concern in the ranks of the defender, particularly when *Australia II* proved a dominant force in the Louis Vuitton challenger eliminations. Conner, especially, was spooked – so edgy about his own prospects in the Defender trials that he played one of his aces-in-the-hole to ensure progress and cut a confidential deal with the New York Yacht Club. That deal allowed Conner to acquire multiple rating certificates for *Liberty* in different sailing configurations, which meant he could select a performance set-up that best suited the conditions on a particular day. It was legal, but it was sneaky.

The highly colourful Tom Blackaller and the youthful Gary Jobson, campaigning *Defender* on their own account, were left seething by the NYYC's part in this duplicity.

Jobson, tactician on Ted Turner's winning defender *Courageous* in 1977 and now doing the same job for Blackaller in the 1983 defence trials elaborated:

> 'We go into the competition believing it's a fair deal. If we sail our boat around the course faster than Dennis Conner, we'll be the defender. What we don't count on, though, is that Dennis has gone and convinced the NYYC that they will have a better chance at defending against this radical boat, Australia II, if they have a deal with him to allow multiple measurement certificates.'[8]

Even the Aussies, great respecters of Conner, were unimpressed. Veteran crew member and Bond's America's Cup project manager John 'Chink' Longley observed:

> 'Dennis [Conner] is one of the greatest fighters you can imagine but he was so spooked by our boat he was like a cornered animal and he pulled

out the last shot in his locker. We jokingly called it his three-card trick but quite frankly, that was pretty poor form, to pull that one against his own people.'[9]

All of this became mere background clutter, however, when a new rumour exploded over a Newport that was already sensing history in the making. The magic keel, it was claimed, was the work of the Dutch technicians at the Netherlands Ship Model Basin (NSMB) and not of an Australian, as the rules required.

The NYYC reacted immediately, sending Richard S Latham, a member of the club's America's Cup selection committee, to Holland to investigate. Armed with a couple of pages of searching questions, his mission, if the allegations were correct, was to acquire proof that the Dutch, and not the Australians, had designed *Australia II*. He left empty-handed and, without a smoking gun: the NYYC had no case to make. The club, however, remained super-suspicious and made several more attempts to uncover evidence of skullduggery by the Aussies.

Finally, with the Cup match just two days away, a decision had to be made: disqualify the challenger or shut up and race. The debate was fierce – the reputation of the Cup and the Club were on the line – and, in the process, the 1983 America's Cup match came within a whisker of being cancelled amid rumours that Alan Bond was threatening to sue NYYC for $US500 million if the 1983 match didn't happen.

On the evening of 13 September 1983, less than 24 hours before the match was due to start, the NYYC's America's Cup Committee met in the private confines of *Summertime*, the luxury motor yacht owned by committee member and former winning America's Cup skipper Bus Mosbacher. This was just two hours before the traditional America's Cup captains' meeting in the Vanderbilt Mansion, one of Newport's array of imposing stately homes from grandeur days past.

The question before those assembled was whether to reject *Australia II* as a legitimate challenger because, NYYC was convinced, she did not meet the 'constructed in the country to which the Challenging Club belongs' requirement in the America's Cup rules. Everyone present was fully familiar with the lengths to which their club had gone to uncover evidence that *Australia II*'s revolutionary winged keel and, in fact, the boat itself, contravened that requirement because they were the work of the Dutch at NSMB/MARIN, and not of Lexcen.

Put simply, on that fateful evening the committee was being asked to cancel the 1983 America's Cup match, when the stage was set and the audience, from all parts of the world, was already in town and ready to party. And the club came within a whisker of doing so.

Vic Romagna, secretary of the committee, in chapter 9 of *Upset: Australia Wins the America's Cup* (a 1983 Nautical Quarterly book by Michael Levitt and Barbara Lloyd) recounted: 'We were in a tight spot. We didn't want to appear to be spoiling it [the America's Cup match] for the sake of spoiling it, but we were convinced the Australians had overlooked nearly every rule.'[10]

According to Romagna, the discussion went around the group until finally there was nothing more to say. It was clear where everyone stood and, if a vote had been taken there and then, the outcome would have been 5–4 not to race. But there was no vote. Romagna declined to say how the members aligned themselves, but he made his own views clear: 'We didn't have the guts to stand up and say we won't race ... so we just folded up our tents and went off into oblivion.'[11]

The committee's legal counsel, San Francisco lawyer James Michael, was another in favour of booting out the challenger. Like Romagna, he felt the club had a duty, as trustee under the America's Cup Deed of Gift, to see that the rules were upheld, regardless of public opinion. Michael intimated to trusted journalists that the members who backed down (from voting not to race) were concerned about the outcry if the NYYC, at that late moment, declined to meet the Australian challenger. Almost in the same breath, however, he conceded that the committee's biggest problem all summer long had been its inability to convince the media and public of the legitimacy of its reservations over how the Aussies had gone about designing their boat.

The course of least resistance had some powerful support, not least that of the respected Arthur J Santry Jr, who would become NYYC commodore in 1986. Santry explained to author Doug Riggs, for the book *Keelhauled: Unsportsmanlike Conduct and the America's Cup* (Simon & Schuster, 1986), that when dealing with an expensive world event that drew enthusiasts from all around the world, you couldn't simply cancel it at a moment's notice.

This led Michael to observe in *Keelhauled*: 'The officers of the club, led principally by Arthur Santry's very strong position in the matter, decided that the public relations aspect of the situation overrode all the other considerations and, therefore, we should go forward.'[12]

Mosbacher, NYYC vice-commodore at the time, saw it differently. His view (as expressed in *Keelhauled*) was that the decision (or the non-decision) to race stemmed from 'the almost overpowering dedication of those trustees and flag officers and members of the club present to the fact that the club is made up of men who are sportsmen and gentlemen, and should deport themselves as such, even if they know they are being cheated or had.'

The 1983 match did, then, go ahead – and the outcome was a lot closer than anyone predicted. *Australia II* ultimately prevailed, winning the best-of-seven contest 4–3, but to do so she had to come from 1–3 down and then perform miracles to retrieve a hopeless situation in the final race.

Warren Jones extrapolated:

'We'd fought back from 1–3 down and the score now was 3–3. But, it looked as though it had all been in vain as we approached the second-last mark [in that final race]. We were trailing Dennis by a great distance [57 seconds, to be precise]. To all intents and purposes, we were done.

Normally, when you are racing 12-Metres and you are coming around a mark first, you always protect your position relative to the wind, or place yourself between the breeze and your opponent so that he can't get to that breeze first. And there's an old saying that goes with that strategy – when you have the opposition in jail, locked away in an unfavourable position, swallow the key. Well, Dennis forgot the basic rules of covering your opponent, and he forgot to swallow the key. Rounding that penultimate mark first and turning downwind for the final time, strangely he just waffled off on starboard gybe, more or less down the middle of the course, and allowed Australia II *to go hard right, sailing a faster angle. He even gybed away on port for a while, giving* Australia II *even more of a chance to find something different in the way of breeze out to the right.*

Dennis then gybed on to starboard to come across to the right-hand side and get back into position, and gybed back on to port, intending to close the door on rounding rights for the final turn. But he was too late. Liberty's 57-second lead at the last mark was gone. He gybed again, right in front of Australia II, and now the magic of Benny's winged keel was there for all to see. Australia II sailed lower and faster than her rival and broke through her lee to lead by 21 seconds going into the final beat to windward. It was the most dramatic and fateful pass in America's Cup history. And Dennis was locked in jail and we were swallowing the key.'[13]

Australia II covered every move that *Liberty* made up the final beat and crossed the finish line 41 seconds clear, ending the longest winning streak in sport. Afterwards, in interview, the key players had this to say.

Alan Bond: 'Dennis and the NYYC had the champagne on the end of the jetty. They expected it to be 4–1.'

Warren Jones: 'If something had broken and we had lost that series 4–1, we would have discredited the best 12-Metre that [until then] had ever been built.'

John Longley: 'It would have been a tragedy for us to have lost. And we so nearly did. We so nearly did.'

In Newport on that fateful evening, amid wild celebrations, Bond ordered *Australia II*'s winged keel to be revealed. As the boat, this time minus skirts, was lifted clear of the water, there for all to see was the upside-down keel shape, wings and all, in camouflage blue and white. Almost unnoticed, Dennis Conner quietly clambered across some dinghies to an adjoining dock and walked off into the darkness, in tears. Later, he recounted:

'I didn't know anything about other sports – I didn't surf, ski or play tennis. All I lived and breathed was the America's Cup. It was my whole life, all I thought about, to the exclusion of anything else. So, when the Aussies came up with a clever yacht design and did such a good job campaigning that yacht, and the Cup was lost – I wasn't just disappointed. I was devastated. I didn't really know what to do other than go home and put a pillow over

my head. I am usually full of life and energy but I just did not want to get out of bed in the morning … I wanted to hide … it just seemed like the end of the world.'[14]

More than a year later, doubts about *Australia II*'s eligibility persisted among members of the New York Yacht Club who still perceived there to have been 'improprieties' on the part of Alan Bond and his team.

The well-informed Barbara Lloyd reported a new claim that further obfuscated the issue. Leading Dutch aerospace scientist Joop W Slooff allegedly claimed that the innovative keel on the 12-Metre *Australia II* was his design rather than the work of Australian yacht designer Ben Lexcen who, in turn, disputed this, countering that the Dutch scientist had merely run a computer analysis program for him.

Slooff, then 43, was director of the theoretical aerodynamics department at Amsterdam's National Aerospace Laboratory. Of his involvement with the design, he said that he hadn't spoken out during the races because there seemed to be no point: 'It wasn't to anyone's advantage to make a whole lot of fuss … I thought it was no use. There was too much heat at the time. Now it doesn't matter.'[15]

The Slooff claims, however, failed to gain traction and Keelgate went quiet. For the next 25 years the whole controversy appeared to have died through lack of interest or of any supposed new evidence of chicanery. Until, that is, in 2009, Peter van Oossanen dropped a bombshell.

In an article in *Professional BoatBuilder Magazine* (October/ November 2009), and also in a report on ABC National Television, he categorically claimed that Lexcen did not design *Australia II* nor her winged keel:

'We at MARIN made the drawings for the upside-down keel. Ben [Lexcen] had nothing to do with it. He wasn't even here when we tested it. The only contribution he made was that at some stage towards the end of his visit here in Holland he made a bit of a sketch of what perhaps an upside-down keel with winglets attached might look like. That was his only contribution.'[16]

Following up on the article, the *Sydney Morning Herald*'s Rick Feneley, on 14 October 2009, wrote:

> 'A boat designer has blown the whistle on a "lie" that allowed Australia to seize glory in the 1983 America's Cup: the claim that Ben Lexcen invented the winged keel that helped propel Alan Bond's yacht Australia II to victory.
>
> The Dutch naval architect who worked with Lexcen, Peter van Oossanen, has confirmed what the Americans alleged but could not prove 26 years ago. The true designers of the keel, with its critical winglets, were his Dutch team and Dutch aerodynamicist Joop Slooff. Lexcen, he said, had played only a minor role, contributing perhaps 5 or 10 per cent. There was an argument that Australia II should have been disqualified because the rules said competing yachts had to be designed by residents or citizens of the country they represented.
>
> Dr van Oossanen said from his home in Wageningen in the Netherlands that Lexcen had not been in the Netherlands at "the Eureka moment" in the development of the keel.
>
> He said he remained Lexcen's close friend until his death of a heart attack in 1988, and he still regarded him as a "true Australian hero", but at 65 – and having become an Australian citizen in 1990 – he had grown tired of what he believed to be the airbrushing of the Dutch contribution from history.
>
> "Ben was a nice guy," he said. "He had a flair for things, a flair for shapes. But he wasn't a scientist and he wasn't able to understand the full physics of what was going on. He left to go back to Australia on 20 June 1981 before the vital tank tests. The role he played was a minor one. Ben did things by feel and intuition, but in the America's Cup that will get you nowhere. It is a very scientific thing."
>
> For keeping the secret, Dr van Oossanen claimed, Alan Bond had said to him words to the effect: "We'll look after you." After the America's Cup win, $US25,000 appeared in his bank account: a gift from Mr Bond, which he now regarded as hush money.
>
> Didn't the Dutch involvement mean that the Australia II syndicate cheated? "Yes," Dr van Oossanen said. "If everything had stayed the same, I would have taken this to my grave. But they are writing us out of history."

He said Lexcen did not design the boat's key elements – the small hull over an upside-down keel and winglets. They were not even his ideas.

"We are talking about the underwater hull – the part of the design that made the boat go faster and win the America's Cup. When we conducted the first vital tank tests with the upside-down keel, and we saw we had 25 per cent less lift-induced resistance and tonnes of extra speed, that was the Eureka moment. Ben wasn't there."[17]

Van Oossanen's accusations caused outrage in Australia. Ben Lexcen was a national hero, and this attack on his memory (he died from a heart attack on 1 May 1988) was bitterly resented. Feneley was, however, prepared to listen to what the Dutchman had to say and, later, asserted: 'Had the guy been clearly vengeful, clearly unconvincing, I probably wouldn't have written a word. But … there was plenty of correspondence to establish the Dutch involvement and the critical Dutch role in the winning design.'[18]

He recalled his first interview with van Oossanen: 'I must have spent two hours on the phone with him … and by the end of that conversation I am struck. This is a very compelling story … this is a man who clearly isn't just making stuff up.'

But why resurrect all this after 25-odd years have gone by?

'The point is that he [van Oossanen] felt the Bond team was airbrushing him and the Dutch team from history.'

The *Professional BoatBuilder Magazine* article and Feneley's follow-up, syndicated to other leading Australian newspapers, prompted a hard-hitting response from Bond's *Australia II* project manager, John 'Chink' Longley, who wrote to the respected online newsletter *Scuttlebutt* on 19 October 2009:

'I … worked closely with Warren Jones and Ben Lexcen in the early days of the Challenge, when the design work was being done. Together with John Bertrand, who had already been appointed skipper, that was it – the four of us. John lived in Melbourne so in the Perth office during that amazing time there was only Warren and me. Both Warren and Ben are now dead, so that leaves me to tell what was going on in June 1981 when the breakthrough design was created.

To help my memory of the facts, I went down to the Western Australian Maritime Museum and dove into the seven filing cabinets of documents that we donated to the WAMM when the Bond syndicate was wound up in 1990.

It is all there waiting for some PhD student to sieve through and come up with the definitive story … I went straight to the file labelled 'Designer' and almost immediately I found documents that contradict some of Peter van Oossanen's claims [that he designed the winged keel].

Claim 1, made by Peter van Oossanen on ABC National Television last week: "Ben wasn't even interested in the radical design…" There is a letter in the file, dated 9 February 1981, from Ben Lexcen to Warren Jones, setting out in detail why he wanted to use the Netherlands Ship Model Basin (NSMB) and asking for support in funding a tank-testing program. The main reason, he stated, was that the NSMB had the capacity to test very large models and were very good at it. In his letter, he states: "I have some novel ideas I would like to try in the keel area, which would be quite revolutionary, and if they work out would be quite a big breakthrough. But only with models of this size can we try these ideas."

This was written well before Ben ever went to Holland, but Peter van Oossanen says he [Ben] was not interested in innovation. Of all the statements that Peter van Oossanen has made recently, this was the most bizarre. Ben's middle name should have been Innovation.

Claim 2, made in the Professional BoatBuilder Magazine *article and reproduced in* Scuttlebutt: *"Ben had nothing to do with it. He wasn't even there when we tested it." There are a number of letters and telexes that totally refute this claim. In a telex to Warren Jones, dated 22 May 1981, Ben says: "Keel III a big advance. About to take yachtdesign [sic] into space age. Darth Vader looks good in computer in 3 Dimension. Will test on Wednesday 10 June. Can't return to Land of Oz untill [sic] 17 June. Need Brass and conversation." Darth Vader was Ben's code for the winged keel.*

A letter from NSMB, signed by Peter van Oossanen, dated 2 June 1981, says in part: "The NLR keel, with and without appendages, will be tested on June 9 and 10, 1981. I have recommended to Ben that he should stay at least one week more [till 17 June 1981] to enable us to go through all the results together." At this stage, Ben had already been at the NSMB for four months and the design programme was already six weeks behind schedule.

By telex, dated 9 June 1981, Warren says to Peter van Oossanen: "*Agree that Lexcen must remain until final configuration agreed thus leaving you to complete your formal report, which is required by Alan Bond by earliest possible date.*" Then, a telex from Ben to Warren, dated 15 June 1981: "*Going to Germany to meet John Bertrand's Professor … Be back at tank Thursday and Friday, come home Saturday.*"

These telexes clearly show that Ben was in Holland through all the critical stages of the breakthrough keel's design and testing.

Claim 3, in the Pro BoatBuilder *article, van Oossanen says:* "*We did the final set of full-scale loftings, the final hull design, the final keel design. It was all done by us.*" In a file [at WAMM] marked Keelgate, *there is a telex from Peter van Oossanen to the Head of the NSMB, Dr MWC Oosterveld, dated 21 September 1983, which was midway through the America's Cup finals off Newport, RI.*

In it Peter van Oossanen advises his superior how to respond to Mr R Latham [representing the NYYC]. *It is a long telex but there is one critical paragraph that says:* "*The heart of the matter is, as I see it, that the conclusion you arrive at from Dr Peter van Oossanen's description of NSMB's activities concerning* Australia II, *differs from Dr Peter van Oossanen's and my own conclusion from his description. Your conclusion is that NSMB should be considered as having participated in the design of* Australia II. *Ours is that NSMB acted in a testing capacity and did not participate in the design. From our own conclusion, it follows that in our opinion Mr Lexcen is the sole designer of* Australia II. *An opinion we have openly expressed.*"

So, in Peter van Oossanen's own words, he told his boss that Ben designed Australia II. He was therefore either misleading his superior then … or us now, when neither Ben Lexcen nor Warren Jones are alive to refute his claims. The sad thing about all of this is that we have always acknowledged that the technicians, including Peter van Oossanen, played a part in the evolution of Australia II – how could they not? Ben spent four months in Holland surrounded by the NSMB personnel.

… Finally when the full-scale lofting of the boat arrived from Holland and was laid out on the floor of Steve Ward's shed in Cottesloe,

I and Steve watched as Ben spent days crawling over the lofting floor fine-tuning the lines. Later he did the same with the keel lofting before the plug was made.

Peter van Oossanen, Joop Slooff and other technicians and computer programmers at NSMB all had a role in the evolution of Australia II, *but it was Ben Lexcen who was the team leader and designer who pulled together the whole package from the tip of the keel to the truck of the mast.'*[19]

Interviewed for *Exposed*, van Oossanen repeated and elaborated on his October 2009 claims, saying that when Lexcen arrived in Wageningen [in May 1981], no programme as such had been decided on, and he refuted some of Longley's claims, stating:

'I never said to anyone that Ben did not have an interest in innovation. I told the Sydney Morning Herald *that Ben was not interested in the alternative keel project which I initiated with the Aerospace people in Amsterdam [Slooff]. He [Ben] didn't believe in it because of the very radical ideas Slooff and I had. He was keen to test two conventional keels – one that was thicker allowing for more lead ballast further down in the keel (affording more stability) and one with a leading edge that had less sweep. He prepared drawings for those keels while we were testing the* Australia 1980 *model in May 1981. He then left for one of his trips.*

He started showing an interest in what we were doing when Slooff reported that the computer calculations pointed to a relatively large gain in performance in the case of the upside-down keel fitted with crude winglets. He then started to ask questions and take an interest and, after the tests of his two conventional keels, he agreed that we should build the upside-down configuration and test that too. That was just before he left to return to Australia.

John Longley was thus incorrect about the four months that Ben was at Marin. It was no more than 5 weeks. After he left we refined the keel (reducing its size and optimizing its shape), which required the testing of two further models, and we completely modified the aft portion of the hull, removing the bustle and shortening the rated waterline to the minimum of 44 ft. The last model was tested in September after Ben was long gone.

You need to remember that it would take at least 2 weeks to make a new model of the keel or to make changes to the hull and so on. So, all-up, the programme lasted some 5 months.

John Longley continually refers to the telex exchange that I had with my superior at MARIN in August 1983 which refutes the claims about the Dutch involvement. The fact of the matter is, however, I was a team member as much as anyone else [in the Australia II campaign]. I had, with an assistant Bert Koops, written the total software package that was used for analyzing the performance of the boat and we had a telemetry link that allowed me to log the performance (speed, wind angles, heel angle, rudder angle, etc) of Australia II on the computer on board of our tender Black Swan. I was on board Black Swan during every race and, so, I spoke to Warren Jones and Alan Bond every day. So, I was completely aware of everything that was happening and on a number of occasions Warren handed me the text of a message that he wanted to telex to my people at MARIN, in my name. This was by no means a secret and I was not in a position to disagree. I didn't want to, anyway, because of my loyalty to the team.'[20]

According to van Oossanen, the topic of wings on keels didn't come up until, he thought, mid-April 1981, by when it had become quite clear that the 'upside-down' concept was highly promising. There was, however, a drawback in that their keel developed a big tip vortex at the bottom of the appendage and a lot of energy was lost in that vortex.

When Slooff became aware of this, he advised van Oossanen that NASA aerodynamicist Dick Whitcomb, in the USA, had recently applied for a patent on what he called winglets, to be fitted to aeroplane wings to resolve tip vortex issues. Slooff recommended that testing winglets of that type, fitted to the upside-down concept keel, would be really worthwhile.

Van Oossanen was well aware of the influence of end plates – little flat surfaces – fitted to the bottom of keels of yachts, but the aerospace laboratory people explained that Whitcomb's winglet concept was totally different in that it developed special lift forces that generated their own flow, counteracting the natural tendency of a wing to develop a tip vortex. The winglets fitted to the would-be *Australia II* keel would be totally different to anything that had been done before in yacht design and would resemble nothing of that ilk.

Then, on 27 July 1981, Bond, Bertrand and Jones visited the MARIN facility. Van Oossanen recalled:

> 'Joop Slooff and I took them through all the work that had been done, commencing with the calculations on the keel shapes and all of the model testing. We then detailed the "upside-down" keel with winglets and explained that a 12-Metre with such a keel would, depending on wind strengths, be at least 3–5 minutes faster around the track in Newport conditions. John Bertrand said he didn't believe it and the Australians would look foolish if they turned up in Newport with a keel like that on their boat. But, according to van Oossanen, Bond and Jones really liked what they were hearing: "Maybe Ben had explained that we were on to something."[21]

Van Oossanen was asked why he had waited 25 years before breaking his silence on all of this. He explained that, when he was in Melbourne in March 1983, for *Australia II*'s final workouts before she was shipped to the USA for the Cup challenge, Jones had taken him aside and made it clear that he (van Oossanen) could never take any credit for his team's work on the design of *Australia II* and her keel.

> 'I accepted that. I knew and understood what the nationality rules, the rules for the designer, were all about and I said to him, "That's fine, because we are quite happy to have the role, to have been given the role, that we have." Warren made me sign a statement that we could never own up that we had done the keel and the hull, that in effect we would always have to maintain that Ben was the designer. I signed it and that was the end of it. The quid pro quo was that the Australians would keep a low profile on any design issues. They would not be involved in any books claiming that Ben was the designer, nor would they cooperate with other people doing that. It was as simple as that, and I kept my promise for 25 years. It was only when people like John Bertrand, Jim Hardy and John Longley started writing newspaper and magazine articles in support of Ben's nomination to the America's Cup Hall of Fame [Lexcen was inducted posthumously in 2006] that things changed. They were saying that the

Dutch had nothing to do with the concept [for Australia II*] and that Ben did everything. They even said that Ben came over here [to Holland] to carry out tests and told our engineers how to do them. Which is just stupid, if you think about it.*"[22]

Van Oossanen reflected on the lengthy saga. It maybe was strange to be revisiting it 'all these years later', with Warren Jones also dead (he died on 17 May 2002, after a massive stroke). It was, he said, 'a bit like having to own up to something bad.' He was not proud of the fact that, at certain times, he had concocted untruths in order to keep his word to Jones but, he claimed, 'what I am telling you now is the real story, the truth.'

In his book, *Australia II and the America's Cup: The Untold, Inside Story of The Keel* (published in March 2016), Slooff is at pains to emphasise the veracity of his version of events, which, he says, is based on his working notes, photo albums and scrapbooks of that period.

The Slooff version, which mirrors very closely that of van Oossanen, details how, in late April 1981, his department in the Dutch National Aerospace Laboratory (NLR) became sub-contractor of the National Ship Model Basin/MARIN working on the *Australia II* project.

Van Oossanen outlined to him that he wanted a number of 'candidate keel configurations' analysed by NLR, using its computational fluid dynamics (CFD) computer programs. He (Joop Slooff) was 'free to propose whatever keel shape I consider promising' provided its shape conformed with the 12-Metre design rule and fitted within the approved budget.

Slooff claimed he stressed, at a meeting with van Oossanen, on 16 or 17 April 1981, the importance of investigating upside-down keels and also mentioned 'the possibility of applying winglets' at the bottom of the keel. He noted that Ben Lexcen was not at that particular meeting – 'He is still in Australia'.

On 24 April 1981, he met with van Oossanen and his 'co-worker' Bert Koops and showed them a 'first, rough "on the back of an envelope" sketch' that he's made, of an 'upside-down' keel with winglets. On about 6 May 1981, he met again with van Oossanen, this time at the NSMB with Ben Lexcen present, and a definitive list of keel configurations to be analysed computationally was agreed. The list included 'upside-down' keels, one with winglets that was tested in the NSMB/MARIN towing tank on 10 June 1981, with van Oossanen, Slooff and Lexcen all in attendance. That keel showed the potential to be a design breakthrough. Further testing after Lexcen had returned to Australia yielded the promise that Bond's new yacht with winged keel should be 5 minutes faster around a full America's Cup racecourse than the 1980 *Australia* – a massive gain.

Why, after all this time, was Joop Slooff again breaking his silence to claim ownership of *Australia II*'s keel design?

Because, he said, the Australians claimed that the winged keel was the work of Ben Lexcen and because, publicly, 'they ignored that I existed'. Even after 32 years, the world had the right to know the facts.

Asked whether the Bond group broke the America's Cup design rules, or the intent of those rules, when delivering *Australia II*, Peter van Oossanen, with hardly a pause, replied:

- Yes, in terms of the aft part of the hull, which the Dutch had 'totally redesigned' after Lexcen went home to Australia;
- Yes, in terms of the keel , which was, he said, designed with very little input from Lexcen.

'So,' he added 'the intent of the rule was not lived up to, was broken.'

Moreover, if he was apportioning credit for the design of *Australia II* and her magic keel, it would be to:

- the NSMB, for proposing the upside-down keel in the first place;
- the NSMB, for taking the crude wing concept that they found in the patent, and that was proposed by the Aerospace Laboratory, into a refined shape with the right wetted surface area;
- Joop Slooff for suggesting winglets;
- and the NSMB for the fact that the aft end of the hull was so substantially refined.

Unprompted, he added: 'Certainly, however, Ben Lexcen should be seen as the designer of record. He was also the leader of the design team and gave us total freedom with respect to the way the whole programme went.'[23]

In the conclusion to his 2016 book, Slooff says that Lexcen had full design responsibility and the Bond group had the courage to pursue something that was very radical and unproven. Victory in 1983, therefore, 'remains an Australian success' even if the concept and the 'mechanic details' were his.[24]

John Longley's view was unchanged, as he wrote in the 19 October 2009 letter to *Scuttlebutt*. The design of *Australia II* was the work of Ben Lexcen:

> '*Peter van Oossanen, Joop Slooff and other technicians and computer programmers at NSMB all had a role in the evolution of* Australia II, *but it was Ben Lexcen who was the team leader and designer who pulled together the whole package, from the tip of the keel to the truck of the mast.*'[25]

The Aussies loved (and still do) the amiable 'Blinky Ben' Lexcen and took to referring to him as 'a genius'. They believed (and still do) that, unquestioningly, the boat and keel were his work. There are, however, some Australians who aren't so sure.

Sydney Morning Herald journalist Rick Feneley:

> '*It was an exciting time. I was a cadet at News Limited at the time … and when the Prime Minister of the day puts on his technicolour dream coat and tells the employers of Australia they'd be bums if they expected everybody to turn up to work the next day, well – I was enjoying that as much as anybody else. People got swept up in the whole thing and they probably didn't give a thought to who designed the boat. It would be 27 years or something before Australia really got to grapple with the idea that Ben Lexcen, who had been accepted as the designer, may not have had the critical role that we all assumed he had.*'[26]

So, armed with all the above information, who, then, did design the history-making *Australia II* and her magical keel?

The Dutch may have taken their time to claim credit but there can be no denying the sincerity and integrity of Peter van Oossanen and Joop Slooff. The indications are that, while not mortal enemies, they aren't, either, bosom pals. According to Joop Slooff's book, they have met only twice since the big happenings in Newport. That would almost certainly rule out collusion on facts, dates and events. Yet, they offer almost identical accounts of what went down in those fateful days and they make a compelling case for having inspired and scientifically developed many of *Australia II*'s key design attributes.

The same, however, must be said of Lexcen and the Australians.

John Longley is almost the last man standing, a solid and much-respected stalwart of the *Australia II* campaign. The telex trail that he introduced from the Western Australian Maritime Museum archives strangely contradicts some of the 'facts' that van Oossanen and Slooff have presented. How much, therefore, have the 'facts' been influenced by time and 'spin'?

For instance, in his 19 October 2009 letter to *Scuttlebutt*, Longley referred to a telex from van Oossanen to the head of the NSMB, Dr MWC Oosterveld, dated 21 September 1983, in which the Dutch scientist says: 'From our own conclusion, it follows that in our opinion Mr Lexcen is the sole designer of *Australia II*...'

Longley observed: 'So, in Peter van Oossanen's own words, he told his boss that Ben designed *Australia II*. He was therefore either misleading his superior then ... or us now.' Longley didn't, however, countenance van Oossanen's claims that the telex in question was dictated by Warren Jones who, astutely as always, was defending Australia's position and marshalling its resources.

In their 1983 book *Upset: Australia Wins the America's Cup* (rightly regarded as the definitive work on Keelgate), Michael Levitt and Barbara Lloyd quote Lexcen saying:

> 'They [the Dutch technicians] were just doing what I told them. Sometimes they'd tell me things back. How the hell can you stop them from telling you things? It's like in a jury – "Well, disregard that remark..." You can't disregard that remark. If someone says, "I think this could be a good idea," you can't say, "Well, I didn't hear that." The situation at the tank puts you almost under conditions that would contravene the spirit of the bloody ruling [that the boat must be designed by a national of the country of challenge]. As far as I'm concerned, if you can use the tank, then you can talk to the people at the tank.'[27]

If you read between the lines, Lexcen might have been conceding that *Australia II*'s final design attributes might have been the product of collective bright minds working in a fertile environment. In that environment, some of the proprietary lines might have become blurred. At the same time, there clearly are hints of proprietary differences between Messrs van Oossanen and Slooff, although van Oossanen makes it very clear that the all-important winglets on *Australia II*'s keel were Slooff's inspiration.

A decade later, when Team New Zealand hired American Doug Peterson to be a key player in its design team for the 1995 America's Cup in San Diego, he made comparable observations to those of Ben Lexcen. Fresh from a similar role in Bill Koch's *America*³ programme, which produced the 1992 Cup winner, Peterson moved to Auckland in time to establish New Zealand residency and qualify to work as a Kiwi under the modern interpretation of the Cup's nationality requirements.

A very honourable person, Peterson made it clear from the outset with Team New Zealand that he would not divulge any of A^3's proprietary design information – and he never did. He decided, however, that a person can't unlearn what s/he has learned. So, he salved his conscience by not allowing design pursuits that he knew, from his A^3 experience, were dead ends.

It was another take on the point that Lexcen had sought to make – you can't unlearn what you have learned – and if you are in a design environment or testing facility such as a towing tank, the various technicians are going to talk to you, and you are going to talk to them – and the conversation is not going to be about the weather. So, certain lines get blurred.

Having said all that, hindsight indicates that the Australians recognised that, in the winged keel, they had a winner. But they also had a potentially serious rules problem that was not theirs to control. If van Oossanen is to be believed – and why shouldn't he be? – they, rather clumsily, tried to address that by imposing a confidentiality agreement on the Dutch. Medium/longer term, that was never going to work and, inevitably, a version of the 'truth' leaked out. But the savvy Warren Jones, according to Slooff, at the end of a meeting on 23 September 1983 in his [Warren's] Newport office, said: 'The facts can be released after a few months.'

Asked whether the design of *Australia II* was legal, Dennis Conner replied:

'Whether it was legal or not, it makes no difference now. In similar circumstances today, if Ben Lexcen was the principal designer and in charge of all subcontractors, if he got van Oossanen and/or Slooff to help him with the winged keel, that would be okay.

But the interpretation of the rules in those days [1983] was that the boat had to be designed by a countryman, in which case having Slooff and/ or van Oossanen design the winged keel was outside of those rules. It should not be forgotten, either, that while it was Alan Bond's money that made it all possible, Warren Jones was the brains of the outfit and it was Warren who outfoxed the New York Yacht Club and Dennis Conner … a brilliant guy, very smart, savvy, keen, tough. To my mind he, ultimately, was the guy responsible for winning.

I'm not sure who picked Ben Lexcen to be the designer but he was an obvious choice and John Bertrand was a great sailor, but without Warren Jones they never would've made it. He kept the New York Yacht Club at bay with all the battling over the design of the boat.'[28]

So, the question of who really did design *Australia II* and her magic keel will probably never be answered definitively. Ben Lexcen, Warren Jones and Alan Bond have now all passed away, and it is left to the likes of Longley to fight their corner. The Dutch have fired their shots, some of which found targets, but the damage is editorial only.

Perhaps, then, it is time to close the book on Keelgate and allow the last word to the man who was mostly on the receiving end throughout the long-running brouhaha. Conner: 'It doesn't really matter now, does it? It doesn't really matter. The Aussies did what they did and they won the America's Cup. So, good on you, Australia, and good on you, Alan Bond, and good on you, Warren Jones.'[29]

03

THE DEED OF DISCONTENT

Keelgate is, arguably, the biggest controversy in Cup history involving the Deed of Gift and the interpretation of that now-ancient document. But it certainly hasn't been the only example of what can happen when a set of event guidelines, drafted in days gone by with the very best of intentions and sporting objectives, are put under a modern microscope and subjected to the machinations and pressures of competitive sport as we know it today.

To trace the origins of the Deed, you have to go back to different times, to the early 1800s when, on the crest of the Industrial Revolution, on both sides of the Atlantic, large fortunes were made by the pioneers in manufacture and transportation (principally steamboat ferries and railroads). When they died, they left those fortunes to offspring who were just as competitive but more relaxed about the great wealth into which they had been born – and about how they spent it.

They have been described as 'hard-living, hard-riding and hard-swearing, rich amateur athletes' who could 'wager, sail, shoot and ride with equal skill – yet kind-hearted and extremely hospitable'. With time and money on their hands, they turned to sport, notably horse and sailboat racing, to fill their days, and bet huge sums of money (even the equivalent of $US1 million in today's currency) on the outcome of sporting events.

The membership of the New York Yacht Club in those early times was almost certainly a reflection of American, particularly east coast, society – brash and ambitious, confident and highly motivated, living in an environment in which extraordinary fortunes could be made in short periods of time. We're talking here of men such as shipping and railroad tycoon Cornelius Vanderbilt III, Standard Oil founder John D Rockefeller, steel pioneer Andrew Carnegie and banker and General Electric founder J Pierpont Morgan – 'The Men Who Built America'.

To these people, and to the young America in general, anything was possible in times of explosive opportunity. American clippers were dominating the tea trade between China and Britain. American inventors had produced the telegraph, the sewing machine and the rotary printing press. Thomas Edison and Nikola Tesla (championed respectively by JP Morgan and George Westinghouse) had established the way to the first commercial electrical energy distribution networks. American railroad mileage had increased by 7,000 miles since 1840.

Enter two individuals who were contemporaries and very much of that time – John Cox Stevens and George Lee Schuyler.

Cox Stevens, according to the New York Yacht Club archives, was from 'one of the more remarkable families in US history'. His grandfather was a member of the Continental Congress, and his father, John Stevens, a Revolutionary War colonel turned entrepreneur and inventor of steam engines and boats. The colonel and his three sons developed the first steam ferry to cross the Hudson River, and one of their ferries, *Phoenix*, delivered to Philadelphia on her own bottom, in 1809, was the first steamer to go offshore.

In 1804, 19-year-old John Cox Stevens steered the first propeller-driven boat and, soon after, built the sailing yacht *Diver* in which he raced fishing boats and ferries up and down New York Harbour for wagers. Philip Hone, mayor of New York in 1825–1826 and later a celebrated diarist of early times in America, once said of Stevens: '… he was a railroad and steamship-line promoter and man about town – a mighty good fellow and a most hospitable host.'

A passionate sportsman, Stevens was elected the first commodore of the New York Yacht Club, which he instigated and which was founded aboard his yacht *Gimcrack* in 1844. The NYYC wasn't the first yacht club in America (clubs in Boston and Detroit lay claim to that distinction), but it did become the country's pre-eminent sailing institution. Its first clubhouse was located on the Stevens family's property at Hoboken, New Jersey.

John Cox Stevens had two younger brothers – Robert Livingston Stevens and Edwin Augustus Stevens. They were just as competitive as he, and the trio's gambling excesses were legendary. For instance, before a horse race in 1823, the three of them bet all their cash, their diamond stick pins and their gold watches on their horse *Eclipse* in a match with the southern champion Sir Harry. Eclipse won by a nose, and John later became president of the prestigious Jockey Club.

Robert L Stevens was the more mechanically talented of the three and he had the primary role in the design of the family's 97-foot sloop *Maria*. The brothers, however, collaborated on the designs of their yachts, usually trying them out in model-testing on nearby streams. It is estimated that they spent in the region of $US100,000 on experiments and improvements to *Maria* in the 20-odd years that she was owned by the family. Robert also drew the lines of several Stevens steamships, invented the T-shaped railroad track and a percussion artillery shell that could be fired from a canon (the rights to which he sold to the US government).

Edwin, the youngest, who also went on to become the commodore of the New York Yacht Club (1859–1865), spent approximately $US1 million on an ironclad gunship, designed by brother Robert, which was called the *Stevens Battery*. A revolutionary, steam-powered, high-speed vessel, she was never completed and was finally sold for scrap. When he died in August 1868, Edwin left $US650,000 in his will to found the Stevens Institute of Technology on family land in Hoboken. The facilities included a towing tank in which, in later years, models of America's Cup defenders were tested.

George L Schuyler, a civil engineer with steam ferry and railroad interests, was the grandson of General Philip John Schuyler, of Revolutionary War fame. Born in Rhinebeck, New York, on 9 June 1811, he (according to an article in *The New York Times*):

'*... early settled in this city and received his education at private schools and at Columbia College. In the early part of Mr Schuyler's business career, he* *was one of the chief owners of the old steamboat line to New-Haven and was also interested in the New-York, New-Haven and Hartford railroad. His means being such as to allow him to gratify a strong taste for yachting, he naturally was one of the number of gentlemen who, in 1844, organized the New York Yacht Club, and he had retained his active interest in it to the day of his death.*[1]

Stevens and Schuyler, in fact, exemplified the club member described (in chapter 2 – *Down-under Plunder*) by Bus Mosbacher after the non-vote on the eligibility of *Australia II* when he said '… the club is made up of men who are sportsmen and gentlemen, and should deport themselves as such, even if they know they are being cheated or had'.

Stevens and Schuyler were close friends so it surprised nobody when, in 1850, the former invited the latter to be a member of the syndicate he was putting together to commission and build a new schooner – to be called *America* – that would cross the Atlantic and seek high-stakes matches against the cream of England's sailing establishment (Edwin A Stevens was another member of that syndicate).

America was designed by George Steers, who had made a reputation for himself with some of the fastest pilot boats of the day. Built at William H Brown's yard, on the Manhattan bank of the East River, at about 12th Street, her probable principal dimensions were 112 feet length overall (including bowsprit), 89 feet 10 inches on the waterline, 22 feet 10 inches beam, 11 feet draught and 10 tons displacement – *probable* because there were a number of versions of those figures and different measurements were achieved in different states of trim. Brown's quoted price to build her was $US30,000 but delays and renegotiation reduced that figure to $US20,000. Additionally, if *America* did not prove a winner, the syndicate need not accept her.

Her owners were John Cox Stevens, his brother Edwin A Stevens, Colonel James A Hamilton and his son-in-law George L Schuyler, Hamilton Wilkes (the NYYC's first vice-commodore) and non-yachtsman John K Beekman Finlay.

The New Yorkers were looking forward to a bit of sport, literally at the expense of the Brits, but they were also thrilled at the prospect of raining on Prince Albert's parade with a prime example of their embryo nation's emerging technological and manufacturing might (*America* would arrive in Britain in time for Prince Albert's 1851 Great Exhibition in London, the first international exhibition of manufactured products).

While under construction, the schooner was visited by the British ambassador, who mentioned the experience to his friend Lord Wilton, the commodore of the Royal Yacht Squadron in England. Wilton, in turn, wrote to *America*'s owners offering the club's hospitality if they did bring their schooner to Cowes, on the Isle of Wight, where the squadron was headquartered. Stevens replied and mentioned the 'sound thrashing we are likely to get by venturing our longshore craft on your rough waters'. The gamesmanship had begun!

America set sail across the Atlantic on 21 June 1851 and, on 11 July, arrived at Le Havre in France where she was joined by the Stevens brothers and Colonel and Mrs Hamilton, who had crossed the Atlantic by steamer. The schooner was spruced up for her debut in English waters and the opportunity was taken to replenish dwindling wine stocks in anticipation of the 'entertainment' that awaited in Cowes. She sailed for the Isle of Wight on 24 July, and the following day was making slow progress into the East Solent where she found, lying in wait for her, the crack English racing cutter *Lavrock*. The Royal Yacht Squadron might well have offered all hospitality but its members were not going to be caught napping when the inevitable wagers were negotiated. They wanted some indication of *America*'s capabilities.

The mood aboard *America* changed. The syndicate had been put on notice by a dubious *New York Tribune* editor, Horace Greeley, who had warned: 'The eyes of the world are on you; you will be beaten and the country will be abused, as it has in connection with the Exhibition … if you do go and are beaten, you had better not return to your country.' Now, here was *Lavrock*, tacitly laying down the gauntlet. Challenge equally tacitly accepted, the pair hardened up in a light westerly and, close-hauled, made all speed to Cowes. Before the brief skirmish was over, *America* had worked out from under and astern of *Lavrock* to a position ahead and to windward – attributes that every racing yachtie yearns for in his/her vessel.

Cox Stevens later wrote that they allowed *Lavrock* to get about 200 yards ahead and started in her wake. The schooner then slowly edged to windward of the cutter, sailed over the top of her rival, and beat her to Cowes by one-third of a mile after six miles of sailing. It was all a bit indecisive, because *America* was well burdened with the residue of her stores and equipment for the Atlantic crossing (not to mention the generous new supply of wines taken aboard in Le Havre), while *Lavrock* was (reportedly) towing her longboat tender. But there was no disguising *America*'s speed.

The British viewed the sleek, black-hulled visitor as 'piratical'. With her low freeboard, sharp clipper bow, wide beam amidships and full stern, she was completely different to everything they were used to, and there was immediate, wild speculation about her propulsion.

Waiting to welcome the Americans in Cowes were a number of officers and senior members of the Royal Yacht Squadron, among them the 83-year-old Marquess of Anglesey, a squadron stalwart since its founding in 1815. He was invited aboard *America* when she dropped anchor off West Cowes.

The Marquess, or Henry William Paget, was a formidable personage who had distinguished himself as a cavalry commander in a number of major battles, including the Flanders Campaign, in the French Revolutionary War, and the Peninsular War. In 1815, during the Hundred Days of Napoleon, Paget led the charge of the heavy cavalry against Comte d'Erlon's column at the Battle of Waterloo. One of the last cannon shots fired that day hit him in the right leg, which subsequently had to be amputated. Legend has it that the Duke of Wellington was close by at the time, and when Paget exclaimed: 'By God, sir, I've lost my leg!', Wellington replied, 'By God, sir, so you have!'.

According to his aide-de-camp, Thomas Wildman, during the necessary amputation of what was left of his 'lost' limb, Paget smiled and said, 'I have had a pretty long run. I have been a beau these 47 years and it would not be fair to cut the young men out any longer.' He had an articulated artificial limb fitted, and a few weeks after the battle was made Marquess of Anglesey.

Keen to discover the performance secrets of the Yankee schooner, the Marquess stumped around *America*'s deck, taking in the differences to the British norm, but he departed little the wiser in terms of where *America*'s speed came from. His son, Lord Alfred Paget, whose 56-ton cutter *Mona* would soon be racing against *America* was, however, heard to declare: 'If she's right, then we must all be wrong.'

By the time of *America*'s visit, our hero Lord Anglesey was a much-respected member of the Royal Yacht Squadron and, per his appointment as 'Captain of the Castle', was ensconced in his official residence, Cowes Castle – the imposing structure overlooking Cowes Roads on the north-westerly point of the Isle of Wight, built in 1539 as part of Henry VIII's chain of coastal defences against the French. The comforts of the fortification were upgraded in the 19th century to sumptuous country-house level.

Following Anglesey's death in 1854, and that of his successor Lord Raglan in 1855, the government reviewed the future of the castle and decommissioned it. It was then leased, first to Lord Conyngham and next to the Royal Yacht Squadron (RYS), whose old clubhouse was on the nearby site that is occupied today by the Gloster Apartments. The RYS first raised its burgee over the castle on 6 July 1858 and remains in residence to this day.

America's arrival attracted enormous interest, not only among yachtsmen, shipbuilders and boatmen of Cowes but also among the local population, and there was spirited debate about the lines of the visitor. *The Illustrated London News* said: 'As a model, she is artistic, although rather a violation of the old established ideas of naval architecture.' Word of the *America/Lavrock* encounter spread quickly and did not assist Stevens and his syndicate in their quest to line up some meaningful, high-stakes matches. For the next several weeks, the schooner languished in Cowes without a taker, moving a *Times* newspaper correspondent to observe that the reaction of English yachtsmen was like 'the agitation which the appearance of a sparrowhawk on the horizon creates among a flock of woodpigeons or skylarks', and to question their 'pith and courage' and their dedication 'to our national naval spirit'.

In an attempt to make a match more inviting, Cox Stevens offered to race any yacht for 'any sum from one to ten-thousand guineas'. James Steers, the brother of *America*'s designer, described the sum (the equivalent, perhaps, of $US800,000 today) as a 'staggerer'. Meanwhile, as *America* waited in vain for challenges, the rumours grew, and James Hamilton wrote of 'a very great impression at Cowes that *America* has a propeller, which is ingeniously concealed'.

More time slipped by, with Cox-Stevens spurning matches for purses or against opposition that he did not deem worthy until, with the end of the racing season not too far distant, he faced the prospect of returning to the USA without hoisting *America*'s sails in anger. Finally, he relented and accepted a Squadron invitation for *America* to contest the 53-mile Around the Isle of Wight race, which would be the final event in the club's annual five-day regatta. The date was to be Friday 22 August 1851. The race would be 'Open to Yachts belonging to the Clubs of all Nations' and there would be no time allowances (handicaps). At stake would be a new trophy, called 'The RYS £100 Cup' (the £100 refers to the cash prize that was also at stake, as opposed to being the price charged by Robert Garrard for the trophy's manufacture, as popular myth will later have it).

There has always been confusion about the trophy's original name. The promotional bills for the race appear to show what, since time immemorial, has been the recognised unit sign for the British pound. But the same sign was, whether correctly or not, sometimes also used for the guinea. It is quite feasible, therefore, that the RYS intended the cash prize at stake in the famous race to be 100 guineas for, in those days, a guinea was considered a more gentlemanly amount than £1; you paid tradesmen in pounds but gentlemen in guineas, although the two were not precisely interchangeable in terms of value.

To add even more confusion, the official website of the Royal Yacht Squadron refers to: '… the Royal Yacht Squadron's race round the Isle of Wight for a Cup of One Hundred Sovereigns' and notes that 'the Cup is often referred to mistakenly as the Hundred Guinea Cup, by which name it became known in America where it was subsequently engraved … the Americans seem to have used pounds (sovereigns) and guineas interchangeably.'

Whatever the prize money or the official name of the trophy, a total of 15 yachts – seven schooners and eight cutters – were at the start lines on that historic August day. There were two lines, one for the cutters and another, 300 yards to the west, for the schooners. Thousands of spectators lined the Cowes' foreshore and crammed the rails of the estimated 100 or so spectator yachts and passenger steamers that would follow the action.

The race started precisely at 10am with the yachts, as was the custom, anchored in pre-designated positions. The tidal current was strong and *America* rode over her anchor, with the result that she had trouble clearing it and was last away.

The first leg was downwind, heading east, and in very light airs *America* hooked into a building westerly and quickly caught the fleet ahead.

She was fifth around the first mark, No Man's Land buoy in the East Solent, and took the lead on the reach towards the Nab Lightship.

Next came a 15-mile upwind leg to St Catherine's Point at the most southerly tip of the Isle of Wight, then it was a reach in the English Channel to the Needles, at the western extremity of the island. *America* revelled in the upwind work and then the reach to the turn, through the Hurst Narrows, back into the waters of the Solent. A running log from the deck of *America* noted that the schooner rounded the Needles, 9 miles from the finish, at 5.40pm. Here, the wind dropped and the yachts began to struggle. It took the schooner until 8.37pm to reach Cowes and cross the finish line – a winner.

While passing Alum Bay, just inside the Needles, *America* encountered the royal yacht, the 223-foot *Victoria & Albert*, with Queen Victoria on board. *America* dipped her ensign and crew hats were doffed in a show of respect for the British monarch. Popular myth has it that Queen Victoria later asked who had won the race, and was advised that it was *America*. She then enquired who was second and was told, 'Ma'am, there is no second'. But there most certainly was a second, and a close one at that. The 84-foot cutter *Aurora* (Thomas Le Marchant), the smallest boat in the fleet, finished somewhere between 8 and 24 minutes after *America* (her finish time was not recorded accurately). It was almost dark, and *America*'s log had the gap at 20 minutes. Had the race been decided on handicap, *Aurora* might have won and, as a consequence, yachting history would be completely different.

Our friend the Marquess of Anglesey, so amazed by *America*'s performance, hurried aboard the schooner again, this time determined to spy the propeller that was the rumoured source of *America*'s speed. He hoisted himself over the transom for a better look into the waters at *America*'s stern but he was a touch too eager and overbalanced. Only a quick tackle of Anglesey's good leg by Cox Stevens saved the Marquess from a closer, wetter look at the schooner's supposed secrets.

Finally conceding that the Yankees had not cheated, Anglesey lamented: 'I've learned one thing. I've been sailing my yacht stern foremost for the last twenty years.'

Almost as a precursor of things to come in the controversy-fuelled future of the new trophy, there was a protest against the result of the race. The Solent, through which *America* was racing, is a comparatively

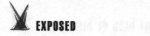

shallow stretch of tidal water that separates the Isle of Wight from the southern mainland of England. It is about 20 miles in length, varies in width between 2½ and 5 miles, and is strongly influenced by a unique tidal system: it experiences four tides per day and its tidal streams are frequently strong and complex, with a variety of concealed obstacles – submerged shingle banks, rocks and shoals – providing further navigational challenges. In its coverage of the big race, *The Times* newspaper described the course to be sailed as 'notoriously one of the most unfair to strangers that can be selected'.

The usual course, when racing clockwise around the Isle of Wight from Cowes, was to leave to starboard the Nab Lightship in the East Solent on the way out to the English Channel. The lightship marked the Nab Rock and reefs that fringe the Solent's deep-water eastern access/egress. However, there was nothing specific relating to this in the printed sailing instructions received by Robert Underwood, the British pilot recruited by the US Consul in Southampton to provide *America* with essential local knowledge of the tricky waters. The instructions given to *America* (and others in the fleet) only required contestants to round the Isle of Wight, inside No Man's Land buoy and Sandhead buoy, and outside the Nab. A different set of sailing instructions delivered to other contestants, however, required them to round the Nab Lightship.

America, in accordance with the course instructions delivered to her, rounded a white buoy, inside the lightship, shaving several miles off the distance sailed by those observing the 'usual' instructions. Among those that stood away to the north to round the Nab itself was the 392-foot three-masted schooner *Brilliant*, owned by George Holland Ackers. He protested against *America* for failing to go outside the lightship. When the facts emerged, however, Mr Ackers withdrew his protest and *America* was confirmed the winner.

In the year of her vaunted Great Exhibition, Britain had been humbled in her own special domain – the ocean – and one noted Englishman was quoted saying: 'We have had "Britannia Rules the Waves" over our door for a long time, but I think we must now take down the sign.'

News of the victory sparked unbridled celebration back in the USA where the orator and statesman Daniel Webster, in a speech to the

Massachusetts House of Representatives, proclaimed: 'Like Jupiter among the Gods, *America* is first and there is no second.'

Back on the Isle of Wight, where Queen Victoria had a summer home (Osborne House) near Cowes, the young monarch took the opportunity to visit the black schooner that was at the centre of so much attention, during which she appeared to be more concerned with cleanliness than with mythical propellers. She ran her handkerchief over a galley shelf and, when she saw that it was dustless, had every crew member issued with a gold sovereign and gave *America*'s skipper, Dick Brown, a gold watch.

Completely devoid of any sentimentality, Cox Stevens promptly sold *America* for £5,000 ($US25,000) to 39-year-old army captain John de Blaquiere (the 4th Baron de Blaquiere of Ardkill in Londonderry, Northern Ireland), and returned home to New York and a grand reception. He died just six years later, in June 1857, aged 72, but not before he'd persuaded the NYYC, in 1853, to vote for a prize of $US500 for the winner of a race 'open to yachts of all nations, provided one foreign yacht be entered for the race'. The proposed event did not occur but the seed was sown and the idea was resurrected in the year of Stevens' death.

The surviving members of the *America* syndicate soon tired of passing the '£100 Cup' around among themselves and some wanted to have the trophy melted down for commemorative medals so that all could have a memento of the 1851 victory. George Schuyler, however, was against this and proposed instead that the Cup be presented to the New York Yacht Club as a trophy intended to encourage international competition – a cause that had been hatched in lengthy discussion with the now deceased Cox Stevens. Their idea was to invite challenges from foreign yacht clubs to race for the trophy that was now, in the name of the winning schooner, known as 'America's Cup'. This proposal was accepted and Schuyler was given the responsibility of committing to paper the terms for the deliverance of the Cup to the New York Yacht Club – the Deed of Gift – that would be filed with the Supreme Court of the State of New York. His first version of that deed was written in 1852 but inadvertently not delivered to the NYYC until 1857.

Schuyler, at the behest of NYYC, then twice amended that Deed (in 1882 and 1887) and it is the latter (the 1887 Deed) that remains the authority in Cup affairs to this day (amended in 1956 only to accommodate smaller 12-Metre yachts in more austere times post-World War II).

The preamble to that version reads:

> *'This Deed of Gift, made the twenty-fourth day of October, one thousand eight hundred and eighty-seven, between George L Schuyler as the sole surviving owner of the Cup won by the yacht AMERICA at Cowes, England, on the twenty-second day of August, one thousand eight hundred and fifty-one, of the first part, and the New York Yacht Club, of the second part …'*

And the fundamental terms declare: *'This Cup is donated upon the conditions that it shall be preserved as a perpetual Challenge Cup for friendly competition between foreign countries. Any organized Yacht Club of a foreign country, incorporated, patented, or licensed by the legislature, admiralty, or other executive department, having for its annual regatta an ocean-water course on the sea, or on an arm of the sea, or one which combines both, shall always be entitled to the right of sailing a match for this Cup, with a yacht or vessel propelled by sails only and constructed in the country to which the Challenging Club belongs, against any one yacht or vessel constructed in the country of the Club holding the Cup …'*

A 1988 review by San Francisco attorney and yachting authority James Michael provided invaluable insight into the Deed and what Schuyler intended when he drafted and then amended the same. Michael was a former president of the United States Yacht Racing Union (USYRU) and legal counsel to the St Francis Yacht Club, as well as being a member of the New York Yacht Club in the 1970s and 1980s, and legal adviser to its America's Cup committee. An ardent student of the Deed of Gift, Michael had privileged access to the NYYC's library and its treasured documentation of the history of the Cup, including Schuyler's successive Deeds of Gift and his detailed letters explaining the reason for the various requirements and any changes made. He wrote:

> *The original gift of the Cup to the New York Yacht Club was made by the co-owners of the yacht America in a letter written in May 1852, but inadvertently not delivered to the Club until July 8 1857; thus, it is usually referred to as the 1857 Deed.*

A second deed, executed by the last surviving donor, George L Schuyler, dated January 4 1882, replaced the first, and, in turn, was replaced by the present deed, dated October 24 1887, again executed by George L Schuyler. It was amended in 1958, primarily to reduce the minimum waterline requirement to 44 feet so that 12-Metres could qualify.

To gain a correct interpretation of the present Deed and its application … requires not only a careful reading of its terms, but also an understanding of the reasons why the donors chose those terms and, as well, made changes in them over the years. Fortunately, the history of the Deed is well documented, particularly in the writings of the same George L Schuyler.

When the Deed and its history are thusly examined, it will be seen that the donors had an abiding concern that a challenger should have a fair and sportsmanlike match for the Cup. This concern stemmed initially from America's own experiences in England, as is chronicled in a letter by George L Schuyler published in the New York Spirit of the Times *on 15 April 1871.*

America had gone to England expecting to sail a match on mutually acceptable terms, with the best yacht the British could offer. Instead, because America roundly defeated one of their best in an informal skirmish during the last few miles as she approached Cowes, no one in England dared risk a match with her.

Finally, she was invited to race against 17 yachts of the Royal Yacht Squadron around the Isle of Wight (two of the 17 were, in fact, non-starters). That was the usual course for the annual regatta of the Squadron, a course, however, which Schuyler's letter states 'is notoriously one of the most unfair to strangers that can be selected, and, indeed, does not appear a good race ground to anyone, inasmuch as the current and tides render local knowledge of more value than swift sailing and nautical skill'.

America won that race and what became the America's Cup, and Schuyler observes that 'when the owners of the America *sat down, fresh from these experiences, to write their letter of gift', no candid person would think 'it very likely that any contestant for the Cup, upon conditions named by them, should be subjected to a trial such as they themselves had considered unfair and unsportsmanlike.'*

... *When Schuyler rewrote the Deed in 1882, he added a provision which protected a challenger from having to compete against more than one defender.*

In the original 1857 Deed, the donors sought to prevent a one-sided match in favor of the defender, as follows: 'The parties desiring to sail for the Cup may make any match with the yacht club in possession of the same that may be determined upon by mutual consent; but in case of disagreement as to terms, the match shall be sailed over the usual course for the annual regatta of the yacht club in possession of the Cup.'

The donors believed, Schuyler's letter continues, that if a challenger's proposals were not acceptable to the defending club, counter proposals would be made which 'would be satisfactory to any fair-minded sportsman', but failing that, 'We therefore could decide no better plan, for what we supposed would be resorted to only in the last extremity, than to name for the course over which a match should be sailed the one used by the club in possession for its annual regatta.'

A second consideration, in assuring fair treatment of the challenger, was a matter of self-interest. As Schuyler states, 'should we lose the Cup and go after it a second time', the New York Yacht Club, having then switched from defender to challenger, could avail itself of those protections.

In the matches up to 1887, many of the races were sailed on the New York Yacht Club's 'inside course', which included the waters from Hoboken to Southwest Spit. These confined waters and the currents, shifting winds and heavy traffic of New York Harbor made this course, in the words of Lawson's History of the America's Cup, *a 'bad course at best, and a source of hot anger and fierce discontent to British skippers'.*

When rewriting the Deed in 1887, George L Schuyler recognised that 'annual courses', such as the Royal Yacht Squadron's and the New York Yacht Club's 'inside course', did not guarantee a fair match; thus he deleted the reference to them. Nothing in the history, however, suggests that he intended to permit the venue to leave the defending club's home waters and, as already observed, the continuation of the qualifications required for a club to challenge suggest the contrary.

In a letter by George L Schuyler to the New York Yacht Club in July 1890, he comments on the reasons for the change in the definition of the courses, as follows: 'The matter which I thought of greatest importance,

*when the new deed was drawn up, was that of courses. I wanted it so
arranged that in case of a disagreement as to the conditions of the races,
the boats would race in the sea without time allowance, and thus avoid the
possibility of a challenger being left to the mercy of a club course where she
would not have an equal chance to win.'* [2]

It is clear, then, from the measures Schuyler took to protect the
challenger and to ensure fairness of racing for the America's Cup,
that the treatment the donors (the owners of *America*) experienced
in England still rankled greatly despite the passing of time. It is also
notable that, in the embryo days of its tenure of the Cup, the New
York Yacht Club had problems providing early challengers with
the fair contest that Schuyler envisioned and went to great lengths
to enshrine in his Deed. An air of retaliation prevailed, in which the
club and its members did not enhance their reputations for good
sportsmanship.

The first challenger, for instance, the British schooner *Cambria*, was
granted a one-race match only and had to compete against 17 NYYC
schooners on the club's unfair inside course. She was subjected to some
shameful interference by the massive spectator fleet in the confines of
the narrow harbour, and was soundly beaten. If that was good enough
for *America*, it was OK for *Cambria*, eh?

Then, when Ashbury returned a year later with *Livonia*, and
negotiated a one-on-one match, as Schuyler intended, in a best-of-
seven series, the NYYC again pulled a fast one by insisting it would
be represented by four of its best schooners and reserving the right
to select which one it would use on a given day. It was another
discreditable performance by the NYYC, and Ashbury, again on the
receiving end, returned to England convinced that the Americans had
dealt their cards off the bottom of the deck. An embarrassed George
Schuyler agreed with him and had to remind the club of its obligation,
under the Deed, to provide a challenger with a fair and sportsmanlike
contest, competing on equal terms. It would, however, be another 16
years and five challenges before Cup affairs achieved more equitable
foundations.

It is, though, also noteworthy that in the 147 years since the first
match in 1870 and through 35 challenges, the Deed has been before

the New York Supreme Court for interpretation and rulings on just four occasions. The respective orders of the Court are as follows:

> The Order of 17 December 1956 removed the requirement that contestants had to 'sail, on their own bottoms, to the port where the contest is to take place'; and reduced the minimum waterline length for single-masted vessels from 65 feet to 44. These changes were made to facilitate the switch to more affordable, smaller 12-Metre yachts post-World War II.
>
> The Order of 20 September 1984 (the so-called 'Arm of the Sea' interpretation) ruled that: 'Chicago Yacht Club is clearly a substantial club which conducts a major annual ocean-water race on Lake Michigan, a body of water included in the Great Lakes, which qualify either as seas or an arm of the sea.'
>
> The Order of 8 April 1985 accommodated the Royal Perth Yacht Club's win in 1983 by allowing Cup matches to be sailed in the southern hemisphere between 1 November and 30 April.
>
> The Order of 2 April 2009 ruled that a challenging yacht club, to be within the Deed's eligibility requirements, must have held at least one qualifying annual regatta before it submits its Notice of Challenge to a Defender, and that it will continue to have qualifying annual regattas on an ongoing basis.

To provide some perspective for all of the foregoing, when *America* raced around the Isle of Wight in 1851:

- It had been only 36 years since the Yankees secured their young country's freedom in the 1812–1815 war with Britain (the 'second war of independence'). In the process of that conflict, the Americans, with a new breed of big frigates designed and built in the former British colony, inflicted several notable victories at sea over the supposedly invincible Royal Navy.
- The completion of the American Transcontinental Railroad was still eight years in the future, so the pioneers were still pushing railway lines right across their part of what we now know as the North American continent, taming the still-wild frontier and, in the process, discovering and tapping the extraordinary natural wealth of this vast new land.

- The American Civil War was still 10 years in the future.
- It would be another 25 years before Lieutenant Colonel George Armstrong Custer and the Seventh Cavalry would meet their demise at the Battle of the Little Bighorn.

It should not, either, be overlooked that blue-water ocean racing, as opposed to offshore racing (as in the America's Cup), is said to have had its beginnings in the same period, and the wealthy and sportingly aggressive young men of New York were central figures, while gambling again was the instigating force.

In this particular instance, in the autumn of 1866, financier George A Osgood and tobacco baron (and racehorse aficionado) Pierre Lorillard Jr, after a most enjoyable dinner at the prestigious Union Club, started boasting about the relative merits of their racing yachts – Osgood's 106-foot, 206-ton, full-keeled schooner *Fleetwing* and Lorillard's 105-foot, 206-ton, centreboard schooner *Vesta*. Finally, they determined that there was only one way to decide which was the better – a race across the Atlantic for stakes of $US30,000 a corner, winner takes all.

When the 25-year-old James Gordon Bennett Jr learned of the race, he persuaded Osgood and Lorillard to accept his 107-foot, 225-ton, full-keeled schooner *Henrietta* as a third contestant – and the 'pot' swelled to an unbelievable $US90,000 ($US9–15 million in today's money).

Bennett was the son of newspaper magnate James Gordon Bennett Sr, a Scottish immigrant who, in 1835, founded *The New York Herald* newspaper, building it from the ground up and using blatant sensationalism to make it the most widely read daily in America. Bennett Jr took over control of the *Herald* in 1866 – the same year in which the famous first race across the Atlantic occurred.

It was said of Bennett Jr that, in an age of outlandish eccentrics, 'perhaps no high-society New Yorker was as consistently and astoundingly eccentric – or as influential – as James Gordon Bennett, Jr'. He first arrived on the New York scene as a teenager commanding a luxury yacht (courtesy of his father), and distinguished himself in the highly competitive yacht-racing scene as a very talented skipper and seaman. At age 16, he became the youngest ever member of the New York Yacht Club, and in 1861, now aged 20, volunteered his newly built schooner *Henrietta* for the US Revenue Marine Service during the Civil War (he was commissioned as a third lieutenant).

It didn't seem to matter much to Osgood and Lorillard, and now Bennett Jr, that they were proposing to race across one of the roughest stretches of water in the world (the North Atlantic), in the depths of winter and in low-freeboard race yachts, though the hulls of *Henrietta* and *Vesta* were strengthened, shelters were built over the cockpits and the tillers were replaced with worm-gear steering wheels. Bennett hired the very experienced Samuel 'Bully' Samuels to skipper *Henrietta*, while Osgood brought in Dick Brown, skipper of the schooner *America* in the 1851 Hundred Guinea Cup race in England. However, Brown resigned three days before the start of the race for being listed below the navigator, Albert Thomas, who took over as captain. *Vesta* was skippered by George Dayton.

The race began on 11 December 1866, just seven weeks after the Union Club dinner, with Bennett, now the publisher of *The New York Herald*, the only one of the three owners to actually sail the race. It would seem that it was worth the effort, for *Henrietta* won in 13 days, 21 hours and 55 minutes, finishing on Christmas Day 1866, and Bennett pocketed the $US90,000 purse.

Of that first transatlantic race, contemporary yachting author and sailing historian Captain Roland F Coffin, in his book *The History of American Yachting*, wrote:

> *The great race from Sandy Hook [December 1886] across the ocean to the Needles, Isle of Wight, was the most remarkable contest ever entered into either on land or water. That vessels of the size of these schooners should cross the ocean at any time of year, was considered somewhat hazardous, but that they should cross in the dead of winter, added immensely to the risk.*
>
> *Had they been especially prepared for an ocean voyage by having their spars reduced before starting, it would still have been considered something of a feat to have crossed the Atlantic in the month of December, but that they should start with racing spars and canvas to go across at racing speed, was something which all seamen would have considered imprudent.*
>
> *… It was the most remarkable yacht race ever sailed, whether as regards the length and nature of the course, the season of the year, the amount of*

money involved, or the result ... for it was this race which lifted American yachting to a level with any in the world, and placed the New York club on an equality with the Royal Yacht Squadron of Great Britain.[3]

Coffin went on to opine that, in those days, boat owners of the New York Yacht Club 'were practical yachtsmen; that is, they sailed or knew how to sail, their own craft':

As we have seen, American yacht owners had been yearly becoming more adventurous. The old club [inshore] course had become too limited for them, and they had laid out a race track, a part of which was on the ocean. This had not satisfied them, and they had sailed races of hundreds of miles out on the ocean entirely, and on one occasion the track of a race had encircled Long Island.

Of the proposed transatlantic race, Coffin observed:

It is said that this ocean match was originally made as an after-dinner inspiration over the wine; but although this might have been true as to two of the gentlemen engaged in it, it certainly was not as to the third, for he came in subsequently, and after there had been ample time for consideration. The probability is, that inasmuch as the two gentlemen who first made the match were enthusiastic yachtsmen and keen sportsmen, they needed no other inspiration than their own love of sport, and had no other.

Of the race itself, Coffin wrote:

We know that they had a fine, fair start, and the result shows how wonderfully well they were navigated. The Henrietta *won, having sailed 3,106 miles in thirteen days, twenty-one hours, fifty-five minutes. The* Fleetwing *was second, having sailed 3,135 miles, in fourteen days, six hours, ten minutes. The* Vesta *(fastest of the three) came last, having sailed 3,144 miles in fourteen days, six hours, fifty minutes. She was the only centreboard boat, and on the day before their getting in with the land, was ahead of both of the others; a blunder on the part of her navigator in not allowing sufficiently for the strength of Runnell's current, caused her to fall in to leeward of the Scilly Islands with a southerly wind, and a more cruel blunder of her channel pilot caused her to run past her port in the channel and lost her the second place, showing once more that 'the race is not always to the swift'.*

The worst fears of those who questioned the wisdom of racing across the North Atlantic in winter were vindicated when *Fleetwing*, at 9pm on 19 December, took a huge sea aboard while scudding before a hard gale. Eight crew were washed over the side, only two of whom were recovered. Coffin's somewhat inadequate comment was: 'The boat was then obliged to lay to for five hours, under her double-reefed foresail.'

In 1871, Bennett Jr became the commodore of the New York Yacht Club and, in that capacity, was embroiled in the machinations of the first challenger for the America's Cup, Britain's James Ashbury.

04

THE LITIGIOUS BRITS

The early challenges for, and the first 30 years of, the America's Cup were contentious to say the least, and generated a reputation for intrigue and disagreement that is still current today.

It probably is no coincidence that eight of the first ten challengers, between 1870 and 1899, were British, and that five of those challenges were wracked by controversy as a result. The Brits were probably still coming to terms with the fact that America was no longer a colony and old habits persisted – the former colonial 'masters' still seeking to deal down to their recent subjects. At the same time, the new Americans were likely to be prickly and sensitive, stubbornly intent on showing those former 'masters' that this was a brave new world in which the Brits no longer ruled.

Those positions and attitudes were very much in evidence in the challenges from England – by the cantankerous James Ashbury (1870 and 1871) and then again by the obdurate Earl of Dunraven (1893 and 1895). Sadly, these two gentlemen brought out the worst in a pretentious New York Yacht Club and so coloured the territory for their countrymen and the Cup as a sporting contest.

Both Ashbury and Dunraven certainly had some grounds for complaint about the defender, and had good points to make about how the new contest should be run, prompting important changes to the way things were done. However, the manner in which they conducted themselves clearly irritated the New Yorkers, who resisted all/any challenger input until they had asserted their authority – at which point they invariably made significant concessions.

In between their four Cup campaigns was the 1887 challenge of the Royal Clyde Yacht Club, which only added to the acrimony when it dragged through the mud the name and reputation of eminent Scottish yacht designer George L Watson.

JAMES LLOYD ASHBURY

Born in 1834, Ashbury's grandfather was a shoemaker but his father, John, turned his back on the family business and became a wheelwright – just when railways and railroad travel were really taking off. According to the website Grace's Guide to British Industrial History, 'in about 1840' John began business 'in a small way' at Knott Hill in Manchester, England, building railway wagons. Then, in 1847, he opened a large manufacturing facility at Openshaw, near Manchester and built railway carriages, in addition to wagons, under the name of the Ashbury Railway Carriage & Iron Company.

He was later joined in the business by his 16-year-old son, James, who had studied engineering for three years at what is now Victoria University, Manchester. They made a good combination – John concentrating on the core business, while James focused on new business development (international in particular) and marketing. Within ten years, the company was manufacturing railway axles, wheels and turntables as well as carriages and wagons, and grew into a force in the industry, in its prime employing more than 4,000 workers.

John died in 1866 and James inherited £400,000, along with the business. Like his contemporaries on the other side of the Atlantic, James was more liberal in his pursuits and spending than his deceased father. The young Ashbury was keen to circumvent the constraints imposed by Britain's unyielding class structure and unashamedly used his wealth and yachting challenges to further his political and business interests.

In 1867, he bought the 105-ton schooner *Leonora* to provide a leisure pursuit as a diversion from business, but young James was competitive and was soon eyeing more exciting sailing options than cruising. Accordingly, for the following season he ordered, from Michael Ratsey of Cowes, the 108-foot schooner *Cambria*, designed and built to be the fastest racing yacht afloat, showing that James had quickly and shrewdly come to recognise that ownership of such large yachts facilitated serious social advances, enabling him to join prestigious yacht clubs, including the Royal Thames and Royal Harwich. This provided him with a better social base from which to operate, particularly as he was interested in only the highest level of politics and had decided to run for parliament (he was unsuccessful with his first attempt, in 1868, but was persuaded to stand again in 1874, when he was elected for the Brighton constituency).

In 1870 Ashbury mounted, with *Cambria*, the first of his two challenges for the Cup, and followed up in 1871 with the newly built 127-foot schooner *Livonia*. Before his 1870 challenge, he beat his new friend and sporting rival James Gordon Bennett Jr in a race across the Atlantic, from Ireland to New York – Ashbury in *Cambria* and Bennett in his 124-foot schooner *Dauntless*.

Ashbury's dealings with the NYYC regarding the America's Cup were fractious from the start – he trying to ignore Schuyler's Deed of Gift and dictate his own terms, the club adhering strictly to Schuyler's conditions for a match. In October 1868, Ashbury wrote to NYYC inviting it to send to England the following year its champion schooner, to contest races organised by the Royal Yacht Squadron (of Cowes, Isle of Wight) and the Royal Victoria Yacht Club (of Ryde, Isle of Wight) before then racing across the Atlantic to New York against his yacht *Cambria*. On arrival, Ashbury would race the same American vessel around Long Island – two races out of three for the America's Cup. He also advised that, because they were shunned in England (as unseaworthy), he would not race against centreboarders.

The NYYC declined, on the grounds that Ashbury hadn't challenged in the name of a yacht club, as the Deed required, so he responded with the proposal that he would represent 'one of the several royal yacht clubs' of which he was a member but under certain provisions. If he were successful and took the Cup back to England, his defence would be over a 300-mile course 'in the (English) Channel or any other ocean'. Again, he was rejected, on this occasion because the NYYC judged that he was trying to circumvent the provisions in Schuyler's Deed and write his own.

By now it was August 1869 and, with nothing settled, there was not enough time left in the New York racing season to accommodate an Ashbury challenge. So, he notified the NYYC that *Cambria* would race *Dauntless* to New York in March 1870, which meant that he would be able to race for the Cup on 16 May of that year – 'over a triangular course from Staten Island, 40 miles out to sea and back' and '… no centreboarders'. Again, he was seen as trying to dictate his own terms for a match and NYYC told him that the club could not deviate from the provisions in the existing Deed. Oh, and by the way, those provisions specifically allowed for centreboarders, which were very much favoured for racing in New York, with its harbour shallows.

Ultimately, Ashbury had to accept that the inflexible NYYC was not going to change its stance on the Deed, so he nominated the Royal Thames as his yacht club and a match was scheduled for 8 August 1870. First, though, in July 1870, *Cambria* raced *Dauntless* from Kinsale, on the south-eastern coast of Ireland, to the Sandy Hook lightship, off the entrance to New York Harbor. She sailed the 'northern course' and completed the 2,917 miles to Sandy Hook in 23 days, 5 hours and 17 minutes, beating *Dauntless* by the very close margin of 1 hour, 43 minutes. *Dauntless*, sailing the slightly longer 'middle course', completed her 2,963-mile journey to Sandy Hook in 23 days, 7 hours. It should be noted, however, that two days into that journey, on 6 July, *Dauntless* had lost two crewmen overboard while endeavouring to take in a flying jib. This resulted in a ship's boat being launched, in huge seas, and crew searching for two hours before having to concede the task was hopeless and presume that the two men had drowned. Following this delay, which may have cost her the race, *Dauntless* resumed her journey. Back at the Sandy Hook finishing line on 27 July, the victor, Ashbury, now had just 12 days in which to prepare his vessels for the America's Cup match.

Monday 8 August 1870 – a day that had been 19 years in the making – saw the New York Yacht Club about to defend for the first time the trophy it won off the Royal Yacht Squadron in 1851, and there was vengeance in the air. *Cambria* was not racing one similarly sized opponent, as Schuyler envisaged when he wrote his Deed of Gift, but 17 schooners from the New York Yacht Club's fleet, including James Gordon Bennett Jr's *Dauntless*. If Ashbury wanted the America's Cup, *Cambria* was going to have to win it the hard way, just like *America*, by beating everything the defender could send against her. An indication of the feelings within NYYC on the chosen course of action was that only the then commodore, Henry G Stebbins, voted against it.

Cambria didn't stand a chance, even if she were the fastest schooner there – which she wasn't. That distinction went to Franklin Osgood's 84-foot centreboard schooner *Magic*, designed by Richard F Loper and skippered by Andrew Comstock. She led from start to finish and went down in history as the first successful defender of the Cup – the first in what would turn out to be a very long line. *Cambria* finished the race 27 minutes behind *Magic*, eighth across the line and tenth on corrected time. Her cause was not helped by some scandalous, drunken conduct in the huge spectator fleet, or by other contestants who clearly didn't know much, if anything, about yacht-racing rules.

New York Yacht Club historian John Rousmaniere later observed:

On the all-important first leg, she [Cambria] is put about half a dozen times while on starboard tack by boats on port tack, and a collision damaged her topmast shrouds. Her fore-topmast eventually broke and hit Ashbury a glancing blow. He did not protest, but Commodore Stebbins soon had a summary of the racing rules printed up and distributed to his squadron, many of whom barely knew starboard from port, much less that starboard tack had right of way. Owners then knew little about the rules and their professional skippers did not care.[1]

After all of his arguing and strangely arrogant behaviour throughout that long-running fracas over terms for the match, Ashbury took his defeat with a style that endeared him to New Yorkers, who loved a plucky underdog. He further enhanced that popularity when he accepted the NYYC's invitation to race the rest of the season in its fleet. The crowning moment in this unexpected upturn in his endeavours was to be accepted by the upper echelons of society when the US president, Ulysses S Grant, took breakfast with him aboard *Cambria*, at Newport, Rhode Island.

EXPOSED

While investigating railroads in the USA, before returning to England, Ashbury commissioned a new, bigger schooner from designer/builder Michael Ratsey. He was already planning a challenge in 1871 with what would be the 127-foot schooner *Livonia*, and it is almost as though he had also decided 'no more Mr Nice Guy', for he went after the NYYC on all fronts. His primary target was the Deed of Gift, which now, he told friends, he no longer regarded as a document worthy of 'an equitable, sportsmanlike interpretation'. Instead, he deemed it a 'purely legal construction'.

First up, he consulted lawyers and attacked the NYYC's interpretation of the word 'match'. Despite his lengthy endeavours to draw the NYYC into a one-on-one race for the Cup, he had already been the victim of the NYYC's rather contradictory interpretation of what Schuyler intended. He communicated his concerns to his friend James Gordon Bennett Jr, who was now the NYYC's commodore, and the club sought the advice of George Schuyler, who replied with:

> I think that any candid person will admit that when the owners of the America *sat down to write their letter of gift to the New York Yacht Club, they could hardly be expected to dwell upon the interpretation of the word 'match,' as distinguished from a 'sweepstakes' or regatta; nor would they think it very likely that any contestant for the Cup, under conditions named by them, should be subjected to a trial, such as they themselves had considered unfair and unsportsmanlike ... It seems to me that the present ruling of the club [to sail a fleet against a challenging vessel] renders the America's Cup trophy useless as a challenge cup ...*

Score one to Ashbury.

On 24 March 1871, the NYYC accepted Schuyler's interpretation but resolved 'that we sail one or more representative vessels, against the same number of foreign challenging vessels'. Schuyler must have been disappointed for, on 15 April 1871, he wrote to NYYC to chastise it for the 1870 defence against *Cambria*. In his letter, Schuyler expressed his strong convictions that the actions of the New York Yacht Club in requiring the lone British challenger to race against a large fleet of defending yachts was a clear departure from both the letter and spirit of the Deed of Gift.

He pointed out that the Deed calls for a 'match' and he emphasised the 'cardinal principle' that a match 'means one party contending with another party upon equal terms'. And he added: 'I cannot conceive of any yachtsman given six months' notice [then required] that he will cross the ocean for the sole purpose of entering into an almost hopeless contest for this Cup.' Score two to Ashbury, though strangely he accepted the NYYC proposal and immediately tackled other terms in the Deed that he would have liked changed – including the requirement for a challenger to give six months' notice of a proposed match.

By May of 1871 the NYYC might then have been excused if it considered the worst to be over with and everything now in order. Not on your life. Ashbury was just catching his breath and on 12 August, with *Livonia* about to depart for New York, he hit NYYC with another proposed departure from Schuyler's Deed that was an obvious response to NYYC's ploy to use more than one defender.

He wrote to advise that he would arrive as the representative of 12 clubs and proposed that he would sail one race for each of those clubs. He again refused to race against a centreboard defender and suggested that, since NYYC's fleet included a number of racing-keel yachts of the same size or larger than *Livonia*, the club should select one that was as close as possible to *Livonia* and use that vessel for its defence. If *Livonia* won a majority of the races, the Cup would go to the club under whose flag he sailed the last race.

Now he really was dictating to the NYYC, and he went further still, telling the NYYC that its club course was unfair for a foreign yacht and should be discarded, proposing 'we sail from a mark boat off Sandy Hook Point, three times around the Sandy Hook Lightship and back'. This time, it was the NYYC's turn to surprise. It agreed to 12 races (or any other number that might be mutually agreed) while rejecting the multiple-club proposal on the grounds that Ashbury's challenge was in the name of the Royal Harwich Yacht Club only.

Moreover, there was a sting in the tail of NYYC's agreement. It gave Ashbury what he was seeking in terms of a one-on-one match race but advised that NYYC would be represented by four schooners from its fleet and, only on the morning of a given race, would it decide which of the four defenders it would use on that day.

Ashbury was winning some battles but he was losing the war and, ultimately, he accepted a best-of-seven match, in the name of Royal Harwich Yacht Club – *Livonia* against any one of the four nominated NYYC schooners – racing alternately on the club's course and the outside course that Ashbury had laid down (20 miles to windward and return).

If the contest had been lively on the shore, it really hotted up when they finally got racing, in a match between Ashbury's 127-foot keel schooner *Livonia* against whichever was chosen of NYYC's nominated yachts: *Columbia* (Franklin Osgood), a 108-foot centreboard schooner; *Dauntless* (James Gordon Bennett Jr), a 124-foot keel schooner; *Sappho* (William Douglas), a 134-foot keel schooner; and *Palmer* (Rutherford Stuyvesant), an 111-foot centreboard schooner.

The first race was in light winds on the 35-mile NYYC course. The NYYC selected Osgood's light-airs flyer, *Columbia*, which led from start to finish and won by 25 minutes, 18 seconds across the line, and 27 minutes, 4 seconds on corrected time.

It was blowing a moderate gale for race two – a 40-mile windward-leeward race – and, surprisingly, *Columbia* again got the nod to defend. For some reason, the race committee set a course that was 10 miles shorter than that agreed and, worse, the printed race instructions did not specify how the yachts were to round the single turning mark. *Columbia*'s owner, Franklin Osgood, noticing the rounding omission, checked with the committee boat and was told to leave the mark on either hand. The same instructions weren't, however, given to Ashbury, who decided to leave the mark to starboard, as was the norm in England when specific directions were not provided.

The wind backed after the course had been laid so that the race became a broad reach, on port, followed by a fetch back, on starboard. Arriving at the turn with a 1 minute, 10 second lead, Ashbury duly left the mark to starboard and, in boisterous conditions, executed a long, slow gybe to minimise the considerable danger to his spars and sails. *Livonia* emerged well to leeward of the mark and hard on the wind for the return leg. *Columbia*, in turn, left the mark to port and simply tacked around to head into the return leg nicely to windward of her rival with sheets slightly started. It was all over. She sailed straight on by *Livonia* to win by 5 minutes, 16 seconds across the line and 10 minutes, 35 seconds on corrected time.

Predictably (and correctly), Ashbury protested. *Livonia* was in a position to win but for the decisive mark rounding. The race committee first tried to claim that the instructions given were clear, but that was obviously not the case. Then it tried to defend itself with a lengthy and immaterial dissertation on the controversy over whether *America* should have rounded the Nab Lightship in the 1851 race. Bewilderingly, the race result stood and *Livonia*, officially, was 0–2 down in the match. Ashbury, however, was keeping his own scorecard and had it all even 1–1.

More strong winds for race three – a 35-miler on the NYYC course – and all four defenders were in a mess, springing leaks, straining masts and blowing out sails in the willing conditions. And that was before the start, by when only Osgood's *Columbia* was a going concern and she hadn't got a full racing complement. A scratch crew was thus drummed up and *Columbia* was sent out to meet *Livonia*. Her sails weren't reefed, despite the near-gale, and what followed was almost inevitable. *Columbia* broached and staggered around the race track, nearly capsizing, breaking rigging, blowing out sails and badly scaring her crew, until her steering broke and she lay rolling helplessly in the rough seas.

The crew used axes to break open the steering box and rig an emergency tiller so she could get underway again, but by now *Livonia* was a speck in the distance ahead. *Columbia* limped home 19 minutes, 33 seconds behind the challenger, 15 minutes, 10 seconds astray on corrected time. That was it for *Columbia*; William Douglas's *Sappho* took over for the next two strong-wind encounters. It was 2–1 in the match on the official scorecard (1–2 on Ashbury's).

Race four was another 40-mile windward-leeward race, which *Sappho* won by 30 minutes, 36 seconds across the line and 30 minutes, 21 seconds on corrected time.

Race five – another 40-miler, but this time on the NYYC course – was won by *Sappho* again, by 26 minutes, 36 seconds across the line and 25 minutes, 27 seconds on corrected time. That should have been the match – 4–1 to the American defenders – but no, Ashbury didn't agree. He still believed that *Livonia* had won the second race because of *Columbia*'s incorrect mark rounding, so the score now stood at 3–2 in the defender's favour. He advised the NYYC that he would be at the start line on the following day, ready for the next race, and would sail over the course of 20 miles to windward (or leeward) and return, whether or not there was any yacht to meet him. Moreover, he would do the same on the day after that.

The following day, 24 October, *Livonia* raced a private match against the NYYC commodore's schooner, *Dauntless*, over a 20-mile windward-leeward course and was beaten by 10 minutes, 31 seconds. One can only wonder what Machiavellian games Bennett was playing, but Ashbury claimed that because *Dauntless* was not an entry nominated by the club, he had sailed over the appropriate course alone and could claim the race. Accordingly, on his card the score was now 3–3.

The next day, 25 October, saw another private encounter between *Livonia* and *Dauntless*. Wind and seas were up to a stage at which the mark boat couldn't leave the harbour. Ashbury advised the club that this meant another win for *Livonia* since there was no boat on the line to meet him. Thus he had won the America's Cup by beating the defender, 4–3. Where's my trophy?

Singularly unimpressed, the NYYC acknowledged receipt of his letter without comment and turned its back on the troublesome Englishman, who in the space of 12 months had gone from hero, breakfasting with the president, to zero, heading home dubbed an inappropriate social climber.

Back in England, Ashbury published a paper outlining all the wrongs to which he felt he had been subjected in New York. To the copious amount of correspondence between him and the NYYC, he added an opinion written by a person claiming to have been illegally wronged by the same unsportsmanlike organisation. This was a bridge too far for the NYYC, which had put up with more than its share of Ashbury's questionable behaviour. It thus wrote to the Royal Harwich Yacht Club and to the Royal Yacht Squadron refuting Ashbury's allegations, accusing Ashbury in its letter to the Royal Harwich of behaving in an ungentlemanly manner, causing offence: 'He looked for an unworthy motive behind every action and for evidence of concealment and lack of candour behind every explanation.'

Coincidentally, Ashbury seemed to have had enough of yachting – or certainly of the America's Cup. He focused again on politics and business, winning and then losing a seat in parliament and travelling widely. In the course of those travels, in the spring of 1883, he visited

New Zealand, liked what he found and planned to return to buy land and become a sheep farmer. Storm clouds of a different kind were gathering.

Using promissory notes, Ashbury bought an estate on the outskirts of Christchurch in the South Island and, mysteriously, sent out a musician by the name of Zimmer to manage the newly acquired property. The appointment was a disaster and, by the late 1880s, the farm was unsustainable as a business and heading into bankruptcy. Ashbury, trying to sort things out from faraway Britain, withheld payment on his promissory notes and ended up embroiled in legal proceedings, in Britain and New Zealand, with the man who had sold him the estate. These proceedings dragged on for the best part of five years and, by the mid-1890s, Ashbury's finances were shot and his health began to suffer because of the stress he was under. He died on 3 September 1895, in much-reduced circumstances.

SCOTTISH PRICKLES

The 1887 challenger, another from the UK, was a 108-foot 6 inch-cutter designed by George L Watson and owned by a Royal Clyde Yacht Club syndicate, headed by the club's vice-commodore, James Bell. She was skippered by Scotsman John Barr, whose younger brother, Charlie, was also on the crew. Charlie later emigrated to the USA and went on to achieve legendary Cup status by helming three consecutive successful NYYC defenders.

Like *Australia II* some 96 years later, *Thistle* raised the hackles of the New York Yacht Club when she was built behind extremely tight security, and finally emerged from her boatshed with her underwater shape and keel completely hidden by a timber-and-canvas structure that, according to one observer, made her look like 'a big, white, oblong box'. Watson went to these lengths in order to keep secret, for as long as possible, *Thistle*'s all-important waterline length and, once he had arrived in New York, he cleverly fed the flames of acute media and public interest by planting the lines of others of his designs.

The New York Yacht Club had been promised only that the challenger's waterline length would be 85 feet. It was then outraged when, as usual, both yachts were officially measured prior to the event and it transpired that the challenger's waterline length, instead of the promised 85 feet, was in fact 86.46 feet.

NYYC historian John Rousmaniere later wrote:

> *Perhaps if the Scots had been less blatantly secret about their boat, the yacht club would have reacted more calmly; after all, the time allowance system would easily compensate for the difference. But the issue seems to be larger than mere measurements ... honour, trust, and, if we may be a little cynical, the New York Yacht Club's control over the America's Cup are at stake, and the British – especially George Watson – are allowed to feel the full chill of the club's cold fury.*[2]

Moreover, just as happened 96 years later when Keelgate rocked the event, some club members even suggested cancelling the match.

George Schuyler was called in to investigate. The now 76-year-old elder statesman of the Cup decided that, while there had been 'remarkably inaccurate information' provided by Watson, there was no evidence of intentional dishonesty on the part of *Thistle*'s owners. There followed some caustic opinion pieces in the local press but the furore died down and attention switched to the eagerly awaited clash between what, on paper anyway, appeared to be two very well-matched vessels. Sadly, that didn't prove to be the case.

Thistle's opponent was the 107-foot centreboard cutter *Volunteer*, the latest and greatest from Boston designer Edward Burgess, skippered by the formidable Hank Haff. Burgess had already produced two successive, successful defenders for General Charles J Paine and his Bostonian followers, who mounted the defence in the name of NYYC – the 94-foot centreboard cutter *Puritan*, in 1885; and the 100-foot cutter *Mayflower*, in 1886. Paine, a general in the Union Army during the American Civil War, was another who had made his personal fortune in railroads. A keen and knowledgeable yachtsman, he managed his sailing campaigns with military precision in what came to be regarded as the forerunner of modern America's Cup defence operations.

In race one, in the best-of-three match, the wind averaged only 8 knots, putting local knowledge on the NYYC's inshore course at a premium. *Volunteer* trounced *Thistle* by 19 minutes, 28 seconds across the line and 19 minutes, 23 seconds on corrected time.

In race two, a 40-mile windward-leeward race on the 'outside' course in 12 knots of wind and a considerable sea, the margins were 11 minutes, 55 seconds across the line and 11 minutes, 49 seconds on corrected time, again in favour of *Volunteer*. On the 20-mile beat to windward, the boats were equally matched in terms of speed, but *Volunteer*, with superior sails, was consistently pointing higher. On the 20-mile downwind return leg, *Thistle* was faster by 2 minutes, 25 seconds but couldn't claw back all the time lost to the beamier, lighter centreboarder on the beat. General Paine was now the first defender in the Cup's short history to win three defences in a row.

George Watson explained the loss by saying that he had cut *Thistle*'s underbody away excessively, seeking to reduce wetted surface and so resistance through the water. As a result, *Thistle* made too much leeway when pressed by her immense sail area.

COMETH THE EARL

While George L Watson's waterline length error was undoubtedly an embarrassing mistake on the part of the highly regarded Scot, there was nothing accidental about the unprecedented controversies generated by the next two British challenges (in 1893 and 1895), or about the ruthless manner in which the challenger, the Irish-Anglo nobleman the Earl of Dunraven, went about his business, even accusing the New York Yacht Club of cheating.

Windham Thomas Wyndham-Quin, the 4th Earl of Dunraven and Mount-Earl, KP PC (12 February 1841–14 June 1926), styled Viscount Adare between 1850 and 1871, was a man of many parts: Irish landowner, racehorse breeder, Oxford graduate, Conservative politician, soldier, war correspondent, entrepreneur, adventurer, sportsman, yacht designer and environmentalist. At age 26, after serving as a lieutenant in the 1st Life Guards cavalry regiment, he became a war correspondent for London's *Daily Telegraph* and covered first the Abyssinian War (1867–1868), then the Franco-Prussian War (1870–1871). He subsequently served with distinction on active duty in the Boer War (1899–1902).

Dunraven succeeded his father in the earldom in 1871, inheriting the 39,000-acre Adare Manor estate at Adare, County Limerick.

He took his seat in the House of Lords the same year and was Under-Secretary of State for the Colonies from 1885 to 1886 and again from 1886 to 1887.

The earl was an avid hunter of wild game and, in 1872, visited America where he met and befriended 'Buffalo Bill' Cody and 'Texas Jack' Omohundro, who acted as his guides on buffalo and elk hunts. In his autobiography, *Past Times & Pastimes* (published in 1922 by Hodder & Stoughton), Dunraven said: 'I must certainly have arrived in this world with strong proclivities for open spaces and the "out of doors". The rolling prairies and the ocean have always appealed strongly to me.'

In particular, the young earl loved the American north-west, with its endless great plains and good hunting – so much so that in 1874 he decided to make the whole of Estes Park, in Colorado, his own private hunting preserve. By stretching the provisions of the Homestead Act and pre-emption rights, Dunraven claimed 15,000 acres in the present-day Rocky Mountain National Park, endeavours that came to be described as 'one of the most gigantic land steals in the history of Colorado'.

His land grab ran into a lot of opposition as more and more settlers arrived and disputed what he was doing, but he controlled 6,000 acres before he changed direction and ventured into tourism. In 1877, he opened the area's first resort, the landmark Estes Park Hotel, which was an early version of a Dude Ranch.

Despite the success of this venture, in the late 1880s a disillusioned Dunraven turned his back on the area and left for good. This abrupt about-face, walking away from something that he had mastered or just grown tired of, seems to have been a personality trait. There is ample indication in his biography of a highly competitive, multi-talented and fiercely focused individual who didn't do things by halves. There are also hints of 'it's my way or the highway', as evidenced by his land grab and tourism excursions.

Of one of the early examples, Dunraven wrote:

I loved music, the violin. On that divine instrument I became fairly proficient, and came near to devoting my life to it. But the sea was the master-passion, and one fine day I had to come to a momentous decision.

The violin requires suppleness and delicacy of the hands and fingers, and handling ropes, rowing, and other outdoor games and sports are incompatible with that necessary condition. It was not easy to decide but after a struggle, the tarry rope beat the fiddle-string, and I never touched the violin again.

So, given his competitive nature, when Dunraven turned irrevocably away from the prairies and focused again on his love of the sea and sailing, it was no surprise that his focus was now on racing yachts for all he was worth and, ultimately, competing for the sport's great prize – the America's Cup.

Dunraven first sailed rented boats on the River Isis while an undergraduate at Oxford University. He then bought 'a disused Cardiff pilot boat' 'for a very small sum' and fitted her out 'partially'. He joined the Royal Cork Yacht Club – 'the oldest yacht club in the three kingdoms' – and purchased a small cruising yacht, called *Windsor*, which he rechristened *Cripple* – 'because I was continually getting ashore and having to hold her up on two wooden legs'.

He was perfectly content just mucking about in boats and developing seamanship and boat-handling skills. With a couple of mates as regular crew, he explored the coastlines of Devon and Cornwall and then ventured as far afield as the Channel Islands and the west coast of Ireland. At this juncture, he discovered the plains of North America and his energies found a new direction: 'The sea treated me very well – it always has; but I gave it a long rest. Other interests, other pursuits arose, and it was not 'til many years later that the sea called to me again.'

When he got that call, as was his wont, he studied yacht design and became an accomplished, if amateur, naval architect. He worked his way up through a succession of yachts, some of which he designed himself, until in 1888 he challenged for the America's Cup in his first *Valkyrie* – 'a composite ship, 75 feet on the waterline. I was in hope of a race for the America's Cup for 75-footers, but it was declined. I don't know why; possibly for a good reason.'

Dunraven, surely, would have known that reason. His challenge was through the Royal Yacht Squadron and he chose to assume that, if successful, he and the RYS would not have to enforce the terms of the NYYC's Deed of Gift. There was a lengthy trail of correspondence between the RYS, then Dunraven, and the NYYC, in which the earl ultimately admitted to being ignorant of a new edition of the Deed, enacted by George Schuyler on 24 October 1887 [the 'Third Deed'], and apologised to the RYS for inadvertently misleading the club.

It is difficult to understand how a man of letters such as Dunraven, a war correspondent to boot, could be guilty of such an oversight. The Deed is fundamental to the contest, always has been, and Dunraven surely knew that. Was he, then, trying it on even before having a challenge accepted? When the NYYC advised the Squadron that the assumption was quite wrong, the challenge was withdrawn, and nothing more was heard from the earl until he again challenged for a match in 1893.

The 1887 Deed was the result of the NYYC realising that arrangements for America's Cup matches would need to be a lot more formal, with the requirements of the Deed of Gift clarified, so as to pre-empt future controversy or, at least, nip it in the bud. The club appointed a committee, including three-times Cup winner General Charles Paine, to draft a new version of the Deed for George Schuyler to approve and sign.

While the two originals were mere informal letters of transfer, the Third Deed was a legal document clearly drafted by lawyers and full of contractual legalese. It also contained some new requirements: the notice-of-challenge period was increased from six months to ten months; centreboarders would always be eligible; and the contentious NYYC inside course was dumped. From now on, all Cup races would be sailed on ocean courses free of headlands.

One other important change attracted the most adverse reaction. In order for the defender to better match the vessel challenging, and ensure fairer competition, the NYYC (and any future trustee of the Deed) would henceforth require not just the waterline length of that vessel but also its draught, waterline beam and extreme beam. There was strong criticism of this, on both sides of the Atlantic, based on the view that a challenger would be giving away all of his performance features before, perhaps, his boat had even been built. Despite this, the invariably fair-minded Schuyler signed off the new edition and it became law as far as all future challenges were concerned (and still is today).

Dunraven, however, really was ignorant of all this, or he chose to ignore the Deed's fundamental role in achieving 'friendly competition between foreign countries'. In either case, he embarked on a lengthy and complex exchange of correspondence with NYYC that left the club dumbfounded by his proposals to sidestep the Deed and agree new terms for a match. His seemingly endless raft of proposals included one to have three Americans and three Englishmen meet at a suitable location – Paris might suit – to determine new rules and draw lots to decide a new race venue. The earl, of course, got nowhere and ended up where he should have started – accepting the Third Deed as the terms and conditions for his match.

And so, in October 1893, Dunraven's 117-foot, George Watson-designed cutter *Valkyrie II* went to the start line off New York against the NYYC's 124-foot Nathanael Herreshoff-designed centreboard cutter *Vigilant*, managed by wealthy New York banker/yachtsman C Oliver Iselin.

The outcome was 3–0 in the defender's favour. The first two races were relatively easy for *Vigilant*, which won the first by 7 minutes, 36 seconds across the line (5 minutes, 38 seconds on corrected time) and the second by 12 minutes, 23 seconds (10 minutes, 35 seconds on corrected time), without being at all stretched. She was, however, really put to the test in race three. Both yachts had gear problems heading out to the course and the start was delayed an hour, by which point it was blowing 20 knots and gusting higher. The deep-keeled *Valkyrie II* had the edge over her centreboard rival on the 15-mile upwind leg and led at the turning mark by 1 minute, 55 seconds. It was now blowing 25 knots for the 15-mile run home, and *Vigilant* threw caution to that increasing wind. Shaking out the reef in her main and piling on more sail, she tore off after the earl, with her mast bending scarily under the strain. She stormed past *Valkyrie II*, which had already blown out two spinnakers, and won by 2 minutes, 13 seconds across the line and by just 40 seconds on corrected time. *Vigilant* averaged nearly 12 knots and was 4 minutes, 8 seconds faster than *Valkyrie II* down that crazy final leg, causing the huge crowd of spectators to go wild. It was game, set and match and the America's Cup as an exciting sporting spectacle had finally come alive. The earl could go home with his head held high and his intransigence at least temporarily forgotten.

It didn't, however, take his lordship long to burst that bubble. His incessant letter writing began almost immediately with Dunraven lamenting (legitimately in this instance) the spectator fleet interference to which *Valkyrie II* had been subjected in the 1893 match. The NYYC later took meaningful steps to address this continuing embarrassment, but it was much less accommodating when Dunraven tried once more to circumvent the Deed and negotiate different terms for a second challenge.

Again, the earl's various proposals were rejected and, on 6 December 1894, the Royal Yacht Squadron, on his behalf, tendered an unconditional challenge under the terms of the Third Deed. This was accepted by NYYC on 14 January with the date for the first race set for 7 September 1895. Dunraven's challenger this time was the 129-foot George Watson cutter *Valkyrie III*, a big, Yankee-style skimming dish that turned out to be some 3 feet beamier than the defender.

Nathanael Herreshoff designed the NYYC's yacht, which was the 125-foot cutter *Defender*, and C Oliver Iselin was again the campaign manager. *Defender* was a narrower-keel yacht and was the first non-centreboarder to represent the USA in the Cup since *America* herself in 1851. It's almost as though the pair had swapped opposite ends of the design spectrum and this added to the already great interest in the best-of-five series, prompting the NYYC to appeal to 'those in charge of vessels attending America's Cup races' to keep at least half a mile away from the competing yachts, even when to leeward of them, to leave a clear space of at least half a mile around the start line and a quarter mile at turning marks, and to observe the instructions of patrol boats flying white flags. The club's pleas, however, fell on deaf ears and the race yachts were badly hampered when they went to the line for the start of race one, when it seemed like the whole of the city of New York wanted a ringside seat on the water.

That first race, on 7 September 1895, started in a 6–8-knot easterly breeze and there was little between the two yachts on the upwind leg. *Defender* led around the mark by 1 minute, 56 seconds and stretched out downwind to win by 8 minutes, 20 seconds across the line and 8 minutes, 19 seconds on corrected time.

Dunraven complained to the NYYC's America's Cup committee that, in his opinion, *Defender* was floating 3–4 inches lower in the water than when she was officially measured for the match. He claimed that the resultant increase in her waterline length was a significant 'three to four feet' and he believed the change had been made without the knowledge of *Defender*'s owners. Given that a boat's speed is a function of its waterline length, these were serious assertions.

Dunraven demanded an immediate re-measurement and the following day, Sunday 8 September, the vital statistics of the two yachts were checked again. The differences identified were negligible. *Defender*'s waterline was ⅛in longer than it was when it was recorded on official measurement day, while *Valkyrie III*'s was 1⁄16in longer – meaningless numbers in terms of relative performance.

Race two, on 10 September, was a triangular course with 10-mile legs. There was a light southerly breeze for the start and both yachts were reaching hard for the line, on starboard tack, when they were baulked by a steamer in their path. *Valkyrie III* held up to windward, to pass across the bow of the interloper, while *Defender* took her stern. When the pair closed again, they were level and travelling at the same speed, and a coming together seemed unavoidable.

Valkyrie III luffed hard to avoid contact, but it was too late. The end of her main boom hooked *Defender*'s topmast shroud and wrenched the wire rope out of the end of the spreader. As the unsupported spar bent off to leeward, a protest flag was immediately displayed. *Valkyrie III* continued on her course and crossed the start line 1 minute, 2 seconds ahead of her wounded rival. She rounded the top mark with a lead of 2 minutes, 50 seconds, the breeze having freshened to 10 knots.

Despite her damage, *Defender* gained slightly on the tight reach that followed and, after the gybe at the final mark, was then able to set full sail and make big inroads on the broad reach to the finish. *Valkyrie III* held on, though, and won by 1 minute, 16 seconds across the finish line (47 seconds on corrected time).

At the ensuing protest hearing Dunraven claimed that the overtaking *Defender* caused the pre-start collision by luffing into *Valkyrie III*. Photographic evidence, however, proved him wrong and the protest committee ruled in favour of *Defender*. Iselin sportingly offered Dunraven a re-sail but the offer, correctly, was declined. The protest committee, having awarded the race to *Defender*, could not possibly recognise a rerun. That evening, Dunraven advised the NYYC committees that, unless the course was properly cleared, he would not sail the next race.

Two days later, on 12 September, in very light and shifty airs, the scheduled start of race three was delayed by 15 minutes. At the 5-minute gun for the restart, *Valkyrie III* was cruising around the line with minimum sails bent on. There was little happening on her deck although the earl was visible, scanning the scene through binoculars. At the start gun, *Defender* set a spinnaker and managed to fill it. *Valkyrie III* ambled up to the line under mainsail and jib only, luffed slowly around the lightship and headed back into New York Harbor. For her, the match was over. *Defender* sailed the course and finished just inside the six-hour time limit to claim a 3–0 victory.

A disillusioned Dunraven returned to England and vented his spleen in a long communication that was published in the yachting pages of *The Field* (a country and sports magazine) on 9 November 1895. He again pointed the finger at *Defender*'s waterline length.

The Times of London took Dunraven's side and thundered: 'The general impression … is that no efforts, however strenuous, except on the part of the Cup trustees could possibly secure a fair race under conditions on which they feel themselves bound to insist … It is a most unpleasant story.'

The Sun, in New York, came out strongly against the earl, claiming: 'The people of the United States will ask for no refutation of Dunraven's slanderous and blackguardly suggestions of actual cheating by the syndicate that owns the *Defender*. He is a quitter and cad and should be expelled from the New York Yacht Club.'

The earl's allegations of irregularities in the measurement of *Defender* caused outrage in the NYYC and the club acted swiftly to clarify matters, calling a special meeting on 18 November to review the situation. The clubhouse was packed and the members appointed a high-powered committee 'to represent NYYC and take any action that is proper' in the matter. That committee included pillars of New York society, such as banker J Pierpont Morgan (who would become club commodore two years later), a fact that reflected the club's concern.

When advised of these developments, Dunraven cabled his intention to sail for New York on 8 December aboard the *Germanic*, to appear in person before the committee. The Royal Yacht Squadron was also notified of the investigation and was asked if it would stand by Lord Dunraven or repudiate the charges he had made. The RYS declined to be involved. The controversy, it replied, was a personal matter for Dunraven.

Among the expert witnesses summoned by the committee were naval architect Nathanael Herreshoff and consulting engineers. The former had calculated that it would take 13 tons of additional lead ballast to sink *Defender* enough to lengthen her waterline by a foot, and the absurdity of Dunraven's claims became apparent. Iselin was thus cleared and Dunraven, on 19 February 1896, resigned his NYYC membership.

It transpired that, on 10 September, after the dramatic events of race two, the earl had put pen to paper to advise the NYYC's America's Cup Committee: '… it is with great reluctance that I write to inform you that I decline to sail *Valkyrie III* any more under the circumstances that have prevailed in the last two races.' He described conditions on the start line, pressed by moving steamers in the same space as the race yachts, as 'exceedingly dangerous' and he would not again 'risk the lives of my men or the ship'. Dunraven added that:

> '… today on the reach home, eight or nine steamers crossed my bow. Several were to windward of me and, what was worse, a block of steamers were steaming level with me, and close under my lee. I sailed nearly the whole distance in broken, tumbling water in the heavy wash of those steamers. To race under those conditions is, in my opinion, absurd and I decline to submit myself to them again.'

It would seem, however, that the spectator fleet issues, scandalous as they had become, were not the main reasons for Dunraven's discontent. He was inwardly seething that the race two start line protest decision had gone against *Valkyrie III*, maintaining that *Defender*, the overtaking boat, had been in the wrong. But even that wasn't his main source of unhappiness. That lay in his utmost belief that *Defender* had been re-ballasted following her official measurement prior to the start of the match, and that he and others in his entourage had witnessed that re-ballasting. As a result, he was 'positively certain she was sailing at least a foot beyond her proper length'.

This was a serious claim. If Dunraven was to be believed, the Americans had disdainfully added weight to increase performance, after the yachts had been officially measured. In other words, the Americans had cheated and, again, if Dunraven was to be believed, this had taken place without the knowledge of *Defender*'s owners. If that was in fact the case, who authorised or ordered the changes? Even if you ignored the potential consequences in terms of standing and reputation in society, loading 13 tons of illicit ballast aboard a race yacht and into her bilges is not a straightforward undertaking; it would require a high level of duplicity, almost certainly including the collusion of the designer – in this case, the highly respected Nathanael Herreshoff.

It was all too far-fetched. While Dunraven was due a fair amount of sympathy for some of the treatment he had received at the hands of the New York Yacht Club and its committees, and for the interference to which *Valkyrie II* had been subjected by the spectator fleet, his allegations of American cheating didn't bear scrutiny and smacked very much of a desperate man who didn't like the game if it wasn't played his way and, as he had done before, he left the scene.

He didn't, however, go quietly, instead using his biography to outline his views on international competition in sport and aim some parting shots at his old adversary, the New York Yacht Club. He wrote:

I am not sure that I like international contests. In such matters as yacht-racing, polo, golf, and so on, I think they tend to demoralise sport by turning it into a serious business in which national prestige is at stake, and to convert amateurs, playing a game for the game's sake, into professional specialists struggling for their country's sake.

Moreover, there are ethics in sport, as in everything else, and though rules are in all cases identical, and are equally observed, different peoples view a game from different angles, and misunderstandings may occur.

In those days [the early days of the America's Cup], the course was very badly kept. Excursion steamers thronged it and hampered the yachts badly. Not purposely I dare say, for steamer captains did not understand the effect of their lofty vessels upon the wind, and were anxious to give spectators their money's worth. Their unwelcome attentions were probably impartially bestowed, but it would be only human nature if a skipper was meticulously careful not to interfere with his own side. That has all been altered, I believe, and latterly courses have been admirably kept.

The protest that it was my duty to make against the Defender in 1895, created an amount of excitement that could not have been exceeded if someone had deliberately hurled an insult at the American nation. The tide of feeling ran very high. It was a curious, serio-comic experience.

The London Stock Exchange cabled New York that they hoped that, when war was declared, excursion steamers would not get in the way of our Fleet; and the New York Stock Exchange replied that in the interests of a fair fight they hoped our warships would be better than our yachts.

All very funny, but not funny to me, for though I found many very good friends, I did not have a pleasant time; and the matter was more serious than comic, for indeed it really looked as though a protest about a yacht race was going to cause serious estrangement between two nations. When I went over to attend a very belated enquiry, I was smuggled out of the liner at Sandy Hook. My good friend Maitland Kersey took lodgings for me close to the New York Yacht Club, where the enquiry was held, and I was under close police protection.

A protest has nothing to do with motives or responsibilities. It is a mere question of facts whether so and so happened or did not happen, whether this or that was or was not done, whether the protest was frivolous or justified; but when facts became submerged in a great wave of emotion, they are lost sight of and a protest became absurd.

I don't say whether evidence was or was not withheld, but I am very sure that not one of the American crew of the tender in which we lived would have dared to give evidence against the Defender had they wished to do so. Well, I am not going to reopen that question, even to myself. But I thought at the time, and I think still, that to raise a game, or a race, to such a pitch, is not conducive to real sport.

Somewhat at odds with his (sometimes) lengthy and fond reminiscences of cruising experiences, Dunraven was almost dismissive of his two Cup challengers. Of *Valkyrie II*, he recounted simply:

In 1892 I built, Valkyrie II, and raced her the following year. In the same year Britannia, almost a sister ship, and by the same designer, was launched for the Prince of Wales, and she was my principal and most dangerous antagonist … Valkyrie II had to give up racing early in the autumn of 1893, to get her jury rig fitted to cross the Atlantic to race for the America's Cup that autumn … [she] did not win the Cup.

And, of *Valkyrie III*:

… She also crossed the Atlantic and contested the Cup in 1895, but came home without it. She was broken up about five years later.

05

WIN WITH PLEASURE, LOSE WITH A SMILE

Starting with its controversial win over James Lloyd Ashbury's *Cambria* in 1870, the New York Yacht Club successfully defended the America's Cup 24 times over a period of 113 years before it finally tasted defeat, in 1983, at the hands of Alan Bond's *Australia II*.

The 25 challenges (including *Australia II*) came from just three countries – the United Kingdom (16), Australia (7) and Canada (2).

The most controversial and litigious were those of James Ashbury, in 1870 and 1871, and the Earl of Dunraven, in 1893 and 1895. So it would have come as a mixture of surprise and relief to the New Yorkers when the next two British contenders for the Cup turned out to be absolute gentlemen who, between them, would challenge for the Cup seven times over a period of 31 years, and help inject some much-needed decorum into the event before World War II put everything on hold and nearly spelled the end for the Cup.

The first of these Brits, with five successive challengers, was the New York Yacht Club's all-time favourite challenger and America's most popular loser – the genial grocer from the Glasgow tenements, Sir Thomas Lipton.

The second was aviation industrialist Sir TOM Sopwith, a racing-car driver, yachtsman, speed-record holder, balloonist, pioneer pilot and engineer.

Sir Thomas Johnstone Lipton has been poorly served by most of those seeking to portray the history of the America's Cup and the succession of leaders of industry that have populated its colourful history. Names such as Cox Stevens, JP Morgan, the Rothschilds and the Vanderbilts are tossed around with relish, while that of Lipton is almost disdainfully consigned to the loser pile – albeit in an exalted position.

Lipton though, possibly as much as anyone else in the distinguished list of defenders and challengers, personified the competitor that George Schuyler et al had in mind when they gifted the Cup to the New York Yacht Club.

While he has been depicted as possibly the world's best loser, Lipton was, in fact, the opposite – a superb winner and achiever in a wonderfully diverse life, who was quoted saying:

> *The actual trophy [the America's Cup] surely is no fabulous guerdon to be st⸱iven for might and main by the finest and most costly racing yachts the world has ever seen. But as is always the case in true sport, the prize itself means nothing – the winning of it everything. Even the fighting for it is good, healthy and internationally stimulating.*

He also observed:

> *I think I can say, with all truth, that it was on the muddy banks of the clay-holes in High Green [in the slums of Glasgow] that I learned one of the greatest lessons in life – how to win with pleasure and lose with a smile.*

Lipton's parents, Thomas Senior and Frances, were 'Ulster-Scots' who had migrated from the Lowlands of Scotland to County Fermanagh, in Northern Ireland. The family had been smallholders in Fermanagh for generations until forced to leave by the potato famine of 1845, whereupon they moved to Glasgow in search of a better living, settling on the south bank of the River Clyde where the man of the house worked as a labourer and a printer. Although there is some confusion as to when and where Thomas junior was born, his birth date appears to have been 10 May 1848, making him the youngest of five Lipton offspring; his older siblings – three brothers and a sister – all died in infancy.

By the early 1860s, the Liptons were the proprietors of a shop at 11 Crown Street, in the Gorbals, where they sold ham, butter and eggs. It was with the aim of supplementing his parents' limited income that young Thomas left school at the age of 13 and found employment as a printer's errand boy and, later, as a shirt-cutter. He also enrolled in a night programme at the Gorbals Youth School. He spent the next 30 years of his eventful life amassing a great fortune, and then the 30 afterwards enjoying, on a grand scale, the fruits of his considerable labours.

In 1864, aged 16, Lipton signed up as a cabin boy on the Burns Line steamer running between Glasgow and Belfast. He was fascinated by life aboard the ship and the tales told by sailors who had travelled to America. When the steamer company let him go – he was given a week's notice for allowing a cabin lamp to smoke and discolour the white enamel of a ceiling – the 18-year-old Lipton wasted no time buying a steerage-class ticket to the fabled USA.

He disembarked in New York and spent the next two years living hand-to-mouth and travelling all over the country, finding work on a tobacco plantation in Virginia, as an accountant and bookkeeper on a rice plantation in South Carolina, as a door-to-door salesman in New Orleans, as a farmhand in New Jersey, and finally as a grocery assistant in New York. This last position, at AT Stewart's progressive dry goods store in Manhattan, was a game changer for the young immigrant. The emporium offered a variety of everyday items not too different from those sold in Lipton's native Glasgow, but displayed them creatively and marketed them cleverly with advertising in the popular press.

It was all very innovative for the day and made a big impression on the young Lipton who, when he somewhat surprisingly returned to Glasgow at the ripe old age of 22, was armed with the new-found knowledge of the grocery trade and the secrets of the American techniques of salesmanship and advertising that were to become his trademark.

He put into practice what he had learned – first in his parents' small grocery business and then, the following year, in the first of his own provisions outlets, Lipton's Market, in the Anderston area of Glasgow.

From those humble beginnings, over the next 20 years he expanded his interests into a chain of more than 300 stores across the length and breadth of Britain, often sleeping under the counter of his latest store while ploughing any profits back into the enterprise. Then, in 1888, having achieved so much in general trade, Lipton turned his attention to tea, the drinking of which had become much more popular in the late 1880s but which was still prohibitively expensive for the average working-class family.

After investigating the trade with the tea brokers in London's Mincing Lane, he decided to tackle the selling of tea using the same methods that had proven so successful in the grocery trade – cutting out the middleman 'with profit alike to myself and my customers'. The only way he could do this was to control the whole production process, so he secretly booked a passage to Australia but disembarked at Colombo, in what was then Ceylon, where he visited the tea plantations for himself and found that the purchase price of tea was only half of what he had been willing to pay. Additionally, Ceylon was closer to Britain than the former traditional supplier, China, and the lower shipping costs this entailed presented another saving that could be taken advantage of.

Lipton moved quickly and soon owned five plantations in Ceylon, meaning he now had the control of the production process that was the key to his business model. Within a year he was selling, at prices the masses could afford, huge amounts of tea in pound, half-pound and quarter-pound packets. Even his 300 shops could not satisfy the demand. 'Lipton's' became a household name and a byword for tea, and the now 40-year-old Thomas was well on his way to becoming a multi-millionaire.

While his parents were still alive, Lipton resisted the logical move to London, which was increasingly the hub of his growing business empire. However, in 1889, when his mother died, followed a few months later by his father, Lipton made the shift south to England's capital. Throughout the 1890s, he continued to prosper, and the close commercial ties he'd forged with America led him to the decision to tackle the tea market on the other side of the Atlantic and expand his operations into fruit farms in Kent, stockyards in Omaha (Nebraska), and packing companies and meat stores in Chicago.

Although he was somewhat reclusive and a workaholic (more the latter than the former), Lipton was a constant philanthropist who never forgot his roots. In another game-changing moment in his life, his charity work brought him into contact with Alexandra, the Princess of Wales, and his natural charm and quick wit – he was an excellent raconteur – endeared him to her husband, Albert Edward, Prince of Wales, the heir apparent of Queen Victoria, and resulted in him becoming a favourite of the British royal family.

In April 1896 Lipton, recently returned from a trip to his estates in Ceylon, read in *The Times* an open letter from Princess Alexandra to Sir George Faudel-Phillips, the Lord Mayor of London, pleading for a different commemoration of the Queen's Diamond Jubilee the following year. Rather than another statue, the princess argued for helping 'the poorest of the poor in the slums of London – let us provide these unfortunate ones, these poor beggars and outcasts, with a substantial meal during the week of the Jubilee celebrations'.

To help launch a fund for the initiative, the princess sent a personal cheque for £100 and Lipton, as he had done many times, offered his support in the form of all the tea and sugar that the Princess Alexandra Appeal could use. Later, on learning from Sir George that only a fraction of the target sum of £30,000 had been received, Lipton took up his pen and wrote a cheque for £25,000 (equivalent to an estimated £2 million today) and handed it to the Lord Mayor with the proviso that it should be an anonymous donation.

This was an extremely generous gesture that would, helped by a shrewd tweak from the marketing genius, change his life forever. Lipton guessed accurately how the press would react; the news of a last-minute, anonymous benefactor would make for compelling headlines. The papers responded accordingly and speculated wildly about the identity of the unknown donor. Lipton, who had already donated in kind and had no reputation for giving out cash, flew under the radar until, after ten days, with the 'hunt' now feverish, he allowed the Lord Mayor to release his name. Now the media really had a story and Lipton had a platform from which to retell the tale of how a self-made man had clawed his way out of the Glasgow slums to become one of the most successful business entrepreneurs in British history.

It wasn't long before Lipton was supervising the organisation of the fund's 'dinners' for 400,000 persons throughout the city. Everyone would get a 1lb meat pie, a 2lb loaf of bread, 4oz of cheese and 8oz of cake, along with ginger beer and lemonade and, of course, Lipton tea. Just to deliver the 689 tons of food parcels to halls around London took 400 removal vans.

The dinner was judged an outstanding success and 'Jubilee Lipton', as he was dubbed, let slip to an eager media that he was engaged on an even more ambitious scheme – the Alexandra Trust and its objective to alleviate poverty by supplying cheap, wholesome food to the poor (he had already contributed a further £100,000 to this new work).

So, just three short months after his return from Ceylon, Lipton was a major celebrity who had earned the very real gratitude of the wife of the future King of England. It was no surprise, then, when Queen Victoria's New Year's Honours List in 1898 included a knighthood for the tea baron – for his services to business (he had already, in 1895, received the royal warrant to supply the Queen with tea).

As though in celebration, the new knight bought himself the luxurious, Clyde-built 1,240-ton steam yacht *Aegusa*, which he renamed the *Erin*. She was 260-foot long and 40-foot wide, with a crew of 40, and would become one of the joys of his life. He recalled in his *Leaves from the Lipton Logs* (henceforth referred to as *Leaves*): 'Looking back now it gives me intense satisfaction to recall the many prominent and distinguished people to whom I had the honour of acting as host aboard my floating home.'

That same year (1898), Lipton, to the surprise of many, floated his company, and he did so Lipton-style with cleverly managed publicity that prompted an unprecedented rush for shares that was dubbed 'The Lipton Scramble' by the *London Evening News*. Applications were received for almost £50m worth of shares and, at the National Bank of Scotland, the police had to regulate the crowds.

As a public company Lipton's continued to prosper, increasing turnover and dividends year after year, with Sir Thomas, now in his fifties, the managing director. However, his view of the world was achieving a wider focus and growing the business was no longer the all-consuming preoccupation that it had always been. He would have to find other outlets for his energies and aspirations and, if the acquisition of *Erin* was possibly a first manifestation of the changing Lipton, the next would trump it completely. The lad from the Gorbals' tenements challenged for what arguably was the most prestigious (and expensive) prize in sport – the America's Cup.

The new century started well for Sir Thomas. On the death of Queen Victoria in January 1901, Lipton's good friend 'Bertie' became king-emperor as Edward VII, with Alexandra the queen-empress, and in March that year, Sir Thomas was elevated by the new King to Knight Commander of the Royal Victorian Order. Then, in 1902, he was created Baronet of Osidge (in the Parish of Southgate, County of Middlesex).

The now public company continued to prosper and it was business as usual until World War I intervened. Lipton was too old to fight but he promptly put his yachts, including the beloved *Erin*, at the disposal of the British Red Cross Society and the Royal Navy. *Erin* was repainted white with a large red cross and re-equipped as a hospital ship. Lipton also helped organisations of medical volunteers and used *Erin* to transport doctors, nurses and medical supplies.

In Serbia during the winter of 1914–1915 and the spring of 1915, several British hospital teams were working with Serbian military when a catastrophic typhus epidemic erupted, killing thousands, with medical staff among the first victims. At the height of the epidemic, Sir Thomas decided to visit the stricken country and sailed, in *Erin*, to Salonika, in northern Greece, from where he completed his journey by train. He asked only for modest lodgings and 'the same meals the common people were eating' under war conditions as he visited hospitals and medical missions. His modesty made him very popular and he was subsequently made an honorary citizen of the city of Niš. The then King of Serbia also created him a Knight of the Grand Order of St Sava.

Later in the war, *Erin*, under her original name, served as HMY *Aegusa*, helping to patrol Mediterranean waters for German submarines. In that capacity, on 27 April 1916, off Malta, she struck a mine and sank, with the loss of six of her crew. At the time, she was trying to save surviving crew of HMS *Nasturtium*, which sank in just 7 minutes after also striking a mine. Lipton lamented: 'My beautiful and historic yacht went to the bottom of the sea, carrying with her, alas, six members of my crew. For the life of any one of these I would gladly have given the ship.'

After the war, Sir Thomas retained nominal control of Thomas J Lipton Ltd, but the change from sole personal ownership to working on behalf of shareholders through the medium of a board of directors was becoming an increasingly uneasy experience. Additionally, in the early 1920s, the marketplace was changing and the chain of 500 Lipton shops that previously had seen no real competition was facing new rivals, in the form of Van den Burgh's, Home & Colonial, Sainsbury's, David Greig's and Maypole.

The almost inevitable happened at the rancorous annual meeting of Lipton Ltd in 1926. Sir Thomas, still managing director and the largest shareholder, was removed from the power chain by his fellow directors, who promoted him sideways to the ineffectual position of Life President: an office without power. For the first six months, Lipton resisted being put out to grass, but finally he bowed to the inevitable and agreed to depart, disposing of his remaining interests in the company for a reputed £2.5 million (£150 million in today's money). He did not, however, relinquish control of his American company, Thomas J Lipton Inc, nor his tea interests in Ceylon.

His foray into steam yachts, followed soon afterwards by the America's Cup, should not, according to the man himself, have come as a surprise; it was more a rediscovery of an earlier passion. In his *Leaves*, he revealed: 'My "debut" as a yachtsman took place when I was about eleven years old! As a matter of fact, I founded a yacht club and was its first commodore.'

It seems he used timber from an old wooden chest to carve, with an old 'gully knife', the hull of a boat to which he added a mast and bowsprit – all complete with rigging. He fashioned sails out of strong paper and carefully carried the finished model to a field near his home that featured several large, water-filled ponds, which were relics of old brick-making operations. There, he launched his first *Shamrock* and 'not only did she float, and on an even keel, but she sailed across the pond like a thing of life at the first time of asking. Not once in all the crowded years that have come and gone since then have I ever recaptured the thrill of the launch and the first "race" of the original *Shamrock*.'

His mates were so impressed that they set to building their own models, 'and soon yacht-racing on the water-holes of the High Green became the order of the day'. A club was formed and the founder of sport and club, young Tommy Lipton, was declared commodore and chief referee (except, of course, when *Shamrock* was a competitor).

He never lost, he said in *Leaves*, the passion for sailboats (albeit, in the first instance, models of the same):

> *Through the strenuous years of building up my business, I had not lost one spark of my early love for the sea. I revelled in my repeated trips to America, for instance, as much for the 'whiff of the briny' as for any tangible rewards of my journeyings. The best parts of my holidays were the hours spent upon the water.*

It was not, though, until 1898 that:

> *I found my thoughts definitely and longingly turning again to my boyhood's passion – to the wind and the waves and the salt spray lashing and a mast bending under a well-filled sail. At all events to the actual possession of some craft which would gratify my zest for the sea and give me more frequent respites from the cares of business. The appeal was almost irresistible. And thus it was that I became owner of the* Erin, *the beautiful steam yacht which, in after, happy years, was to be so well-known all over the world.*
>
> *The acquisition of the* Erin *spelt for me a new joy. Only then did I begin to realize that it is not good for any man to be tied, neck and heel, to his office desk. No matter how hard I worked there was always the complete change and pleasure of a weekend on the* Erin *to break the monotony and to give me fresh vitality. Besides, I found I could have much more companionship on my ship than I could possibly have ashore.*

Calling upon this passion, Lipton challenged for the America's Cup no less than five times in the 31 years from 1899 to 1930 – all with yachts named *Shamrock*.

For the 1899 match, the original, *Shamrock I*, a 128-foot William Fife III design, was built on the River Thames at Millwall by John I Thornycroft & Co. The guideline budget was agreed at £100,000 (an estimated £10 million today) but ultimately cost Sir Thomas double that price before she crossed the Atlantic.

The American defender was 131-foot *Columbia*, designed by Nathanael Herreshoff and skippered by Charlie Barr for a hugely wealthy syndicate that included New York Yacht Club commodore J Pierpont Morgan (arguably the most powerful banker in the world at the time), and his relative Edwin D Morgan, for whom, it was said, acquiring yachts was like your average man buying a paper from a news stand. This was the world that Sir Thomas Lipton had now entered.

In the best-of-five match, *Shamrock I* was beaten 3–0 by *Columbia* after losing her mast in race two, and races one and three by 10 minutes, 8 seconds and 6 minutes, 45 seconds respectively. Sir Thomas told the media: 'The better boat has won, but I have in mind to challenge again' – which he did in 1901 with *Shamrock II*.

While Lipton built a new George Watson-designed 134-footer for his second tilt at the Cup, the Americans opted to again defend with the 131-foot *Columbia* and Charlie Barr. The challenger gained notoriety before her departure for America when her mast collapsed during a trial outing on the Solent, almost on the head of Lipton's friend King Edward VII – news that only heightened interest in the challenge.

Shamrock II was the first Cup boat designed with the help of model-towing in a test tank. With Edward Sycamore at the helm, she was well sailed and fast, and would provide a serious examination of the merits of *Columbia* and Barr. The upshot was the closest match (so far) in Cup history, with an average winning margin of just 1 minute, 52 seconds. *Shamrock II* led around the first mark in all three races, the best of which was the last – a titanic contest in which *Shamrock II* crossed the line just 2 seconds ahead of her rival, only to lose the race by 41 seconds on handicap. The huge spectator fleet roared its delight and Lipton wrote, in *Leaves*:

> *What splendid racing we had that year. I really think that with the slightest shade of luck I might have pulled off a victory. In the last of the series the* Shamrock *crossed the line two seconds ahead of the* Columbia *but lost because of the time allowance we had to give her. That was a sporting finish, if ever there was one. The British boat was freely admitted to be the best and swiftest challenger ever sent over. But as Mr Herbert L Stone says, in his fascinating book describing the races: 'The* Columbia *and Charlie Barr were a hard combination to beat.'*

Before he returned to England, Lipton was elected an honorary member of the New York Yacht Club – 'a very exceptional compliment, which I highly appreciated'.

Lipton was back again in 1903, with the William Fife III-designed 134-footer *Shamrock III*, and this time the Americans didn't take any chances with their defender. A syndicate of New York's wealthiest, including a Vanderbilt and a Rockefeller, commissioned Nat Herreshoff to design and build them what would be the biggest vessel ever to contest a Cup match (a distinction she still enjoys today) – the 'beautiful behemoth' *Reliance*.

Launched on 12 April 1903, *Reliance* was a masterpiece of design and technical genius. When measured at rest, her waterline length was 89 feet 8 inches, just under the 90-foot maximum. However, just above the waterline she splayed out into huge overhangs – 28 feet long at the bow and 26 feet aft – giving her an overall length of 144 feet 8 inches. When she heeled, the overhangs submerged to her true waterline length of 130 feet. She had a scow-like hull with a 25 foot 8 inch beam and shallow draught. Stability came solely from her fin keel that dangled 100 tons of cast lead 19 feet below the waterline. Her mast was as tall as a 20-storey building, her working sail area was 16,160 square feet, her spinnaker pole was 84 feet long and it took a crew of 66 to sail her.

Lipton's preferred designer George Watson was by now tired and ageing, but he helped William Fife III with the design of *Shamrock III*, which, although drafted after extensive tank-testing, owed as much to the traditional art of yacht design as it did to contemporary science. The only *Shamrock* to be painted white – the other four were all radiant Irish green – she looked graceful and fast but she was something of a dinosaur compared with the Herreshoff masterpiece she was about to face. To her credit, though, she kept the racing tighter than most would have predicted in a best-of-five match that, because of a mix of calms, fog and gales, took 15 days to complete. She trailed by 7 minutes, 3 seconds in the 30-mile windward/leeward first race and then by 1 minute, 19 seconds in the 30-mile triangular race two. Then she got lost in fog and failed to finish race three.

Lipton wrote:

Mr Fife produced in Shamrock III *an exceedingly beautiful boat, judged by the standards of these days. She was narrower and much longer than her immediate predecessor and, once more, we all thought that this time, surely, our turn had come ... We had not been long in America on this trip [though] when it was borne in on us that, while we had a good ship in* Shamrock III, *the genius of 'Nat' Herreshoff had built a bigger and a better one in the* Reliance. *The defender was certainly a 'freakish' yacht in many ways, and spread a tremendous amount of canvas – something like sixteen thousand feet, or fully two thousand more than my ship. But that she could travel through the water she demonstrated conclusively by beating* Shamrock III *pointless in all the races of the series. It was not a case of Mr Fife's yacht being a bad boat, but of Mr Herreshoff's being a phenomenally good one.*

There were widespread concerns about what Lipton termed 'freakish' yachts, the so-called 'out-and-outers'. In the 1903 match, for the first time in Cup competition, a race was cancelled due to strong winds – everybody nervous about the lightness of construction and rigs, as designers sought to control displacement. The towering rigs and long overhangs were not seaworthy, and these posed attendant threats to crew safety.

Lipton was aghast at where yacht design appeared to be headed and he delayed a further attempt for the Cup until 1907, when he challenged specifying a boat that would be built to the J-Class rating, which would mean boats of around 110-foot overall length instead of the extremes of the out-and-outers. The New York Yacht Club rejected this challenge with former Commodore Lewis Cass Ledyard arguing that yachts of such 'insignificant power and size' would lower the America's Cup to second-rate status. He was backed by the powerful J Pierpont Morgan, who argued that the Cup should be contested by 'the fastest and most powerful vessels that can be produced'.

Lipton waited another six years before re-entering the fray with a challenge in boats that were 75-foot long on the waterline (the size of a J-Class boat). The NYYC dug its toes in, as it had done so often in the past, insisting that the defender would be 90 foot on the waterline, as allowed under the Deed of Gift. When Lipton saw that he was not getting anywhere, he made his challenge unconditional and, now that it had once again successfully asserted its authority in Cup affairs, the NYYC dropped its own conditions and agreed to 75-foot waterline yachts under the 'mutual consent' provisions in the Deed. Lipton got the boats he wanted; the New York Yacht Club had not lost any authority; and the next match was scheduled for September 1914.

Accordingly, Lipton built the 110-foot Charles Nicholson-designed *Shamrock IV*, which was launched on 26 May of that year and prepared for the tow to New York by Lipton's steam yacht *Erin*. The small convoy was crossing the Atlantic when, on 4 August 1914, Britain declared war on Germany. The crews on *Erin* and *Shamrock IV* learned of the outbreak of what would be known as the Great War via an intercepted radio transmission from a German cruiser. They immediately headed for Bermuda and then on to New York where *Shamrock IV* would sit in a cradle until the 13th match was finally raced, in July 1920. Nicholson had always referred to his purposeful-looking creation as 'the ugly duckling', and by now that term of endearment was even more appropriate because *Shamrock*'s storage cradle had broken and her bow and stern had sagged. That did not, however, appear to hamper her affairs on the water where her opponent was the 106-foot Nat Herreshoff-designed *Resolute*.

Shamrock IV found herself 2–0 up in the best-of-five match. In the 30-mile windward/leeward opener, *Resolute*'s throat halyard parted and her gaff jumped off the mast, forcing her to retire. Then, in the 30-mile equilateral triangle race two, a wind shift turned the course into an extended reach. *Shamrock IV* was first into the building breeze and marched away to win by 9 minutes, 27 seconds across the line and 2 minutes, 26 seconds on corrected time (she had to give her opponent 7 minutes on handicap).

Shamrock IV now needed one more victory to take the Cup and she came desperately close to achieving that in race three, when she held *Resolute* to a lead of just 2 minutes after a hard-fought 15-mile beat to windward and then used her bigger sail area to catch and pass the defender on the 15-mile run to the finish, crossing the line just 19 seconds ahead. However, this wasn't enough to clinch the victory she needed on corrected time. *Resolute* then tied the match with a win on line and handicap in race four to take the match to a fifth-race decider.

The big one was delayed when it blew 25 knots the following day and then proved a disappointment the day after when the deciding 30-mile windward/leeward was raced in shifty, light airs. *Resolute* took the lead on the first leg and stretched out to win by 13 minutes across the line and

20 minutes on handicap. On a day of ultimates, the 13th Cup match was the last sailed off New York (the NYYC thereafter defended the Cup off Newport, Rhode Island); the last sailed on handicap; and the last sailed in gaff riggers.

Lipton wrote in *Leaves*:

> *In the actual races of 1920, we did better than we had ever done before. Of the five races sailed, I won two. One of these victories was due, it is true, to an unfortunate mishap to the defender, which I regretted as much as my opponents. Moreover, when the* Resolute *recorded the first of her three victories, the margin by which she won was no more than the time my ship had to allow her under the then existing measurement rule. So far as pure sailing was concerned, it was virtually a dead heat. And in one at least of the defender's two other victories, rather baffling weather seemed to like us less than it did our opponent. But I did not grumble. It is all in the game. We had had a series of splendid races, and I had, at any rate, the melancholy satisfaction of knowing that in the final result the better boat had won.*

As he planned his fifth (and what would be his final) Cup challenge in 1930, the now 80-year-old Lipton was frail but had lost none of his determination to succeed:

> *My first four Shamrocks all failed – some less completely than others. But in each one of them, my fond hopes were centred. With them I made four attempts to 'lift that old mug' – surely the most elusive piece of metal in all the world so far as I am concerned – but I can truthfully say that in the quest of it I have spent some of the happiest hours of my life. Neither money, nor time, nor trouble – aye, nor disappointment – have marred my joy in the pursuit of it. America's Cup hunting has been my principal recreation for over thirty years. It has kept me young, eager, buoyant and hopeful. It has brought me health and splendid friends.*
>
> *Now my challenge with* Shamrock V *is within appreciable distance of being fought out. As all the world knows, this year's races will be sailed under considerably different conditions from those in former years. Not only will both challenger and defender have been built to the same Universal Rule, but in the construction of the yachts the requirements of Lloyd's Register rules for yachts will have been fully complied with.*

The new rules will ensure that both yachts are not extreme examples of types, and that, broadly speaking, they will be fit for general service as yachts, and not useless for everything else but racing. In my humble opinion this is a most happy outcome of the negotiations that have taken place from time to time, and always in the most friendly and genial spirit since I became a challenger for the famous trophy. One pleasant result of the change will be that public interest is likely to be keener than ever in international yachting, and, indeed, in all branches of yachting. The development is one which was bound to come, and, having come, it will be welcomed everywhere.

This summer, I have spent many weeks on board my new steamship Erin *– yes, I have now another and a larger* Erin *– and it has been my joy to see my* Shamrock V *win many magnificent races all around the British coast against the best of the yachts on our side of the water. What, then, of my very latest challenger? I can truthfully say that Mr Nicholson has turned out a fine boat, and one that has, as I have just mentioned, given evidence of being a fast mover under varying conditions. Her skipper is Edward Heard, of Tollesbury, and we are all hopeful that the struggle will see him at the top of his form. With my old friend and trusty yachting advisor, Colonel Duncan Neil, to lend him the benefit of his shrewd and lengthy experience, I am more hopeful that Captain Heard will distinguish himself.*[1]

The essential parts of what had, over 60 years of defending the 'Auld Mug', become the defence machine were, however, once again coming on line and picking up speed to see off another usurper. Waiting for *Shamrock V* was the 121-foot William Starling Burgess-designed *Enterprise*, which embodied pretty much all of what had been learned in those 60 years of designing, building and campaigning America's Cup defenders.

Burgess was the highly inventive son of Edward Burgess, who designed the successful defenders *Puritan* (1885), *Mayflower* (1886) and *Volunteer* (1887), while her owner/skipper was the formidable Harold Stirling 'Mike' Vanderbilt, whose father and uncle had financed Cup defenders around the turn of the century. These were but two of the second generation of Cup campaigners who had laid and consolidated the foundations of the New York Yacht Club defence dynasty, and they would make their own indelible marks on Cup history in the years immediately ahead. It was, however, a no-win situation for Vanderbilt for it seemed that a nation of Americans wanted Lipton to win.

As the *Enterprise* crossed the finishing line for a straightforward 4–0 victory, Lipton put on his usual brave face but he was 82 years of age and, suddenly, he felt it. Gathering reporters around him on the aft deck of *Erin*, he lamented: 'It's no good. I can't win. I can't win.' He then shook hands with them one by one.

The following day the newspapers agreed that Sir Thomas had lost his bounce, that he looked tired and the sparkle had gone from his eye. The editorial in *The New York Times* accurately summarised: 'If sentiment could have gained the victory, the America's Cup would be in the hands of Sir Thomas Lipton.' In a letter that appeared as the newspaper's editorial in that same edition, movie star cowboy and vaudeville performer Will Rogers urged:

> *What do you say to this? Let everyone send a dollar apiece for a fund to buy a loving cup for Sir Thomas Lipton, bigger than the one he would have got if he had won, contributed to by everybody that really admires a fine sportsman. Send it to, I would suggest, a Lipton Cup Fund in care of Mayor Walker in New York. Let Jimmy buy it and present it on behalf of everybody with an inscription along these lines: 'To possibly the world's worst yacht builder but absolutely the world's most cheerful loser.' You have been a benefit to mankind, Sir Thomas, you have made losing worthwhile.*

The colourful New York mayor Jimmy Walker responded enthusiastically and endorsed the suggestion with: 'There might be some doubt about his ability to win the Cup, but no doubt about his ability to capture our hearts.' Letters of approval flooded in from all over the USA and within ten days $US16,000 had been subscribed – all in single-dollar bills.

When Lipton sailed home on 27 September, he had regained some of his jaunty composure and even promised the press corps that he would be back with yet another challenge. Two months later, he returned to the Big Apple to collect the loving cup. Designed by Tiffany, it was made of 18-carat gold and stood 18 inches high. Its solid-silver plinth had been donated by a consortium of Utah mine owners and the engraved legend read: 'In the name of the hundreds and thousands of Americans and well-wishers of Sir Thomas Johnstone Lipton, Bart., K.C.V.O.'

The presentation ceremony, in the aldermanic chamber of City Hall, was long remembered in New York. The dais and balcony were draped with flags and buntings, the police band played stirring Sousa marches and the proceedings were broadcast live to every corner of the nation. The mayor, soon to be booted out of office in a graft (political) scandal, was in top form and said to Lipton: 'You are the gamest loser in the world of sport. It is not simply a goodwill cup from America. It could not have carried a more widespread affection and admiration if it had come to you from the League of Nations. Take it to your native land where there will be no constitutional impediment to your full enjoyment of it.'

Lipton rose unsteadily to his feet and told the cheering crowd: 'Although I have lost, you make me feel that I have won. But I will try again. Yes, I will try again.' He then paused and, suddenly, sat down. His parting message when, a few days later, he left New York, was that he would challenge again in the autumn of 1931 and would race in 1932. Those close to him, though, knew that the Atlantic crossing to England would be Lipton's last voyage.

Sir Thomas died peacefully in his sleep at his home, on 2 October 1931, just 12 months after *Shamrock V*'s defeat. He was buried beside his mother and father in the Southern Necropolis, Glasgow, thousands of Glaswegians filing past his coffin in St George's Church and huge crowds lining the streets as the funeral cortege made its way to the cemetery.

THOMAS SOPWITH

If Sir Thomas Lipton was, as many believe, the ultimate self-promoter, his successor in the challenger ranks, Sir Thomas Octave Murdoch Sopwith, CBE, was his complete antithesis. Here was a man who avoided public prominence throughout his life, despite achievements that ranged from gaining a gold medal playing ice hockey in the first ever European Championships in 1910 and holding the powerboat speed record of 55mph in 1913, to winning the much-coveted Schneider Trophy – one of the most prestigious annual competitions in aviation – in 1914 with a Sopwith Tabloid floatplane flown by the company's test pilot, C Howard Pixton. He was also awarded a CBE in 1918 and, in 1953, received a knighthood for services to aviation.

A modest man, Sopwith's ability to select the most able managers was much admired, as was his practice of delegating to them control of individual companies while he usually remained in the background, deflecting any attention to the managers of his industrial groups. He always described his successes in business and so many other fields as 'pure luck', but that didn't fool anyone who had glimpsed the real man.

Sopwith was born in Kensington, London, on 18 January 1888 – the eighth child and only son of Thomas Sopwith (a civil engineer) and his wife Lydia Gertrude. He was educated at Cottesmore St Mary Catholic Primary School in Hove and at Seafield Park engineering college in Hill Head. When he was ten years old, while on a family holiday on the Isle of Lismore, near Oban in Scotland, a gun lying across his knee went off, killing his father – an accident that would haunt Sopwith for the rest of his life.

The young man's interest in flying was inspired by American aviator John Moisant piloting the first cross-Channel passenger flight. On 17 August 1910, the cavalier Moisant flew from Calais to Deal in a Blériot biplane, with two passengers – his mechanic, Albert Fileux, and his cat, Mademoiselle Fifi. The flight, only his sixth at the controls, took 37 minutes. His original destination was Dover but he got blown off course by a westerly gale.

Sopwith's first flight was with French aviator Gustav Blondeau, who had opened a flying school at Brooklands, in Weybridge, Surrey. He then taught himself to fly, on a Howard Wright Avis monoplane, going solo for the first time on 22 October 1910. He crashed after travelling 275 metres (300 yards) but improved quickly and on 22 November was awarded the Royal Aero Club's Aviation Certificate No 31, flying a Howard Wright 1910 biplane.

On 18 December 1910, Sopwith won a £4,000 prize for the longest flight from England to the Continent in a British-built aeroplane, flying 272 kilometres (169 miles) in 3 hours, 40 minutes. He used the winnings to set up the Sopwith School of Flying at Brooklands, and followed this move, in June 1912, with the Sopwith Aviation Company. In November of that year, Sopwith Aviation won its first military aircraft order, which necessitated a shift to larger premises in Kingston-upon-Thames.

The company produced more than 16,000 aircraft for the allied forces in World War I, 6,000 of which were redoubtable Sopwith Camels, the most successful fighter aircraft in the long conflict. The Camel's crowning moment came on 21 April 1918 when a young Canadian named Captain AR Brown shot down the greatest air ace of World War I, Germany's Baron Manfred von Richthofen, 'The Red Baron'. That one victory alone secured the Camel's place in aviation history.

Hard times followed the armistice, however, and Sopwith had to pay off creditors and crippling taxes, then liquidate his company. He formed a new, small concern, building motorcycles under the name of his chief engineer and test pilot, Harry Hawker. Then, as the aviation industry slowly recovered, he became the chairman of Hawker Aircraft and started to rebuild his business empire. Despite a slow acceptance of the new technology, the Hawker Aircraft company was successful with several metal biplanes in the mid-1920s. The RAF had no qualms about these machines, and Hawker Aircraft was soon supplying the majority of its inventory, while also becoming an increasingly successful exporter.

Sopwith, in the 1930s, displayed his business acumen with a series of company acquisitions, adding hugely to his aviation portfolio with the purchase of Avro, Armstrong Whitworth and other major firms. His next decision was equally bold. In 1932, when he decided to mount what would become his 1934 challenge for the America's Cup, Sopwith hired a young aeronautical engineer, Frank J Murdoch, to oversee the work of boatbuilder Camper & Nicholsons on the mast and rigging for his Cup challenger, *Endeavour*. The two had raced each other in 12-Metres (in those times, Sopwith was recognised as arguably the best 12-Metre skipper in the world, while Murdoch was a leading Metre-boat sailor in his own right and represented Great Britain in the mixed 6-Metre class at the 1952 Helsinki Olympic Games), and the pair had become friends.

So it was, in late 1936, when Sopwith needed someone to go to Germany to consult with the marine engine manufacturer MAN on the motors to be installed in his new 1,600-ton diesel yacht, *Philante*, he sent Murdoch who, while at the MAN facility, observed large numbers of

U-boat engines under construction. It was the same story with fighters and bombers at the Heinkel aircraft factory. Germany, it was obvious, was preparing for war.

Murdoch wasted no time reporting this to Sopwith who reacted immediately, commissioning 1,000 airframes for the Hurricane fighter that was being developed by his Hawker works, doing so on his own behalf, without any government order. The extra months of Hurricane fighter production that he gained proved a saving factor in the Battle of Britain that ensued.

Sopwith's wartime factories also produced other airplanes that became part of Britain's aviation folklore – including the legendary Lancaster bomber and the Allies' first jet fighter, the Gloster Meteor. Again, however, the post-war years were difficult ones for the British aviation industry as advancing jet-engine and missile technologies created confusion in forward-defence planning. One thing, however, was clear: there were too many small aviation firms in the United Kingdom and, in the 1960s, the Labour government ordered the firms to merge.

Sopwith's Hawker Siddeley group had created some of the finest post-war fighters and bombers but there was no escaping the fact that the British aviation industry, as it had emerged from the war, and despite its ingenuity, lacked the resources needed to compete with the Americans in the brave new aviation world. The major restructuring saw the plethora of household-name aviation companies (de Havilland, Vickers, English Electric, Shorts, Fairey, et al) merged into one or other of two major British aviation combinations that would become BAC (British Aerospace Corporation) and/or its offshoot BAE (British Aerospace).

Hawker Siddeley and the Bristol Aeroplane Company, with a combined workforce of more than 130,000, held out longer than most until, in 1975, the group became a founding component in BAC. By now, the 87-year-old Sopwith was long gone, retiring as chairman in 1963 but continuing to work as a consultant to the company until 1980.

As noted, Sopwith was already a yachtsman of some repute when he mounted his 1934 Cup challenge. He first made his name in 12-Metres, in 1926, with *Doris*, but it was with the Camper & Nicholsons-built *Mouette* that he really hit the heights – winning the English championship four years running (1927–1930) and 75 first prizes in the three seasons.

The combined aviation industry and engineering backgrounds of Sopwith and his main man Murdoch, and the sophisticated technical innovations and advanced instrumentation that they brought to the table, raised the bar when they entered J-Class competition. The first move they made was to buy *Shamrock V* from the Lipton estate. Then, while Sopwith raced the boat through the 1933 season, Murdoch installed strain gauges to measure all the rigging loads (a very innovative move for the day) and built up a large information base that then helped him design the rig for the new challenger, the J-Class *Endeavour*, along with a winch package that included a unique two-man winch that operated like a rowing machine. To all of that, he added on-board wind speed/direction indicators that were a first in sailing, and then raced on the boat to lend his expertise as a sail trimmer and general overseer.

Driving *Shamrock V*, Sopwith proved an excellent big-boat skipper on the English summer circuit, which pitted J-Class against other huge yachts in a kind of travelling circus that went from coastal town to coastal town, racing on short courses before thousands of paying spectators. The financial proceeds went to the professional crews (a successful boat might win $US5,000 in a season), the glory to the wealthy owners. It was a thriving sailing scene, especially when compared with that in America, still in the grips of the Great Depression, where the J-Class boats remained in their cradles. In this climate, the combatants in the best-of-seven 1934 Cup match were Harold Vanderbilt's 127-foot William Starling Burgess-designed *Rainbow* – the only new American boat – defending on behalf of the New York Yacht Club, and Sopwith's 130-foot Charles Nicholson-designed *Endeavour*, representing Britain's Royal Yacht Squadron.

Much of the good work on *Shamrock V*, in terms of developing Sopwith's crew on the English summer circuit, was undone when, on the eve of *Endeavour*'s departure for the USA, Sopwith's professional hands presented him with an ultimatum. They would not sign for the transatlantic passage and the Cup races unless he agreed to pay them substantially more. Sopwith, somewhat unwisely, flatly declined to agree to the demand and gave the men two days to reconsider. In that moment, he probably lost his (and Britain's) best opportunity to win back the Auld Mug. Only two of the hands opted to stay the course. The other 15 declined what Sopwith was offering, packed their kit and left the boat, leaving Sopwith little recourse but to recruit amateur sailors from the Royal Corinthian Yacht Club.

There was a lot of sympathy for the professional hands. In the main, they were professionals from the East Coast fishing fleets, men who understood the sea in all its moods, expert at handling sailboats in all weathers. For them, sailing was not a sport, it was their livelihood and their families depended on it. In the main, they were paid for yachting only until the end of the racing season. Then they had to return to their home ports to secure berths on fishing boats for the winter. With the racing off Newport not taking place until the end of September, they would miss the allocation of fishing boat berths and would have no income to support them and theirs until sailing began again the following spring. Their gripe, really, was not with Sopwith so much as with the system of employment.

Probably much to Sopwith's satisfaction, *Endeavour*, rigged as a ketch and escorted by his motor yacht, *Vita*, sailed for America on the day originally arranged and made good time crossing the Atlantic to Newport, Rhode Island. But Sopwith, valiantly as his 'corinthians' performed, would come to regret the lack of his professionals when the heat came on in the Cup match ahead.

Bristling with innovation, *Endeavour* had looked fast in her own challenger trials and the Brits, growing in confidence, fired the first shot in the psychological war by protesting *Rainbow*'s skimpy accommodations. The supposed issue centred on whether the defender should be required to carry a bathtub, as the challenger did. All was readily resolved by removing the tub from *Endeavour*, but Sopwith had made his point – he wasn't going to be messed with or bullied.

The series got away to a slow start when the would-be first race was abandoned in near-calm conditions. Then *Endeavour* won the re-sail, a 30-mile windward/leeward race, sticking close to *Rainbow* on the upwind leg then sailing away from her downwind to cross the line a comfortable 2 minutes, 9 seconds clear. *Endeavour* also won the next race, a 30-mile equilateral triangle, the quicker boat in the 15-knot breeze and covering carefully to cross the line 51 seconds ahead.

Things were looking bleak for Vanderbilt, and the prospect was even bleaker in the 30-mile leeward/windward race three when the defender trailed by more than 6 minutes at the turn. To make matters even worse, a slight shift in the wind turned the home leg into a tight reach rather than a beat – meaning that instead of sailing hard into the wind and having to tack to progress, *Endeavour* could sail straight to, and fetch (pass on the correct side), the committee boat because the wind was coming from an angle rather than head on. However, the Americans hadn't held on to the Cup for so long without learning a trick or two and, they had won before with a slower boat.

Vanderbilt, as planned, handed over the helm to Sherman Hoyt, because he had the best feel for the boat in light winds, and he immediately started to sail a little high of his course, hoping to hook into more wind. This unnerved Sopwith, who tacked in order to retain control of the situation. It was a bad move. In the light winds, *Endeavour* was now headed away from the finishing line at low speed. When she tacked back, Hoyt headed *Rainbow* down to pick up speed and drove right through *Endeavour*'s attempted cover. *Rainbow* won the race by 3 minutes, 26 seconds. She had come back from the dead to be on the scoreboard at last and, just as importantly, it was Sopwith who had blinked first when the pressure really came on. As is so often the case, it marked a change in momentum in a close match.

That change wasn't immediately apparent as *Endeavour* overhauled *Rainbow* at the first turn in race four – a 30-mile equilateral triangle. There was a luffing (defending position) incident and positional change. *Rainbow* emerged in the lead and, unimpeded, sailed on to win the race by 1 minute, 15 seconds, but *Endeavour* was flying a protest flag as she crossed the line.

It transpired that Sopwith in fact made two complaints. The first involved the start sequence and the obligation of the overtaking yacht to keep clear in order to avoid a collision. The second concerned the luffing incident immediately following the rounding of the first mark. *Endeavour*, the leeward yacht, luffed *Rainbow* hard but the latter failed to respond and *Endeavour* was forced to bear away to avoid a collision. In both cases, both skippers averred that they were in the right but photographic evidence, later produced, showed that it was the defender who was in the wrong.

The relative merits of the incidents didn't, however, matter because the New York Yacht Club's race committee disallowed the protests on the grounds that *Endeavour*'s flag was not displayed immediately the incidents occurred, as the rules required. This prompted an increasingly testy exchange of correspondence between Sopwith and the race committee, along with an uproar – on both sides of the Atlantic. To many, it smacked of the committee using a debatable rule transgression to obviate a very real possibility of the defender being penalised out of the race, prompting the witty observation: 'Britannia rules the waves and America waives the rules.' There was, though, no turning things around.

Whether because Sopwith was unnerved or because a re-ballasted *Rainbow* was now a faster boat, *Endeavour* lost the fifth race by a wide margin (4 minutes, 1 second). The following day, in what proved to be the final race of the match (a 30-mile equilateral triangle), *Rainbow* trailed after the end of the first leg (a 10-mile reach) but gained the lead on the beat of the same length that followed. She then almost lost it all on the run to the finish when Hoyt tried some more unconventional tactics, which, on this occasion, should have cost *Rainbow* the race, but Sopwith failed to take advantage of his opportunities and the defender hung on to cross the line 55 seconds clear and win the match 4–2.

Sopwith promptly challenged again, for a match in the summer of 1937, and this time he didn't just rely on design and technology innovation. He built his boat early, and in 1936 both *Endeavour*s went at it with, it seemed, the same energy and competitiveness that usually gave the defenders an edge.

The new *Endeavour II* proved to be even faster than her predecessor and it was clear to all that the Americans would have to build a new defender. The US economy, however, was in such a state that nobody knew who would pay for her. Ultimately, Harold Vanderbilt grasped the nettle and approached both Starling Burgess and Olin Stephens to jointly design a boat while he tried to raise the money. They went to work with a will, and created one of the greatest yachts in Cup history – the seemingly invincible *Ranger*. They were helped with their task to come up with a winner by the fact that, surprisingly, Charles Nicholson traded the lines of his fast 1934 challenger for *Rainbow*'s plans, gifting the Americans all the detail of *Endeavour*'s many innovations.

The 51-year-old Burgess and the 28-year-old Stephens worked well together. Burgess had dropped out of Harvard to serve as a gunner's mate in the Spanish-American War (1898). Before returning to college, he invented and patented a new type of machine gun. He was swept up in the new wave of aviation and, in 1910, built the first plane to fly in New England (it covered all of 2 miles). A year later, under contract to the Wright brothers, he opened the first licensed aircraft company in America, at just about the time that Sopwith was getting started on the other side of the Atlantic. He built the first seaplane to take off and land on water, and then sold out to Glenn Curtiss and went into partnership with Frank Paine as a yacht designer. In 1928, he designed a remarkably fast schooner named *Nina* that still won races 30 years later. His fascination with new building materials and his individualism drew him to the challenge of the huge J-Class boats and he was especially fascinated by the possibilities of model-testing in towing tanks.

It was in the tank at the Stevens Institute of Technology (founded by the schooner *America*'s co-owner Edwin A Stevens) that Burgess and Olin Stephens worked on testing models of their own designs against those of *Rainbow* and the first *Endeavour*. Stephens was already one of the most successful yacht designers in the world. He had dropped out after one year of study in naval architecture at the famed Massachusetts Institute of Technology (MIT) – his interest was in yachts, not commercial ships – and, after creating some successful daysailers, he drew the lines of a yawl that would be *Dorade*, in which he and his younger brother, Rod, would win the 1931 Transatlantic Race (by two days).

By the time that the designers and Vanderbilt were confident enough to decide on a design, very little money had been raised, but Vanderbilt decided to go it alone. The Bath Iron Works, in Maine, offered to build the yacht at cost but Vanderbilt's commitment still represented more than half a million dollars.

Ranger was huge, powerful and not, traditionally, very attractive. She was 135 feet 2 inches in overall length, displaced 166 tons, had a working sail area of 7,546 square feet and a spinnaker of 18,000 square feet. She was blunt-bowed, flat-sterned and fast, on all points of sail and in all wind strengths. *Ranger* sailed 34 races in her one and only summer in competition, winning 32 of them, by an average of 7 minutes, 44 seconds – or more than a mile. The 1937 match, then, was almost a foregone conclusion despite the gains made with *Endeavour II*.

Remembering 1934, Vanderbilt was apprehensive about the starts, so he sailed conservatively. As a consequence, in the best-of-seven series, *Ranger* trailed after the first two getaways, but still won those two races, both 30-milers, by 17 minutes, 5 seconds and 18 minutes, 32 seconds. Vanderbilt then pulled back on the reins, content to control the starts and then sail *Ranger* well within her capabilities, to win races three and four by 4 minutes, 27 seconds and 3 minutes, 37 seconds respectively. It was all over and there was no shouting. The results board said it all.

Sadly, by 1942, *Ranger* and most of the magnificent J-Class yachts were broken up, piles of metal and lead, to feed the manufacturing furnaces of World War II. The original *Endeavour*, though, was an exception. She ended up derelict in a mud berth up the Medina River at Cowes, on the Isle of Wight, until purchased, ultimately, by the American heiress Elizabeth Meyer, who sent her to the Royal Huisman shipyard in Holland for complete restoration. Meyer retained Frank Murdoch as a consultant on the project and the beautiful outcome of their efforts still graces the sailing scene today, a reminder of the magnificent sailing days of yore.

06

WHY ELSE WOULD YOU DO IT?

Australia II's historic 1983 victory in Newport, Rhode Island, not only sent the America's Cup winging its way to the land down under, it trumpeted a message to the yachting world: 'The walls are down. The Cup is winnable.'

For, in the modern era of the Cup (post-World War II), the New York Yacht Club (NYYC) had turned defences of the Auld Mug into an art form and created the impression that prising the trophy from the clutches of its original (and, so far, only) trustee was 'mission impossible'. NYYC had, after all, disposed of no less than eight challenges in the 22 years since the Cup was first raced in 12-Metres (in 1958) and its 4–1 humbling of Alan Bond's original *Australia* in 1980. Remarkably, in the process it lost only three of 35 races.

In New Zealand, which by now had tackled every other challenge in keel boat racing, and won pretty much all of them, it also meant that the Cup was perhaps geographically close enough to make a Kiwi challenge feasible. For some reason, Newport, Rhode Island, had always seemed a step too far.

The country's senior yachting institution, the Royal New Zealand Yacht Squadron (RNZYS), let it be known that it was keen to hear from any would-be syndicates, but come the 31 March 1984 entry deadline for Australia's 1987 defence, there was only a deafening silence. Commodore Rob Green had to announce that there would be no Kiwi challenge.

Imagine, then, the surprise when, two days later, the list of paid-up entries was released and there among the potentials was RNZYS. Marcel Fachler, a Belgian-born, Sydney-based businessman, had entered in the name of the Squadron and paid the $US16,000 entry fee out of his own pocket. He told the media: 'I can't for the life of me understand why this move did not originate in New Zealand.'

Fachler was a dealer in bullion, futures and commodities and headed a company that had holdings in Hong Kong and subsidiaries in Australia. He was planning to extend his activities into New Zealand and there was little doubt that the America's Cup would provide a high-profile entrée to the New Zealand business community. Fachler denied this was his objective, saying: 'This is totally a New Zealand challenge. I am simply the catalyst to get it off the ground and I'll underwrite whatever funds are needed to do a feasibility study and to establish the organisational framework for a challenge.'

The Ron Holland design office in Ireland was appointed to coordinate early design steps and to lay the foundations for a full-on design project, including towing-tank and wind-tunnel testing. Holland was an expatriate Kiwi who had taken his yacht design talents to Currabinny, on the banks of Cork Harbour in Southern Ireland, to be closer to the thriving offshore racing scene in Britain and Europe. He had set up shop in a converted pigsty directly across the harbour from the Royal Cork Yacht Club. Holland was already a name designer in offshore racing and he was asked to complete, by February 1985, the design of the first of two new Twelves that New Zealand would build, by December that year, for its Cup debut.

A background objective was to have Holland and two of New Zealand's other internationally renowned marine architects, Bruce Farr and Laurie Davidson, work as the challenge's design team. This wasn't immediately achievable so the Holland office took on the early work alone.

In November 1984, Holland journeyed to Auckland for the launch of Peter Blake's maxi *Lion New Zealand*, which he'd designed for the 1985–1986 Whitbread Round the World Yacht Race. His first stop was the office of *New Zealand Yachting Magazine* editor (and co-author of this book) Alan Sefton, who had been part of the steering group for the embryo challenge. Holland had been spending his own money while instigating the design processes and establishing relationships with the likes of the SAAB wind-tunnel facility in Sweden. However, he was near the end of being able to do that, and the real spending was only just starting.

The pair created a shortlist of wealthy New Zealanders who could be approached for support, and high on that list was a young merchant banker called Michael Fay who, with partner David Richwhite, was among the support sponsors for *Lion New Zealand*. Fay quickly grasped the opportunity to promote New Zealand on a world stage but he wanted a lot more information before making a decision on being involved, and insisted on complete confidentiality while he carried out due diligence. While this was being undertaken, he guaranteed Holland $US160,000 to enable the R&D programme to proceed at full speed. Even at that distance, and with only a fleeting involvement so far, Fay recognised that time was now really of the essence.

Fay ultimately agreed to fully back the New Zealand campaign, but it would be done his way, and not that of a yacht club chasing sponsors and making decisions by committee. One other thing: Fay did not subscribe to the prevailing wisdom that you had to serve your apprenticeship and do two or more Cup campaigns before you were ready to seriously consider bringing home the Cup. So, he said, New Zealand would be going to Fremantle to win, not just to participate.

Humphrey Michael Gerard Fay was born in Auckland on 10 April 1949 – a fourth-generation Kiwi. His father, James A Fay, lost both of his parents to a flu epidemic when he was only six years of age, and was then adopted by his uncle, a Queen's Counsel, who later was to be knighted Sir Humphrey O'Leary. Sir Humphrey became not only Michael Fay's grandfather, but the Chief Justice of New Zealand.

Michael Fay graduated from Victoria University in Wellington and, at the urging of his father, entered law school. By the age of 21, he had completed his formal education and was admitted to the bar.

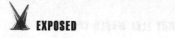

He practised law for a short time, then worked as a truck driver and, next, sold air freight. He soon acquired a large clientele in Wellington only to find that his success was due to quoting prices that were too low. When that job thus ended, he hitch-hiked back to Auckland, intending somehow to go overseas and take a look at the world.

That was 1972 and, as he walked down Auckland's main thoroughfare, Queen Street, he passed an employment agency with a very attractive young lady at the reception counter. Hoping to make her acquaintance, Fay went in and claimed he was looking for a job. That spur-of-the-moment decision sparked a chain of events that, within the span of less than 15 years, would see the then 23-year-old hippie become one of New Zealand's most successful and wealthiest merchant bankers.

Securitibank of Auckland was looking for employees with legal training, and, since Fay was a lawyer, the employment agency was at once able to arrange an interview for him. He donned his one, second-hand suit and headed for the interview, got the job and within six months was appointed the manager of one of the bank's divisions. At that time, Securitibank had only 30 employees; a year later it had 130 and one of those added was David Richwhite, who was interviewed for the job by Fay. As it was late in the day by the time the interview was finished, the pair headed to a nearby bar where they spent several hours getting to know one another. Right from the start, they hit it off and they would become great friends. Richwhite, of course, got the job and became the assistant manager in Fay's division.

Securitibank was growing rapidly and expanding into new fields, some of which involved lending long and borrowing short, a practice that, in the not-too-distant future, would come to haunt more than one financial institution around the world. Fay and Richwhite were concerned, and Fay voiced his objections to others in the bank. Almost inevitably, at a conference of the bank's managers, he was asked to elucidate his concerns and his answers were blunt, suggesting that Securitibank was embarking on a course that would lead to its downfall. Before the day was out, he was fired for being a 'disruptive influence'. His concerns, however, were vindicated when in 1976 Securitibank collapsed in one of the largest financial failures in the history of New Zealand.

Fay, in the meantime, set up his own company, Magnum Holdings. Fifteen months later, he was joined by his former assistant and Magnum Holdings became the merchant bank Fay Richwhite. Right from the outset of their friendship, the pair had talked about the day when they would start their own merchant bank and here they were – 'at the bottom of the heap and with an overdraft of $NZ5,000'.

By 1988, Fay Richwhite had a staff of more than 250 people, was moving into new offices in the latest (and one of the largest) office towers in Auckland (built by Fay Richwhite) and was handling 50–60 per cent of all New Zealand government bonds traded. It had several other offices around the world with still more planned, and it would continue to grow and become the largest and most profitable merchant bank in New Zealand, with Fay and Richwhite ranked the fourth and fifth wealthiest men in the country.

If you asked Fay to explain the dramatic success of the bank, he would first cite the fact that both he and Richwhite had always been committed to working long hours (14-hour days were not unusual) and they had determined to do things differently and not just follow customary procedures. Moreover, their experiences with Securitibank had provided the know-how to 'sense' opportunities when they became available.

When the pair made the call to back New Zealand's first America's Cup challenge, things were not going well on the campaign front. Funding was lacking, important decisions were not being made and there was a corrosive doubt that objectives could be achieved. Fay called together the best minds in New Zealand yachting and, after addressing all the issues and deciding the best way forward, he announced that Fay Richwhite would not only underwrite the entire campaign, but he would personally run the show.

It would prove to be a watershed moment in New Zealand sailing, introducing new standards of planning and operational excellence – not to mention ingenuity and ambition – that would make New Zealand the world power in all aspects of the sport and the marine industry that supported it.

With the new impetus, the dream design team of Davidson, Farr and Holland was achieved and, very early in the piece, they made it clear that fibreglass construction was a highly desirable option. This despite the fact that, so far, nobody in the America's Cup, including the Australians and the Swedes, had been able to convince Lloyd's Register, the classification society for the 12-Metre class, that it was possible to build a Glass Reinforced Plastic (GRP) Twelve – no 'exotics' like Kevlar® or carbon fibre – without it having prohibited advantages in weight distribution and rigidity (over aluminium Twelves).

The New Zealand design team set about the task of convincing Lloyd's that it could be done and finally won the society's approval to proceed. First up, Fay's New Zealand Challenge built identical trial horses, *KZ3* and *KZ5*, that would be shipped to Fremantle, the venue for Australia's defence of the Cup in 1987, for extensive work-up and testing. The data achieved would then be used in the design and build of a third fibreglass newcomer that would be state-of-the-art in every feature and detail, the very best that the resourceful New Zealand marine industry could produce, including rig and sails.

With the 23-year-old Chris Dickson, former world youth champion and match-racing 'gun' on the helm, *KZ5* finished second in the spectacular 12-Metre World Championships off Fremantle in February 1986 – and the yachting world started to pay attention. The new kids on the America's Cup block, with their 'Tupperware' boats, had served notice that they might be a force to be reckoned with. That attention might have switched to concern had the Cup world known that there was a second-generation Kiwi 12-Metre already under way in Auckland that would make *KZ3* and *KZ5* obsolete in almost every way – including race performance.

As it turned out, one challenger did regard the potential Kiwi threat more seriously than the rest and started laying the groundwork for an ambush of New Zealand's fibreglass technology. That challenger was the man whose head, according to Cup mythology, should have been on the Cup's now bare table in the Palm Room of the clubrooms of the New York Yacht Club.

The first Cup regatta outside of the USA, in Fremantle in 1986–1987, is still regarded as the best in the long history of the event – wind and waves aplenty, seemingly eternal sunshine and 13 challengers from seven different countries on the Gage Roads racecourse – and, it didn't take long for controversy to show its all-too-familiar face. Probably the only surprise was that there were no Brits or Aussies involved, nor even the NYYC. This time the protagonist was 'Mr America's Cup', Dennis Conner from the San Diego Yacht Club, displaying much of the campaign ruthlessness that he'd acquired when defending the trophy on behalf of the New Yorkers.

In September 1986, soon after the start of the Louis Vuitton Cup challenger elimination series, Conner's Sail America syndicate fired the first shots at the construction of New Zealand's *KZ7* (nicknamed 'Kiwi Magic'). It was the start of what became known as 'Glassgate' and would be the biggest controversy in what was otherwise a groundbreaking event.

Sail America wrote to Gianfranco Alberini, the commodore of Yacht Club Costa Smeralda (YCCS), from Sardinia – the Challenger of Record for the event – saying it thought there were some shortcomings in the measurement procedures for the regatta, particularly in terms of the make-up of keels and the Lloyd's specifications in terms of the laminates of composite hulls. The San Diegans wanted checks of everyone's appendages to ensure the absence of any substance of greater specific gravity than lead, along with core sampling of all composite yachts to confirm that they complied with the Lloyd's hull-laminate specifications.

It was a thinly disguised shot at the one composite hull in the fleet – that of *KZ7*, which, Conner seemed convinced, did not comply. It transpired that he had also been advised that illegal carbon fibre had been used in the fabrication of *KZ7*'s keel. None of this was true but that didn't matter. Conner was tossing hand grenades to see whether he could get rid of the dangerous Kiwis even before racing started or, at the very least, find out how inexperienced New Zealand would react to external pressure.

YCCS played it by the book and dealt appropriately with Conner's complaints. After careful checks with Lloyd's and its on-the-ground surveyors, it advised Sail America that the construction of the New Zealand boats had been 'very closely controlled and supervised by a surveyor appointed by Lloyd's Register' for that purpose. No materials had been used that were not approved by Lloyd's and the laminate for all three Kiwi boats met the Lloyd's specifications. The YCCS further advised that the measurement committee was being instructed to study a system to control the type and specific gravity of materials used in keels. Checks would be carried out on all yachts that reached the semi-finals of the Louis Vuitton Cup and, should any irregularity be found, the yacht in question would be disqualified and substituted.

When asked, in a Louis Vuitton Cup press conference, if it was true that Sail America was seeking to have core samples taken from *KZ7*'s hull, Conner looked decidedly uncomfortable when he confirmed that Sail America had sent a letter to the Yacht Club Costa Smeralda asking that the construction of 'all composite construction yachts' be checked.

Conner was then asked if the fact that *KZ7* was unbeaten on the water had anything to do with his syndicate's actions, which might be construed as 'sour grapes', to which he replied: 'Well, we're unbeaten too, and I thought this would be a good time to make sure that they are conforming to the rules rather than wait until later – we've been that route before' – a pointed reference to his experience with *Australia II*.

The Glassgate controversy had begun.

Conner's arch-rival, the affable and talented Tom Blackaller, skipper of the San Francisco challenger *USA*, was also on the podium that night and sitting close to Conner in the Fremantle Port Authority building. He jumped to Conner's defence, saying:

> *You guys should take it a little easy on Dennis here. I'd also like to know about that Kiwi boat. I didn't send a letter, but that fibreglass construction and the Lloyd's survey is a very shaky thing and we'd like to know if that [KZ7] was built right too. So I applaud Dennis doing that. I think it's a good thing. These are the first boats that have been raced that are fibreglass and the Lloyd's rules are very, very cloudy. All Dennis wants to know, and I'd like to know too, is whether that boat is lighter in the ends than it is in the middle, and you guys ought to back down and let it happen.*

Nobody could be certain whether Blackaller was serious or whether he was setting up the man he would almost certainly have to beat if he wanted to become the challenger.

Conner was then asked whether his syndicate was accusing the New Zealanders of cheating while, at the same time, questioning the integrity of the Lloyd's surveyors whose job it was to certify that the boats had been built to the rules. The *Stars & Stripes* skipper replied with a terse: 'No comment.'

Could the issue develop into another winged-keel controversy? Conner responded: 'So far as I'm concerned the reason the question is being brought up now is so that there won't be another winged-keel controversy. The matter should be handled right now before the event gets too far, where it can make a significant difference in the event.'

KZ7 skipper Dickson, late arriving at the conference venue and having missed the original exchanges, was asked what he knew of the Stars & Stripes move. He replied that he had not heard of the Sail America syndicate request and was unaware of any controversy over *KZ7*'s construction. 'It's a syndicate issue,' he said. 'I've got 100 per cent confidence in the construction of the boat. It wouldn't have been classified as a 12-Metre if it wasn't up to scratch in every way. I've got every confidence in it – it's a quick little boat.'

Sitting at the back of the hall, his boss Michael Fay read the warning signs. He was only vaguely aware of the Sail America letter that had prompted what clearly was going to cause his syndicate a lot of headaches. A copy, together with a reply from the Yacht Club Costa Smeralda, had been sent to every challenging syndicate as a matter of course but it transpired New Zealand's had gone to the syndicate's dock as opposed to its offices in downtown Fremantle, and their full significance hadn't been appreciated. As a result, Fay had not been advised.

The New Zealand Challenge boss was fast to recover, however, and worked his staff late into the night to review the situation. Sail America's letter to YCCS was dated 16 September 1986, and was signed by Robert Hopkins, the syndicate's measurement representative. It said that the measurement checks requested were 'consistent with the thoroughness of the rest of the measurement process and control parameters that have significant bearing on the performance of the yacht'.

YCCS's Alberini had replied to Hopkins on 29 September saying:

The construction of the plastic New Zealand boats was very closely controlled and supervised by a surveyor appointed by Lloyd's Register for that purpose. Mr Ben Bentley [Lloyd's' chief surveyor from Southampton who was in Fremantle for the pre-regatta checks of the fleet] is quite adamant that there can be no materials in the hulls of KZ5 or KZ7 which have not been approved by Lloyd's Register and that the laminates meet the specifications approved by Lloyd's. For the second problem, the measurement committee has not set out to take samples of the keels and does not have the technology to do so now. Anyway, some samples have been collected and the material appears to be lead. The importance of the matter is such that I agree with you that a deeper investigation must be made in this respect. I am therefore asking the measurement committee to study a system to control the type of material and the specific gravity of the keel at various points during the measurement, which will be carried out, according to Condition 26.4, on yachts entering the semi-finals. A similar procedure may be applied for the plastic hull. Should any irregularity be found, the yacht in question will be disqualified and substituted by the runner-up.

Fay's own technical experts and the syndicate's lawyers were just as clear. The construction of KZ7 was absolutely legal. A lot of time and money had been invested in ensuring this was so, and Lloyd's had reaffirmed this. But was that the true cause of the matter? Was Conner genuinely concerned that KZ7 might not be legal or was he trying to pressure the Kiwis and distract them from the job they were there to do?

With the issue an international news story overnight, Fay called a press conference to clarify the New Zealand position. He would not release the contents of the two letters in question as they were not directed to the New Zealand Challenge, but he confirmed that the Sail America syndicate was seeking a check of KZ7's construction, including the taking of core samples from her hull. Asked if he would allow cores to be drilled, Fay replied:

Over my dead body. New Zealand has complied with all of the requirements for this regatta and KZ7 is a Lloyd's classified 12-Metre.

Lloyd's had a surveyor overseeing every moment of KZ7's construction, just as they did the construction of KZ3 and KZ5. Because we were building the first fibreglass Twelves in the world, the whole process came under the closest scrutiny with checks at every stage of the process. This was after we'd spent many months and a lot of money producing the laminates that would satisfy Lloyd's that we could build a Twelve in glass that would conform fully with the strictest requirements of the rules. I doubt that there has ever been a more precisely built 12-Metre than KZ7 and I find the Stars & Stripes moves at this particular moment in time to be somewhat coincidental, to say the least.

That evening, Malin Burnham, president of the Sail America syndicate, joined the fray and found himself faced by a hostile press who saw the Americans as bullies, worried about their ability to beat New Zealand on the water and trying to sink them ashore. He told the international media:

We are not suggesting that the New Zealand boat be measured any differently from any other boat, our own included. Neither are we questioning the integrity or credibility of the Lloyd's representative appointed to supervise the construction of the yachts KZ5 and KZ7. However, in such a technical construction, we feel that it would be extremely difficult to determine uniformity and the weight of construction without appropriate post-construction testing.

Inherent in all of this is the fact that no individual, in our opinion, has the ability, as a Lloyd's representative or as any other representative, to stand in front of a hull being laid up with fibreglass and resin and opine whether it met the actual specifications, section by section by section, for that hull. It is an impossible task. It should not be done in that way. Our concern is for the very existence and for the future of 12-Metres as a class of racing boat. We don't want to see some new material come in that has some kind of distinct advantage over present construction, which automatically and overnight obsoletes all present boats.

Lloyd's Register was next to react. On 11 October it sent out a worldwide release that read:

Lloyd's Register understands that a claim has recently been made that New Zealand's GRP contender for next year's America's Cup does not comply with two of the requirements of the rules of Lloyd's Register, which embody the latest design criteria laid down by the IYRU [International Yacht Racing Union].

These two requirements are that the construction must (1) not be of less weight nor have a more beneficial weight distribution than the standard aluminium hull on which the existing scantling rules are based, and (2) be of adequate strength and not include materials which are not ordinarily marketed and available, nor include carbon fibre or fibres such as Kevlar®.

Lloyd's Register, as the agreed independent society controlling construction, refutes this claim and can state that the plans and construction specifications drawn up for the New Zealand 12-Metre yacht complied with the rules and were fully approved before construction, and that one of our surveyors [Jamie Course], from the Yacht & Small Craft Department in Southampton, was on hand up to 16 hours a day monitoring the construction throughout the building stages. Accordingly, Lloyd's Register can see no reason for further confirmatory actions such as core sampling of the hull of this contender.

The Sail America case received another setback when the International Yacht Racing Union's (IYRU's) chief measurer Tony Watts was moved to comment:

It is well known … that if there isn't adequate supervision it is quite possible to lighten the ends of GRP construction by not putting in as much resin or maybe leaving out glass. Lloyd's were very much aware of this, as indeed we were in the IYRU, and Lloyd's, with our encouragement and total approval, had one of their surveyors present the whole time the three New Zealand yachts were being moulded. He was very concerned to ensure the material was distributed in accordance with the lay-up specifications that had previously been approved by Lloyd's. So I think it is unlikely that there is any distribution problem with regard to the weight in that boat [KZ7].

Fay observed:

We built a boat which is bullet-proof. We would have been stupid to have done otherwise. If Stars & Stripes think we could be that stupid, then they are badly underestimating us.

Lloyd's then weighed in again with the detail of why they were adamant that the lamination of *KZ7*'s hull was legitimate. Its chief surveyor, Ben Bentley, told Barry Pickthall, from the London *Times*:

No other yacht has ever been surveyed so thoroughly in the history of the society. We are entirely satisfied that the New Zealand boat's weight and weight distribution meet our stringent requirements. Our surveyor worked to the last gram in determining the materials that went into the boat. Tools, buckets, even the plastic sheeting on the tables were weighed at the start of each day and again at night to record wastage. All the materials used in the structure were checked and weighed to ensure that they matched the specifications. Being one of the first glassfibre 12-Metres, we foresaw that this might become a political issue and checked, then double-checked, everything. We are certain the boat is bomb-proof against any claims that it does not meet our standards.

Fay flatly rejected any suggestion that the easy solution to the controversy was to let independent measurers take core samples from *KZ7*'s hull for analysis:

Like hell. We're being had on here and there's a question of principle involved. We've done everything by the book, and it has cost us a lot of time and money to do so. We've got what even the experts regard as the best-built, most closely scrutinised 12-Metre in history. Now you say, 'Let Malin drill holes in it.' Over my dead body. Sail America had plenty of time to query fibreglass construction, yet at no stage through the long build-up to this regatta did they provide any hint that they weren't happy.

I would say the real reason they've had a go now is to try to disrupt the New Zealand effort, to distract us and to put us under pressure. It hasn't worked (a) because we never had any doubts that the boat was right and (b) because our campaign is structured to protect the racing personnel from any such distractions. They've taken up a bit of my time and that of our legal people. In some ways we've enjoyed the skirmish but they have cast doubt on the professional integrity of various of our people – our designers and boatbuilders, for example, not to mention the Lloyd's surveyor and myself. Let's hope it's all done with now and we can get on with the sailing.

Conner and Burnham, and their syndicate, were, by now, the source of ridicule in fiercely proud New Zealand where they were referred to as 'Dirty Dennis, Wailin' Malin and Stirs & Gripes' but, despite all the expert evidence that *KZ7* was absolutely legitimate, Glassgate refused to go away.

During the 8 December press conference that followed *Stars & Stripes'* 32-second defeat at the hands of Blackaller's *USA*, the second of Conner's two defeats in round robin three, Blackaller was asked about his comments in the local press that he would take issues with *KZ7*'s hull but didn't have the time or the back-up organisation to do so. Blackaller replied:

> *I didn't take issue with the Kiwi hull. I think that Lloyd's scantling requirements for fibreglass are probably flawed and I don't have the legal department to press that. We have enough problems ourselves without getting involved. But my own engineers have told me consistently since I've been in this game that you can't build a boat in fibreglass that's light enough and strong enough to compete, because the Lloyd's scantlings prohibit making the boat light enough yet strong enough.*
>
> *None of our engineers thought that that was possible, so I can't believe that they're all wrong. I'm sure Dennis's engineers are telling him the same darned thing – that you can't do that. It's a real tricky business. There is one boat here that's out of a different material and is as fast as hell. There's another which is a wholly different physical concept – which is our boat – that's pretty fast as hell too. So it kind of looks as though, if you want to compete in the America's Cup, you'd better not come in with some garden variety Ben Lexcen copy.*

Sitting alongside Blackaller, the beaten *Stars & Stripes* skipper looked as though he had been drowning his sorrows on the tow back in from the racecourse. Asked whether his engineers had investigated the fibreglass alternative, he replied: 'I beg your pardon. I have a fibreglass muzzle on. I can't tell you that. I'm not allowed to speculate on that.'

Blackaller seized the moment and interposed with: 'I am sure that what Dennis is after is … he's after the fact that there's something screwy in here, something really is not straight.'

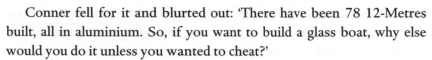

Conner fell for it and blurted out: 'There have been 78 12-Metres built, all in aluminium. So, if you want to build a glass boat, why else would you do it unless you wanted to cheat?'

Blackaller could hardly disguise his glee and chipped back with: 'Whoops, Dennis, oh, oh – I don't think he should have said that.'

'I'll take it all back,' said Conner.

'I don't think you can, Dennis,' replied Blackaller.

The attention now switched to Conner who was asked if his comments represented an accusation that New Zealand was cheating. He replied: 'No, I didn't say that', and, when New Zealand freelance journalist Michael Coupe insisted that he had, Conner retorted:

I'm not going to argue with you. I didn't say that and if you'd like to bet a dollar, I'd be happy to take your money. You are taking what I said out of context. Tommy [Blackaller] was talking about the engineering of the boats and I said, 'Why would you want to build a glass boat based on the facts that you can't do it as strong and as stiff unless you wanted to cheat'. I didn't even mention New Zealand, sir (with heavy, sarcastic emphasis on the sir*).*

Coupe countered: 'You could hardly have mentioned anyone else, could you? There's only one fibreglass boat out there.'

Conner, now thoroughly rattled, replied: 'If you're such an expert on this, why are you sitting out in the audience instead of up here sailing boats? I don't choose to answer any more of your questions.'

Blackaller, who had been thoroughly enjoying his arch-rival's discomfort, was asked how he viewed Conner. His reply was:

I have tremendous respect for Dennis Conner's ability as a sailor. I have been at odds with him for some time about the bludgeon tactics that he uses to try and win races – the $US15 million and three-year programmes. I don't think that's good for the sport. It doesn't prove anything about anything if you just go out and get more money and spend more time. It becomes less a sport then – more a business, or maybe something like the US government.

I guess I'm a little bit at odds with that style of doing things. But Dennis has always been one of the people I respect greatly as a sailor – no question *about that. I just wish to hell that he hadn't turned the sport into something where it costs you $US20 million to compete. We couldn't get our $US20 million this time so we had to take a real hard stab with a revolutionary boat, because that's the only way to compete against $US20 million programmes.*

In accordance with the conditions of the regatta, all four semi-finalists in the Louis Vuitton Cup were resurveyed by an 'agreed' surveyor from Lloyd's Register to reconfirm their classification certificates. The work was carried out by Bob Rymill, the principal surveyor from Lloyd's Register's Yacht & Small Craft Department in Southampton, and involved physical, ultrasonic and gamma measuring tests.

Rymill's report to the YCCS, on 22 December, stated:

I can now confirm that, as the 'agreed surveyor', I have completed my resurvey of the four semi-finalists, in accordance with Condition 24.2, and have issued new Confirmatory Classification Survey Certificates for all of the four semi-finalists. In addition to the above classification aspects, I can also confirm that I have carried out all the necessary physical and electronic testing required to satisfy myself that the scantlings of all four boats are in accordance with the approved drawings and that the weight and weight distribution requirements of the Society's Rules for 12m I.R.C. Yachts have therefore been complied with.

Rymill's work was supervised by an independent representative of the America's Cup measurement committee, Perth naval architect Ken McAlpine, at the request of YCCS. His report to the Challenger of Record said:

I have witnessed the testing carried out by Lloyd's surveyors on all four yachts, have approved the methodology of the physical and electronic measurements undertaken on each yacht. I can confirm that the measured scantlings and weight distribution of each of the yachts comply with the relevant Lloyd's approved drawing in each case. All yachts were treated equally and fairly and Lloyd's were able to obtain all the results that they required.

The Yacht Club Costa Smeralda responded with an official release that stated: 'As organising authority, we have now completed our duties and the semi-finals are starting with four yachts that have been remeasured and resurveyed as prescribed by the Conditions governing the Louis Vuitton Cup.' It noted that: 'A specific clause of the requirements states that a GRP [plastic] construction shall not be of less weight nor have a more beneficial weight distribution nor be less strong than an aluminium yacht.'

KZ7 had again been given a clean bill of health, along with the other three semi-finalists. Did that, finally, mean the end of Glassgate? The answer was no.

Two days later, the French Kiss syndicate, one of the four semi-finalists, questioned the validity of testing in the resurvey. It wrote to Commodore Alberini saying:

In our opinion, the testing might have been conducted using an ultrasonic detector and/or gamma emitter. These two instruments are able to give significant data on the thickness and density of homogeneous materials such as the aluminium hulls of three of the four semi-finalists but are not accurate enough on the composite materials [sandwich-type fibreglass] constituting the hull of the New Zealand challenger.

The French then upped the stakes by threatening to seek a restraining injunction from the New York Supreme Court if 'no appropriate action is taken'.

Fay reacted immediately, telling the media: 'Excuse me for looking angry. I'm not, but I feel very strongly that these questions have been raised [by the French]. I think our position has been fairly tolerant over the last three months, responding to allegations about KZ7's hull, some of them pretty wild. We thought that everything was settled but here we go again.'

Playing a trump card, Fay revealed that, during the resurvey process, at his request, the surveyors had drilled holes in KZ7's hull to enable them to physically measure the thickness of the laminate as a cross-check on their electronic testing.

'The boat was drilled and physical measurement of the hull was undertaken,' the Kiwi boss revealed. 'This process confirmed the results obtained by electronic testing. We will not comment on how many holes were drilled or how big those holes were [they were ³⁄₁₆th inch-diameter holes and there were lots of them]. I just told them the number must be divisible by seven [Fay's lucky number].'

To make it clear to the French that their bluff had been called, Fay provided them with the name and contact details for his legal counsel in New York and asked them for theirs. Moreover, he warned:

The New Zealand position will be quite strong in the future. The boat is legitimate and this has been verified by the most stringent testing, which we agreed to undergo even though we were not required to. I don't intend further to ask our designers, builders, other representatives or employees of the syndicate, or anyone else, to show the sort of tolerance that they have done over the last two or three months when, on many occasions, they have felt justifiably annoyed at some of the comments that have been passed.

In a general press conference soon after, Blackaller observed:

Having the Lloyd's Register of Shipping certify these America's Cup racers is a little bit like having the Royal English Trucking Association certify a Formula One racing car. In point of fact, the high technology of the America's Cup does not lend itself very well to having a shipping company certify the boats. It would be better for the competition if we were allowed to build the boats the way our designers, engineers and scientists want them. We'd have much faster boats that would be stronger and lighter and wouldn't cost so much. And that's a fact.

The Yacht Club Costa Smeralda declined to make any move to reopen Glassgate and, their bluff called, the French withdrew their threat of legal action. Instead, they gave notice that they would protest when *French Kiss* met *KZ7* in the first race of the semi-finals on 28 December. Syndicate chairman French Admiral Rene Marqueze denied that the only reason he was seeking more detail on the New Zealand boat was to ascertain the laminates used in *KZ7*'s hull so that his syndicate could build in fibreglass itself for the next America's Cup.

A Canadian journalist asked whether the other syndicates were ganging up on New Zealand. When Admiral Marqueze denied this, the

Canadian revealed that a survey had been carried out in Vancouver and the consensus of opinion among Canadians was that the Americans and the Europeans were 'running scared' because New Zealand had developed technology that the others didn't have.

In this environment there was hardly time for Christmas.

The Fremantle Doctor – the name given to the fresh, cooling south-westerly sea breeze that prevails through the hot Western Australian summer – was back on duty come 28 December as the first pair of semi-finalists – *KZ7* and *French Kiss* – locked into their pre-start sequence in 18 knots of wind. True to his syndicate's word, Pajot hauled up a red protest flag when the 10-minute gun sounded, but Glassgate would have to wait a few hours. There was racing to be done.

The Kiwis readily disposed of the French contender on the racecourse and the International Jury was just as brutal when it dealt with their protest that evening. Predictably, the complaint was that New Zealand had infringed IYRU Rule 19 and 12-Metre class Rule 26. Without requiring evidence from the Kiwis, the jury took less than two hours to hear and reject the French complaints, finding that: (1) New Zealand (*KZ7*) had a valid rating certificate and so had not infringed IYRU Rule 19; (2) New Zealand (*KZ7*) had a Confirmatory Classification Certificate and so had not infringed Class Rule 26; and (3) that the requirement for a measurement representative (of another syndicate) to be present at remeasurements (of other challengers) did not apply to Lloyd's scantling surveys.

Those decisions really did, finally, bring Glassgate to a close. There was nowhere else for the San Diegans, the San Franciscans or the French to turn but there was still the matter of the Louis Vuitton Cup challenger eliminations to decide, in order to identify the challenger for the 26th America's Cup.

The first parts of that didn't take long. On one side of the semis, *KZ7* made short work of *French Kiss*, winning the best-of-seven series 4–0 by margins of 2 minutes, 46 seconds; 2 minutes, 40 seconds, DSQ and 2 minutes, 44 seconds. Pajot was disqualified from race three, for a port/starboard infringement and collision on the final windward leg of that particular race, gifting a win to *KZ7*.

Stars & Stripes made just as light of it on the other side of the draw, beating Blackaller's *USA* 4–0, by margins of 10 seconds; 3 minutes,

2 seconds; 2 minutes, 23 seconds; and 43 seconds. And so it was that the final series of the Louis Vuitton challenger eliminations was fought out by 'Dirty Dennis', in *Stars & Stripes*, and Dickson, the 'choirboy with the cold blue eyes of a gunslinger' (as Sarah Ballard had described him in *Sports Illustrated*), in *KZ7*.

It was to be an intriguing clash. The New Zealand yacht had proved herself a brilliant all-rounder in winds ranging from near-calm to 28 knots and rough seas. However, Conner had brought a big and powerful boat that was designed and optimised for 'Fremantle Doctor conditions' – strong winds and big seas. At times, she had struggled in the challenger eliminations, needing the skills of the most experienced crew in the regatta to nurse her through when the Doctor failed to show, but the Doctor had begun to make his presence felt in the challenger semi-finals and there was still time for Conner's gamble on winds towards the top of the range to prove a winner.

There were powerful forces at work during the week of the final series – and they didn't favour the Kiwis. Far to the north of Gage Roads, in the Timor Sea, the first cyclone of the season was brewing. When it formed and moved on to the Australian continent, the existing balance of high- and low-pressure systems would be destroyed and the Fremantle Doctor sea-breeze pattern would be broken. The Doctor would lose his sting, probably for the remainder of the summer, and the deficiencies of *Stars & Stripes* in lighter winds would be exposed.

However, satellite weather pictures showed that the system in the Timor Sea was taking its time to develop into the cyclone that the Kiwis needed. For four days in a row, it showed no signs of progressing and, in the meantime, a heat trough lingered inland of Perth, drawing in strong winds from the Indian Ocean off Fremantle. *Stars & Stripes* was in her element and remorselessly ground out a 3–1 lead in the best-of-seven match.

When the cyclone finally did intensify and moved towards the northern coast of Western Australia, the Tropical Cyclone Warning Centre in Darwin allocated it the next name on its list – *Connie* – and on 19 January 1987, the day that Dennis Conner was executing the coup de grace to *KZ7*'s America's Cup hopes by completing a 4–1 win on Gage Roads, his namesake cyclone finally ripped ashore. The eye of *Connie* passed 19 kilometres (12 miles) to the west of Port Headland, a mining town with a population of 17,000 that was lashed by 200kph (125mph) winds and torrential rain.

The following morning, *The West Australian* newspaper's front page sported two headlines. The first read: 'Cyclone Strikes – 200 kph Wind As Connie Clips Town'. The second trumpeted: 'Conner Ends Magic Show'.

The New Zealand Challenge could have added their own somewhat plaintive postscript: 'Connie Kills Doctor – Too Late'. The sea-breeze pattern in Fremantle was broken overnight and never re-established itself with anywhere near the same force for the remainder of the America's Cup regatta.

While international focus was on the Louis Vuitton Cup final, the Australians had finally determined that their defender would be the Iain Murray-designed *Kookaburra III*, which had come out on top of a long and acrimonious qualifier series against Alan Bond's Lexcen-designed *Australia III*.

The *Kookaburra III* campaign owner, Perth department-store mogul Kevin Parry, promptly followed Burnham's lead and sought *KZ7* as a trial horse, and Michael Fay found himself between the proverbial rock and a hard place. On the one hand, there was an agreement between the challengers that the ultimate goal was to win the America's Cup from the Australians and, to this end, the challenger would receive the full support of defeated syndicates. Burnham publicly reminded Fay of this obligation.

On the other hand, it was an agreement to which Fay had not been party, one that had been arrived at before he took charge of the New Zealand campaign. While it was very much in the interests of every other challenger to get the Cup back to the northern hemisphere, there were obvious advantages for New Zealand if the Auld Mug remained in Fremantle. Fay was deliberating the pros and cons when Burnham called in the cavalry.

In Wellington, the Labour government's Minister for Overseas Trade, Mike Moore, received an official visit from the US ambassador to New Zealand while, at the same time, the Bank of New Zealand's chief executive, Bob McCay, and Fletcher Challenge chairman Sir Ronald Trotter (two of the most prominent businessmen in the country) received telephone calls from highly ranked banking figures in America. The messages were quite clear. It would be in New Zealand's best interests if *KZ7* trialled with *Stars & Stripes* and not *Kookaburra III*.

The pressure and the level from which it was coming were indicative of how badly the USA wanted the America's Cup back and of the lengths to which Burnham was prepared to go to get it. Sail America was clearly concerned that Iain Murray and his team might get access to the comprehensive performance data on *Stars & Stripes* that New Zealand would have amassed, along with the benefit of working up against *KZ7*.

But how would Fay justify, to the folks back home, helping a syndicate that had all but accused New Zealand of cheating with their fibreglass boats? And how would New Zealand's nearest neighbour and traditional rival, Australia, view the Kiwis helping Conner to win back the Cup in which the Aussies had vested so much time, money and support?

Fay had already reached his own decision – to make *KZ7* available to the Australians, but none of the performance data on *Stars & Stripes* – when he received a lengthy telephone call from the New Zealand Prime Minister, David Lange. Fay did not divulge what Lange had said, but it was clear the PM considered Anzac blood thicker than North American water – no matter what political and banking muscle Burnham was able to bring to bear.

Burnham's reaction was predictable. He accused New Zealand of reneging on its challenger obligations, but Burnham needn't have worried too much. The Australians hardly made best use of the opportunity to test themselves and their boat against a perfect yardstick. As though they were content to simply have denied Conner some meaningful work-up, their sessions against *KZ7* seemed half-hearted. The New Zealanders remained tight-lipped about the outcome of those sessions but you wouldn't have found anyone in the Kiwi camp prepared to bet on *Kookaburra III*'s chances against *Stars & Stripes*.

For some reason, the Parry people were confident that they had a definite speed edge on *KZ7* downwind and were fully competitive against her upwind. *KZ7*'s crew had seen it differently. Even though the New Zealanders, still bitterly disappointed about their own demise, were less than enthusiastic about having to go out sailing as someone else's trial horse, there was no disguising *KZ7*'s superiority. She had demolished *Kookaburra III* upwind, sailing higher and faster. *Kookaburra III* had proved fast downwind, but against a boat whose crew's interest and concentration were elsewhere. The New Zealand verdict was that *Stars & Stripes* would be too powerful for *Kookaburra III* upwind and that the Australian boat wasn't fast enough downwind to make up for this.

And so it proved. With *Kookaburra III* unable to make the expected impression downwind, Conner wrapped it up in four races straight and became the first man in history to lose the America's Cup and then regain it. The only time *Kookaburra III* looked a threat was in race one when the breeze dropped to 8 knots for the second beat. The Australians gained 39 seconds, but *Stars & Stripes* still led around the top mark the second time by 41 seconds and, with the breeze filling in again to 18 knots, sailed away to win by 1 minute, 41 seconds.

The Doctor was in for race two, blowing 22 knots. *Stars & Stripes* won by 1 minute, 10 seconds, and she went 3–0 up in the next encounter, with victory by 1 minute, 46 seconds in winds of 12–18 knots. With a forecast of light winds, Conner called a layday. Then, in 14–18 knots of wind in race four, *Kookaburra III* held *Stars & Stripes* to a lead of 22 seconds after the first beat and run before Conner opened the taps and eased *Stars & Stripes* away to win by 1 minute, 59 seconds. There was an air of inevitability about it all, with *Kookaburra III* outgunned on most points of sailing and in all but very light winds.

Murray commented: 'He [Conner] just had a bit more than we did. We thought we were sailing better than we've sailed before, but *Kookaburra III* hasn't quite got what he's got, and that's it really.'

The niggling thought in the minds of the New Zealand Challenge contingent that stayed on in Fremantle to watch the Cup match was what *KZ7* would have done to *Stars & Stripes* in the lighter range of conditions that had prevailed for the final four races of the four-month-long regatta. Throughout her campaign, *KZ7* had proved herself the best all-rounder in Fremantle and all the evidence was that she would have been too much of a handful for *Stars & Stripes* in anything less than 16 knots.

However, the races that mattered for *KZ7*, the 4–1 challenger final series, had been sailed in winds that ranged from 18 to 28 knots and averaged 23 knots. It didn't help New Zealand's peace of mind that the breeze died the night of *Stars & Stripes'* final win over *KZ7* or that the Doctor never regained his strength.

TOP LEFT: George L Schuyler, one of six owners of the schooner *America* and author of the America's Cup Deed of Gift (© PPL PHOTO AGENCY)

TOP RIGHT: Sir Thomas Lipton, the New York Yacht Club's favourite challenger (© COLIN M BAXTER ARCHIVE/PPL)

MIDDLE LEFT: John Cox Stevens – founder and first commodore of the New York Yacht Club (© PPL PHOTO AGENCY)

BOTTOM: The schooner *America* won the 1851 race around the Isle of Wight to claim what would become the America's Cup (renamed in her honour) (THOMAS GOLDSWORTHY DUTTON VIA WIKIMEDIA COMMONS)

TOP LEFT: 'The Plunderers' – Warren Jones (left) and Alan Bond plotting *Australia II*'s victory in 1983
(© BOB FISHER/PPL)

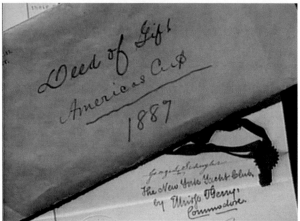

MIDDLE LEFT: The 1887 Deed of Gift that, essentially, still controls the competition today (COURTESY OF THE NEW YORK YACHT CLUB)

BOTTOM: Designer Ben Lexcen on the legendary winged keel of *Australia II*
(© LEO MASON/ POPPERFOTO, GETTY IMAGES)

The 'Plastic Fantastic' *KZ7* in action off Fremantle (© AJS/LK COLLECTION)

A contemplative Sir Michael Fay –
'We challenge you' (© BOB GRIESER/PPL)

Dennis Conner (right) and Malin Burnham with the reclaimed
America's Cup after *Stars & Stripes'* 4-0 victory over the defender
Kookaburra III in 1987 (© AJS/LK COLLECTION)

The controversial 1988 'match' between Sail America's catamaran (foreground) and Mercury Bay's 90ft waterline monohull (© NICK RAINS/PPL)

TOP RIGHT: The line-up for the disgraceful post-match press conference after the 1988 'mismatch' – from left: Tom Whidden (*Stars & Stripes* navigator); Dennis Conner (*Stars & Stripes* skipper); Bruno Troublé (moderator); David Barnes (*KZ1* skipper); Bruce Farr (*KZ1* designer); Peter Lester (*KZ1* tactician) (© AJS/LK COLLECTION)

MIDDLE RIGHT: The 1989 Court of Appeals hearing in Albany (New York) – 'Where in the Deed of Gift does it say that the America's Cup is supposed to be fair?' (© NERNEY)

BOTTOM: In 1995 – the most comprehensive challenger performance in Cup history, New Zealand's '*Black Magic*' (*NZL32*) on her way to a 5–0 sweep of the defender *Young America* (© AJS/LK COLLECTION)

TOP: The 2010 clash between Larry Ellison's trimaran (right) and Ernesto Bertarelli's catamaran. This was only the second time in the Cup's history that mutual consent on match details could not be achieved so the match was raced according to the provisions laid down in the Deed of Gift (© PPL)

BOTTOM: Larry Ellison (third from right) and Russell Coutts (third from left) sharing the moment with fellow 2010 crew James Spithill (second from left) and John Kostecki (second from right) (© BARRY PICKTHALL/PPL)

TOP: The remains of what was the Swedish challenger *Artemis* after the tragic 2013 pitchpole incident that claimed the life of British sailor Andrew 'Bart' Simpson (© NOAH BERGER/ASSOCIATED PRESS)

RIGHT: Bruno Troublé – the mastermind of the Louis Vuitton Challenger eliminations (© JASON HOLTOM/PPL)

BOTTOM: On the foils and low flying in 2013 – the defender *Oracle Team USA* (foreground) chases the challenger *Team New Zealand* on the for-once calm waters of San Francisco Bay (© EZRA SHAW/GETTY IMAGES)

Relations between *Alinghi* owner Ernesto Bertarelli (left) and his skipper Russell Coutts already looked strained in 2009... (© LUCA VITTATA/PPL)

Portugal's Patrick de Barros – badly let down by the Swiss over the selection of the venue for the 2007 America's Cup (© PAULO BARATA)

A close encounter in the 2017 America's Cup match – *Emirates Team New Zealand* (left), scooting downwind while *Oracle Team USA* scampers to clear.

07

I THINK WE'RE IN TROUBLE

If there were any delusions that George Schuyler's admirable values of sportsmanship and fair play were weathering the pressures of professionalism in sport in the 20th century, these were completely shredded on the evening of 9 September 1988 in San Diego.

The post-match press conference that followed the contentious monohull vs catamaran 'mismatch' off the coast of Southern California was one of the most reprehensible scenes in sports history – yet another lowlight in the acrimonious Deed of Gift shoot-out between the defender, San Diego Yacht Club (SDYC), and the surprise challenger, New Zealand's tiny Mercury Bay Boating Club (MBBC). More precisely, between the Sail America Foundation for International Understanding (SAF), supposedly representing SDYC, and New Zealand merchant banker Michael Fay, the challenger on behalf of MBBC.

It was a confrontation that held the Cup captive for two years while the parties hauled their entrenched differences through the entire judicial system of the New York Supreme Court, the legal custodian of the Deed and the trophy. In the process, it subjected Schuyler's Deed of Gift document, enacted in October 1887, to the most exhaustive scrutiny by some of the best legal minds in the USA and New Zealand, before the highest forum in that New York judicial system, the Court of Appeals in Albany, handed down a final decision.

Part of the lengthy argument centred around whether SDYC's use of a much faster catamaran to defend against Fay's 90-foot waterline sloop challenger was permissible under the Deed. Sailing luminaries from around the world bore witness to the court that multihulls are inherently faster than monohulls, and any encounter between the two completely different variations of sailboats would be a predictable 'mismatch'. Nevertheless, in July 1988, New York lower court judge Carmen B Ciparick ordered the two parties to sail their 'match' and, then, if they still had any complaints, to come back and see her.

The news media did not take kindly to Judge Ciparick's decision, or to the prospect of watching a mismatch between a multihull and a monohull for sailing's greatest prize, describing it as a 'judicial cop-out'. *The New York Times* said: 'Imagine Mike Tyson fighting an exhibition match against a kangaroo or, to take a real example, Bobby Riggs playing Billie Jean King. Entertainment value? Sure. A meaningful contest? No.'

The San Diego Union opined that, in terms of the law, it had to be presumed that Judge Ciparick knew what she was doing but, in 'layman's logic', her decision was nonsensical.[1] You couldn't, it reasoned, stage an international sporting contest and decide, after the event, whether the result should count.

The *International Herald Tribune* simply called it 'a charade', saying it was like staging a race between a supersonic jet and a hot-air balloon.[2]

Doyen of the American media, Walter Cronkite, a keen sailor in his own right, said in *The New York Times* that he was convinced the decision was going to result in 'the strangest race ever staged on land, sea or air between humans, animals or machines'. Judge Carmen Beauchamp Ciparick, he said, had 'rendered homage to Solomon' by delaying a decision about the race's legality until after it was over.[3]

Media outrage or not, race the two combatants did – in September 1988, over courses off San Diego that are stipulated in the Deed of Gift in the event the parties to a match can't mutually agree terms for their encounter. And it was very much the prophesied 'mismatch' despite defending skipper Conner muzzling his 45-foot state-of-the-art, winged-sail catamaran *Stars & Stripes* so as not to reveal just how disparate the performance of the two sailboats really was. He still won race one by 18 minutes, 15 seconds and race two by 21 minutes, 10 seconds.

Not content with that, the Sail Americans were out to add insult to injury when they arrived at the media conference and the outcome was described by one seasoned observer as: 'An ugly ending to an absurd match.'

John Marshall, a trustee, vice president and design coordinator for Sail America, fired the first shots when he sniped: 'If it was a mismatch, I think it was significantly because the challenging yacht was not fast, and I know that we have been asked to match her, and I think it is ridiculous to ask myself or any designer to match a boat that is not fast.'

To which the normally mild-mannered, Annapolis-based Bruce Farr, designer of the New Zealand yacht, retorted:

If John Marshall thought the New Zealand boat was not a particularly fast boat, then why didn't he match it with a similar boat that was faster? I suspect the reason was that Sail America couldn't do that so they had to find some other way of beating the New Zealand boat other than meeting it.

Farr, at the time regarded as arguably the most outstanding naval architect in the world, added: 'I find it quite disturbing that the gentlemen on my right, who are supposedly professionals in the industry in which I work, can sit in a press conference and tell lies. That really troubles me.'

To the relief of most, the so-called press conference came to a close. The indignities, however, were not over. Bruce Farr approached Dennis Conner on the now-crowded stage, apparently intent on continuing the exchange. Conner was heard forcefully insisting: 'Clear the stage, Farr, clear the stage! Get out of here, you little shit. You're a loser.'

It was, perhaps, a fitting finale to the most unfair and unsportsmanlike match in the colourful history of the America's Cup and, again, the frustrated media corps didn't like it. San Diego's *Tribune* newspaper summed it up with: 'The entire thing on the part of the Stars & Stripes bunch was totally uncalled for … Marshall could have let it be but chose not to … It certainly was a bad day for yachting. Sportsmanship? Sportsmanship got the beans knocked out of it.'

Barbara Lloyd, of *The New York Times*, wrote that Conner had sailed the race 'like a doctor afraid of a malpractice suit'. While Conner himself observed: 'This was not the most exciting, most pleasant or most rewarding America's Cup I have been in.... I'm not particularly proud of this America's Cup. I'm relieved it's done.'

The follow-up editorials in leading sailing publications were just as disapproving, none more so than that of Bill Schanen, editor and publisher of *Sailing* magazine, who, in his December 1988 issue, under a heading that read 'Mean and Vindictive . . . an embarrassment to American Sailing', wrote 'The Ugly American lives . . . and he's a sailor'.

Schanen ventured that there was never anything pretty about Sail America's handling of New Zealand's unconventional challenge: 'But it was at the post-series press conference – the ritual occasion when worthy winners are gracious – that Conner and company reached a grimy pinnacle of offensive behaviour.'

He said that, through the years, America had had been proudly represented in the America's Cup and recalled one example he had witnessed, on the banks of the Swan River in Perth, Western Australia. On that occasion, its champion accepted the America's Cup 'with humility and grace and warm praise for his defeated opponents'.

'Americans', he said, 'brimmed with pride. The sailor who inspired that pride was Dennis Conner.' Schanen said: 'It was less than two years ago. Funny, it seems longer than that.'[4]

The whole saga started out some two years earlier when, on 17 July 1987, Michael Fay invited himself to lunch with commodore Fred Frye at the San Diego Yacht Club. Frye was accompanied by his vice-commodore, Doug Alford, a lawyer, while Fay had with him his America's Cup legal adviser, Andrew Johns.

As the luncheon was coming to an end, Fay reached into an inside pocket and handed the commodore an envelope. Frye recalled: 'He says, "I'd like to challenge you for a match for the America's Cup ... in a yacht that has a 90-foot waterline and is 120 feet long." I turn to my vice-commodore, Doug Alford, and I say, "Oh shit, Doug, I think we're in trouble".'

News of the audacious challenge was disseminated by a Fay team ensconced in the Beverly Wilshire Hotel in Los Angeles, and an important part of the exercise was to first convince journalists, who had only known the America's Cup in 12-Metre yachts, that you could, in fact, challenge with something else.

The well known and colourful Bob Fisher, yachting correspondent for the British *Guardian* newspaper and columnist for a raft of sailing magazines around the world, was a case in point (but most definitely, not the only one). Fisher took one look at the faxed documentation from LA, and replied: 'Tell Michael, "Nice try".' He was advised to read the paperwork more carefully, including a copy of the Deed of Gift, and he soon realised that the America's Cup was very much not conjoined with 12-Metres.

As with much else in Cup affairs, the modern-day myth was the work of the New York Yacht Club, which, at the time, was probably the only entity that understood the Deed of Gift and what it represented. As the event gained a new popularity in post-World War II years, and multiple challenges became the norm, as opposed to the exception, NYYC adopted a clever practice that pre-empted any unwanted challenges and ensured that the Cup was contested in 12-Metres only, a class of yacht in which NYYC and its members were unquestionably the world's authorities.

To do this, part way through a defence (in those days, off Newport, Rhode Island) the club would formally announce that, should it be successful and retain the Cup, it would defend again in three years' time, in 12-Metres. The rest of the world, yachting journalists and all, simply took it for granted that this was how it was done and that 12-Metres were an integral part of the game.

It wasn't until Kiwi lawyer Andrew Johns actually read the Deed of Gift in 1986–1987 that all was revealed. There was no mention of 12-Metres, not even in the 'Interpretive Resolutions' that accompanied the Deed if/when the Cup changed hands. The requirements were that competing yachts or vessels had to be propelled by sails only and, if of one mast, had to be not less than 44 feet nor more than 90 feet on the load waterline (if of more than one mast they had to be not less than 80 feet nor more than 115 feet on the load waterline).

SDYC commodore Frye readily got to grips with all of this, telling the media:

I think it [the MBBC challenge] is the most innovative that could have been thought up by anybody. I respect Mr Michael Fay and I certainly respect

Mr Andrew Johns, his solicitor, because I find that not only has he crossed all the Ts, he has dotted his Is and minded his Ps and Qs as well. I know this is a bona fide challenge.[5]

That warm and enthusiastic reception changed quickly when Frye advised the club's contracted America's Cup organiser, the Sail America Foundation, of Fay's challenge. Malin Burnham, chairman of the foundation and Conner's mentor, is quoted saying:

I am not going to pay any attention to it. Calling it [Fay's challenge] a publicity stunt is being kind. From what I can ascertain, it is totally counter to the present spirit of the event. I can't even understand what Fay is trying to accomplish here. Maybe he's running a fever.[6]

Burnham then began the outrageous bluff that Sail America would impose on the Cup by outlining what SAF had in mind for San Diego's first defence of the trophy following its defeat of the Australian defender *Kookaburra III* in the 1987 Cup match in Fremantle, stating it would be 'an international regatta in 1991 open to all challengers and interested defenders'. He added: 'We are not going to be influenced by oddball suggestions … Clearly, under the Deed of Gift, challengers do not drive the America's Cup. They never have. They never will.' Within a few days, Commodore Frye was just as combative, saying: 'We're not going to let the Kiwis breeze into San Diego and waltz away with our Cup.'[7]

It was clear that it was the Sail America Foundation, with its principals Burnham, Conner and Marshall, that held the whip hand in defence affairs, and not the nominal Cup holder, San Diego Yacht Club, even though the Deed of Gift states categorically: 'It is distinctly understood that the Cup is to be the property of the Club subject to the provisions of this deed, and not the property of the owner or owners of any vessel winning a match.'

SDYC and SAF had, since February 1987, been embroiled in a long and bitter dispute over the proper interpretation of, and their respective rights under, an agreement they entered into on 1 September 1985. Under that agreement, Sail America was SDYC's representative in all matters pertaining to the 1987 America's Cup match in Fremantle, with SAF undertaking to pay all expenses incurred. The agreement also provided that, if SDYC won the 1987 match, Sail America would become the manager of the next defence of the Cup, for SDYC.

One of the important provisions in the agreement called for the appointment of a San Diego America's Cup Committee 'to oversee and review the future defences of the America's Cup while SDYC possesses the Cup and Sail America is the manager'. Among its duties, the committee was charged with selecting the defending yacht and determining the timing and site of the next match. However, the make-up of that committee was the subject of continuing dispute, which, in turn, became an unseemly battle over the venue for that defence.

The yacht club naturally assumed that any defence of the Cup in its name would be staged in its home waters off Point Loma, even if those waters were noted for lighter winds. For the club, it was a matter of local pride and the financial rewards it would bring to the community and, after all, there is strong evidence in the wording of his three editions of the Deed that this is precisely what George Schuyler had in mind. Sail America, however, had a completely different view that encompassed two compatible objectives. The first was logical, while the second was much less so.

To challenge for, and win, the Cup in the fresh conditions of Fremantle, Western Australia, in 1987, Conner and Sail America trained in Hawaii and accumulated a war chest of technology and know-how on racing 12-Metres in strong winds. It now wanted to exploit that knowledge by holding the defence in a place where fresh winds were again the norm. Hawaii was a front runner, frequently advocated by Conner and Sail America, but other rumoured possibilities were San Pedro Bay, off Long Beach (California), Atlantic City (New Jersey) and even Fremantle (Western Australia).

To many who were following events closely, though, this was but a thin disguise for the real reason for Sail America being prepared to break with tradition (and maybe, even, contravene the Deed of Gift), and that was plain-ol' grubby money. It wanted to sell the venue rights to the highest bidder – for millions of dollars.

SDYC and Sail America were unable to reach a compromise and the matter went to arbitration during which SDYC accused SAF of 'bad faith, unfair dealing, manipulation and attempting to fix the planned

1990–1991 defence in favour of SAF'. The SDYC arbitration brief went on to say:

> *It is repugnant to any sense of fair or friendly sportsmanlike competition, as well as to the Agreement and Deed of Gift, for (SAF) as player, manager and referee to have the opportunity to manipulate the rules, trials, defender selection, and site of the next America's Cup races in order to favour its own yachts and its own skipper. Yet this appears to be precisely (SAF's) intention, however it may protest at this arbitration. To the extent the Agreement is inconsistent with the Deed of Gift, it cannot stand. To the extent that a party attempts to contravene the Deed of Gift, it must be restrained.*

These high-blown allegations by the yacht club, accurate as they might be, would be revealed as cynical contradictions by what was yet to come in this tawdry affair.

On 25 July 1987, an accord finally was reached on the make-up of the seven-man America's Cup Committee, which was to hold its first meeting on 8 August 1987. By that time, six months would have elapsed since SDYC won the Cup back from the Aussies off Fremantle, and the decisions as to the time, place, conditions and type of yachts to be raced in the next match were yet to come. In the interim, around the world, would-be syndicates for the next Cup were forced to sit on their hands, not even able to fundraise without knowing the when, where and in what for their next campaign. Some didn't survive. The Kiwis were prominent among those waiting, but they soon tired of that game.

Andrew Johns, then a young solicitor in the Auckland law firm Russell McVeagh, was already very familiar with the Deed of Gift through the due diligence he'd done on Fay's behalf before the historic decision to build New Zealand's 12-Metres for Fremantle in fibreglass (as opposed to the traditional materials – wood or, in more recent times, aluminium).

Johns recalled:

> *Once we're finished with the Fremantle challenge, Michael [Fay] has a standing army, if you like, waiting for the next event. It's unfinished business and we feel we have at least one more shot [for the Cup] left in us. There are the 12-Metre World Championships scheduled for June or July 1987 in Sardinia, but beyond that there is nothing to plan for.*

It's during this period that we learn that SAF is negotiating with Hawaii – with a chap called Fred Smales – to race the next Cup off Honolulu. I recall going there, at the invitation of Smales, and meeting with the Governor of Honolulu who shows us where the America's Cup village is to be established. It is all part and parcel of Sail America looking for venues, looking to find a lucrative contract to stage the America's Cup in a location outside of San Diego.

At the same time, there is just nothing coming out of the San Diego Yacht Club itself as to the future and, I suppose, we get a little frustrated. I can't remember exactly the day or the reason why the idea of challenging per the Deed of Gift came about but because of the 'Glassgate' business in Fremantle, when Conner accused us of cheating with our fibreglass boats, we have been forced to look very closely at all the documents governing the America's Cup until everything of that ilk is second nature. And when you read the Deed, you don't have to be Einstein to work out what it tells you to do if you want to challenge for the America's Cup, and there's no mention of 12-Metres in which the Americans are so strong.

I broach the subject with Michael. He lights up immediately and calls [his partner] David Richwhite. They confer and then ask me if anyone else knows of my suggestion, because the key element in what I'm proposing – a Deed of Gift challenge in the biggest keel boats allowed – is that you have to be the first challenge received if you want to specify the boats in which you will race.

That's something that the Sail America people either don't recognise, or choose not to recognise – that the America's Cup is a challenge-driven event. In making your challenge, you have to nominate the essential dimensions of the yacht in which you will race. And, in the well-documented view of George Schuyler, the defender is honour-bound to match what you are bringing.

Sail America also chooses to ignore Schuyler's own definition of a match: 'The cardinal principle is that … a match means one party contending with another party on equal terms as regards the task or feat to be accomplished.' His emphasis upon the parties competing on 'equal terms' is consistent with his repeated concerns … that a challenger for the America's Cup should receive a fair and sportsmanlike contest.

So, it really is as simple as that. We get tired of waiting for San Diego to tell us something and that leads to us looking at alternatives. Michael and David decide that the proposal of a Deed of Gift challenge is worth investigating and that's what we do. I spend a lot of time in the library of the New York Yacht Club, the archives of which are steeped in Cup history, and also in the New York Public Library, looking at historical information, old books – finding anything we can about the America's Cup that will shed light on whether this method of challenging is still alive and operative.

When we are satisfied that we have the right of it, the paperwork is completed back in New Zealand and hand-delivered to us in Los Angeles. Then it's off to San Diego for lunch with the commodore. Of course, we don't know whether or not San Diego has what is referred to as a 'hip pocket challenge', an agreed challenge already in place to pre-empt one that might not be so inviting. All we can do is hold our breath. It soon becomes evident, however, that they don't have a prior challenge. Mercury Bay is the first out of the blocks. We are in there.[8]

Michael Fay responded:

You would've had to be deaf, dumb and blind to not realise that this would not be an easy challenge. We are taking a road that hasn't been trodden before. Are we going to do it? Yes. We talk about it a lot and feel it is a good challenge from the New Zealand perspective and a good challenge for the Cup.

Is it aggressive? Yes. Is it too aggressive? For some New Zealanders, yes. Does everybody support us? No. Would we challenge our best friend like that? No. But Dennis Conner? Yes. There are a lot of those elements in it but overall we also feel strongly that it represents a very big chance for the Cup. Twelve-metres have had their day. This is a step forward – an opportunity for the Cup. All that is needed is for San Diego, or Sail America as it turns out, to recognise that opportunity and match us, and we are away into an exciting new era for the event. But they never do, or they choose not to, because they've got another agenda – to make lots of money out of the defence by selling the venue to the highest bidder.

We don't want legal proceedings. We want to race in the biggest sailboats that the Deed of Gift allows. We certainly don't want to go to court to verify the legitimacy of our challenge and the match we are seeking. But Sail America and SDYC leave us with no choice. They stonewall us and refuse to recognise our challenge – as legitimate or otherwise – and label it a 'sneak attack', which, of course, it isn't. So our only recourse is to get the New York Supreme Court to rule on the validity of the Mercury Bay challenge. Then, if the court finds in our favour, San Diego has no alternative. Under the Deed of Gift, it has to defend or forfeit.[9]

On 27 August 1987, Tom Ehman, recently appointed as vice-president and chief operating officer of Sail America, telephoned Andrew Johns to report that the Board of Directors of the San Diego Yacht Club had met and decided to make no response to the Kiwi challenge. The challenge, though, would not be rejected, in case it proved to be valid. Ehman also revealed that SDYC and SAF would formally announce, on 2 September 1987, their plans to go forward with a 1990 or 1991 match in 12-Metres, something the Deed prohibits if the club has already received a legitimate challenge.

The SAF move forced the hand of Michael Fay and, the following day, Friday 28 August 1987, he authorised his US attorney, George N Tompkins, to institute legal proceedings in the Manhattan Supreme Court, which is 'a trial court of original jurisdiction' in New York City. Tompkins, then a partner in the New York law firm Condon & Forsyth LLP, is a graduate of Notre Dame Law School. He is widely recognised in international aviation law and also has extensive experience in appellate litigation, arguing numerous appeals in precedent-setting cases in federal and state appellate courts, including two cases in the US Supreme Court.

The necessary paperwork for the Mercury Bay Boating Club's petition was prepared over the weekend and filed with the New York Supreme Court on Monday 31 August 1987.

The case was assigned to Justice Carmen Beauchamp Ciparick, the daughter of migrants from Puerto Rico. Raised in Washington Heights in Manhattan, she is a 1963 graduate of Hunter College and a 1967 graduate of St John's University School of Law. After progressing steadily through the city's judicial system, in 1978 she was appointed Judge of the Criminal Court of the City of New York and, in 1982, was elected to the New York State Supreme Court.

The Mercury Bay complaint sought three things:

A preliminary injunction restraining SDYC and its agents, including SAF, from soliciting, entertaining or considering any other challenge and from setting the conditions for any match until the one set forth in the Mercury Bay challenge had been decided.

A declaration that the Mercury Bay challenge was valid, and, if not honoured, SDYC would be in breach of its trust and so forfeit the Cup to New Zealand.

A declaration that SDYC had breached the conditions of the Deed of Gift and the agreement it entered into with the Royal Perth Yacht Club (RPYC) when it received the Cup, and therefore that agreement should be rescinded and the Cup returned by RPYC (which was made a party to the action for that purpose).[10]

Judge Ciparick signed an order directing SDYC to appear before the court on 9 September 1987 to show cause why the requested relief should not be granted. The order also restrained SDYC, pending the hearing, from soliciting other challenges or taking steps to set up another match.

Asked for comment, Malin Burnham is quoted saying that the America's Cup is a sporting event, and that the San Diego Yacht Club, even if it found it could gain an advantage under the Deed of Gift, would not take, or even attempt to take, such an advantage. The words were to come back to haunt him.[11]

On 4 September 1987, four days after the Mercury Bay complaint was filed, SDYC filed its own petition with the New York court, which, likewise, was assigned to Judge Ciparick. The petition sought a declaration from the court that SDYC was authorised 'to follow practices and procedures reasonably adopted by it and prior trustees' and for an order 'interpreting, reforming, amending or ratifying a de facto amendment of the Deed' that would allow it:

1   To designate 'a particular class or design rule' under which a match is to be sailed;
2   To set the site of, the dates and times for and the number of races to be sailed in the match;

3   To prescribe a reasonable period of time during which any qualified yacht club may submit a challenge for a match; and
4   To make arrangements for a series of elimination races to select the challenger in the event more than one challenge is received.

In other words – scrap Schuyler's Deed of Gift, which is at pains to safeguard the rights of challengers, and replace it with a Sail America proposal that vests control of everything in the defender. The SDYC petition also asked for a declaration that it was not required to accept the New Zealand challenge.

This attempt to rewrite the Deed was carried out in secret. The original trustee of the Cup, the New York Yacht Club, was deliberately left out in the cold and the SDYC affidavits were all executed between 31 August and 3 September 1987, which indicated that SDYC and SAF were preparing their petition to amend the Deed even before Mercury Bay filed its complaint. It is pure happenstance that New Zealand filed first and both actions were assigned to the same judge, who ordered that copies of all the San Diego pleadings were served on MBBC and RPYC. Thus, the plot was revealed.

If the timing had been a little different, and if SDYC had filed its petition first, a far different scenario would have been in prospect, one in which San Diego filed its petition, naming only the Attorney General of New York as a defendant.

Moreover, since the Attorney General totally endorsed San Diego's proposed amendments to the Deed, the two parties could have jointly gone before the court to have the Deed changed unopposed and the coup completed before the world at large had any inkling that a proceeding to amend the Deed even existed. The America's Cup would no longer be a challenge cup, but one dominated and controlled by the defending club.

While the parties were gearing up for the September hearing, Warren Jones corresponded with Malin Burnham. Jones, still the executive director of Alan Bond's America's Cup activities, was concerned by SAF's surreptitious attempt to amend the Deed. He wrote:

The America's Cup has survived heartily on a mixture of great sailing and controversy. Certainly, the ability of the defending club to administer the event under the original Deed of Gift, which has only been amended in a minor way since its original inception, has been a key ingredient of the event.

We believe it would be tragic if the defending club was to seek to protect its position by altering the Deed of Gift and therefore changing the 'tone' of the event forever. If you close off forever the Michael Fay-style of bid, you will remove the entrepreneurial element which has attracted some of the world's most successful businessmen to the event. Please do not reduce this event to mediocrity and turn it into just another yachting event, which, in my opinion, it is rapidly becoming. Until now it has been the Everest of yachting events in the world.

I do not believe that Michael Fay has any desire whatsoever to win the America's Cup by default. The New Zealanders have proven over recent years that they are amongst the finest yachtsmen in the world.[12]

08

DEFEND OR FORFEIT

At 9.30am on 9 September 1987, Judge Ciparick mounted the bench in the Manhattan Supreme Court to be faced by a dozen lawyers, representing not only the San Diego Yacht Club and the Mercury Bay Boating Club, but also the office of the Attorney General of New York, the City of San Diego, the New York Yacht Club, and the Royal Burnham Yacht Club (of England). Also present were Michael Fay, Malin Burnham and other representatives of the principal parties, along with a host of reporters and other interested onlookers.

Taken aback by the large attendance, Judge Ciparick moved the hearing to her robing room, with only counsel present, and there set the ground rules for what clearly was going to be a bigger affair than she had probably anticipated.

It took until 25 November 1987 for the judge to hand down her decisions, in which she said:

In the face of the Mercury Bay challenge, San Diego asks the court to retroactively interpret or amend the Deed to allow it to ignore the Mercury Bay challenge, to give the defender the right to designate, among other things, the size of the boat, the dates of the races and to organise an elimination series between challengers. In effect, San Diego seeks to have fundamental changes written (or interpreted) into the Deed to take away rights given to the challenger under the Deed, rather than relying on the mutual consent provisions as has been done in the past.

Judge Ciparick then ruled:

Applying the relevant standard, the court finds that the San Diego Yacht Club has failed to make the required showing to justify making truly radical and fundamental changes in the Deed ... For the court to decide otherwise would be to allow the holder of the America's Cup to virtually unilaterally dictate the conditions of future competitions. That result is unjustified in view of the workable Deed and would clearly violate the donor's intent ... Therefore, in the face of a properly tendered challenge, the San Diego Yacht Club, having accepted the Cup pursuant to the terms of the Deed, may either accept the challenge, forfeit the Cup, or negotiate agreeable terms with the challenger.

Sail America's clandestine attempt to arbitrarily amend the Deed had failed and the SDYC had been instructed by the court to defend against a legitimate challenge by Mercury Bay, or hand the trophy back. Despite their posturing and aggressive media statements, the San Diegans had clearly harboured their own reservations and had been preparing the ground for their next moves should Judge Ciparick rule against them.

On 10 November 1987, at the Tuesday Yachtsman's Luncheon of the St Francis Yacht Club, Sail America's chief operating officer Tom Ehman told the gathering that, if it lost in court, Sail America would do whatever was necessary to make sure that Michael Fay had no chance whatsoever of winning on the water – even if there was nothing fair or sportsmanlike about how they did it. The audience of San Franciscan yachtsmen was taken aback.[1]

Then, on 20 November 1987, Ehman was quoted in the *San Diego Union* as saying: 'We'll jimmy the rules to win this thing ... We have our best minds, people like John Marshall, figuring out how to deal with the Kiwis ...'[2] Ehman later denied having said that – 'I was misquoted by the

Los Angeles Times' – but the evidence, including his luncheon statement in San Francisco, did not support that denial and the media were now reporting that various defence options were being considered by SDYC and SAF, including the use of a catamaran and moving the venue to Hawaii.

On 2 December 1987, San Diego Yacht Club and Sail America held a news conference to announce their plans. Commodore Frye, in his introductory remarks, said:

> *The judge told us all that Michael Fay's challenge is a valid challenge, that we must defend on the terms of that challenge or forfeit the Cup, and that she found no reason to vary from the literal terms of the Deed of Gift. This means a race much sooner than 1991, in 90-foot boats.*

Following Frye on the podium, Ehman read to the press a letter, which he had dispatched to Michael Fay, accepting the Mercury Bay challenge and outlining arbitrary terms upon which San Diego intended to defend the Cup and conduct the match. Those terms included the right to choose the number of hulls the defending vessel might have.

The storm clouds were gathering and the press reactions were mixed. In its edition that same day, the *San Diego Union* said that, in the short term, prudence dictated that the SDYC do whatever was necessary to meet and beat the Kiwis at their own game in ten months' time:

> *If that means selecting a site and sailing conditions in which the defender cannot realistically lose, well all's fair in love and war on the water ... If the trophy must be defended against the Kiwis next summer, manipulate the rules to blow them out of the water.*[3]

The next day the same newspaper said: 'What the SDYC thinks is best is to rout Fay – even if it means risking the wrath of worldwide public opinion.'

On 3 December 1987, *The New York Times* noted that the SDYC and Sail America had (finally) agreed to a match with Mercury Bay but had stipulated terms and conditions that would, as-good-as, preclude a challenger win. Their Cup manager Tom Ehman was reported saying that the defender would consider radically different boat options including a catamaran that would assuredly guarantee victory.

On 4 December 1987, the *San Diego Union*, in an editorial entitled 'A Hull of a Mess', took a more restrained position than in its earlier reports and cautioned SDYC/SAF:

> *San Diego's dream of hosting the biggest-ever America's Cup regatta in 1991 should not obscure what is best for the city, the America's Cup and yachting competition. The San Diego Yacht Club appears petulant by compounding the America's Cup difficulties with its all's-fair-in-love-and-war response to New Zealander Michael Fay's successful lawsuit in the New York Supreme Court ... Now that SDYC has agreed to race in larger boats, it is in danger of further tarnishing the America's Cup tradition with a strategy for a rigged, quickie event so that the 1991 regatta can go on as planned. This aggressive response conjures up a fascinating picture, but it threatens to make SDYC, not Mr Fay, the villain in the eyes of the yachting world ... Instead of contentiousness, the SDYC might consider statesmanship ... The San Diego contingent should simply initiate negotiations with Mr Fay.*[4]

That sage advice from a leading newspaper in their own community fell on deaf ears.

Fay recalled:

> *It was frustrating, to say the least. We were doing it one way, in good faith, but we didn't see the same good faith on their part. They never recognised or responded constructively to the opportunity. In simple language, they regarded Mercury Bay's challenge as a threat and their behaviour, their PR strategy, their language – everything – were about trying to gain the high ground, to justify the way they perceived they had to defend in order to succeed. The bottom line was they didn't want to design, build and sail a boat against Bruce Farr. John Marshall led that initiative and mindset. They weren't going to do it because they didn't think they could win that way, so they go the catamaran route.*
>
> *In terms of the head start they always claimed we had in designing and building our boat, I don't think we were, at any stage, more than a few weeks ahead of San Diego. If we were even that, it was because Bruce Farr and Russell Bowler had to come up with a bare-bones concept to give us*

the other dimensions we needed – beam at load waterline, extreme beam and draught – so that we could submit a legitimate challenge. But that's all it was – a bare-bones concept.

Marshall and Sail America would have had everyone, the court included, believe that we'd already started building the boat before we submitted the challenge. One has to ask – how dumb would that have been? We get to San Diego and Fred Frye says, 'Thanks, but no thanks. We've already accepted a challenge in 12-Metres.'

Fleshing out that bare-bones concept, engineering it and then actually building the boat and shipping it to California – all within the time frames we had nominated – was always going to be just as big a challenge for us as it was for them to design and build a boat to match us. The shipping alone clipped the best part of a month off the time available to us. But we were comfortable with that challenge. To us, it was all part of an exciting, new direction for the Cup.

But those time frames and having to produce something better scared Marshall and Sail America, so they turned their backs on what was really required by the Deed and pursued the very high-risk strategy of defending with a catamaran. At that early stage, I was of the view that they wouldn't do that – they wouldn't sail against New Zealand in a multihull just to ensure victory. This was, after all, the America's Cup. How wrong can you be?[5]

On 23 February 1988, MBBC sent formal notice to SDYC saying that, if it attempted to defend the Cup at a venue other than the ocean waters off San Diego, or with anything other than a keel yacht, MBBC would seek forfeiture and to have Judge Ciparick's November 1987 judgment enforced accordingly.

On 9 March 1988, William I (Bill) Koch wrote to Malin Burnham offering to provide a 90-foot waterline monohull yacht to defend the Cup. Koch was the owner of the very successful IOR maxi yacht *Matador* and had, for some time, been engaged in extensive research projects, both on his own and at the Massachusetts Institute of Technology (MIT), which he believed had produced new technologies that would permit the design and engineering, within 30 days, of a very fast 90-foot waterline monohull. He offered to build the boat and present an East Coast team to sail it in a defenders' elimination series.

The offer was rejected by SAF because Koch had no prior experience in the America's Cup. The same Bill Koch, in 1992, would win the America's Cup on behalf of San Diego Yacht Club, with the impressive new IACC class *America³*, a product of his MIT programme, after defeating Dennis Conner for the right to defend.

Koch was not the only one interested in having a chance to defend the Cup in the name of San Diego Yacht Club. David Vietor, an experienced Cup campaigner from the East Coast, had first written to Sail America on 9 November 1987 to advise that his syndicate was prepared to field a 90-foot waterline defender. Thereafter, Vietor met with Tom Ehman and followed up with several more communications asking for a response. His offer, just like that of Bill Koch, was declined.

Cocking a snook to world opinion, Sail America/SDYC proceeded with their intended multihull defence and, on 24 May 1988, unveiled the first of their two new, state-of-the-art *Stars & Stripes* catamarans. Two days later, Michael Fay's *New Zealand* arrived in Los Angeles where the hull and the 160-foot mast were loaded on a barge for transit to San Diego. The 21-foot keel made the journey by road.

On 27 and 28 May 1988, *The Times* of London published a two-part article by its yachting writer Barry Pickthall, headlined 'Conner Finds a Golden Egg in the Cup'. According to Pickthall:

> *Sail America's trustees and officers, including Conner and his design coordinator, John Marshall, stand accused by American sailors not only of 'jimmying the rules' but also of manipulating the defence as much for financial reasons as for sporting ones. We have uncovered evidence of almost $[US]1 million being paid to trustees and officers of Sail America and San Diego Yacht Club while creditors have been made to wait.*
>
> *... In the last three months of 1984, Conner and Marshall, together with two of the club's top officers, Doug Alford, now its commodore, and Sandy Purdon, were paid $[US]119,909 in service and consultancy fees. The following year they were paid $[US]489,469, with Conner taking $[US]175,000 and Marshall $[US]149,597.*
>
> *Only in 1986 when, according to Conner, credit was so hard to come by that even the milk bill had to be paid in cash, did he defer his budgeted*

$[US]10,000 monthly consultancy fee as the tax return discloses. However, Marshall and Purdon continued to draw their full fees and expenses, Marshall receiving $[US]122,202 and Purdon $[US]80,730 … Sail America is under investigation by the US Internal Revenue Service (IRS) following a complaint lodged anonymously last year.[6]

In the second part of the exposé, on 28 May, the Pickthall article continued:

In the money-go-round now structured, Dennis Conner Sports Inc, a marketing company set up after the American skipper regained the Cup, gets 15 per cent of all commercial funds raised. The residue is passed to Sail America, which, according to sources within the Foundation, is committed to placing the first $[US]30 million of its defence budget with the newly formed Stars & Stripes Foundation, the defence syndicate headed by Conner. The power now wielded by this group is highlighted by two outside potential defence syndicates, one headed by David Vietor, the other by William Koch. Both were prepared to build and finance monohull boats similar to New Zealand's challenger but have been shunned by Sail America.[6]

Tom Ehman called *The Times* articles grossly misleading, and said the IRS investigation was only a 'routine audit'. Malin Burnham stated that the articles were 'inaccurate both in substance and in tone'.

The unseemly arm-wrestle lumbered on until finally, on 7 September 1988, off Point Loma, Southern California, the defender, San Diego Yacht Club, unsurprisingly put an end to the speculation and turned up on the start line for the 28th America's Cup in a catamaran. And, now, the whole dispute headed to another level. The best-of-three 'match' between the catamaran defender and the 90-foot waterline monohull was every bit the mismatch that everyone had been predicting and immediately the long-drawn-out affair headed back to court in New York where Judge Ciparick awaited.

On 12 October 1988, the New York Yacht Club, the original trustee of the Cup, filed with the court an affidavit by commodore Frank Snyder stating that the Club had not previously taken a position in the dispute over the legality of the catamaran but after considering the results of the

'so-called match' in September, the Club could no longer avoid doing so.
The affidavit continued:

> *What took place in the waters off San Diego confirmed what so many
> had predicted would be the case. To put a monohull and a multihull on
> the water together is not to conduct a race or competition of any kind.
> For the SDYC to purport to defend with a catamaran what this Court
> had determined was a valid challenge for the Cup by a monohull was,
> therefore, not a defense at all. There was no 'match', as that term is used in
> the Deed of Gift.* [7]

Attached, as an exhibit to Snyder's affidavit, was a paper by respected
yachting historian John Rousmaniere, in which he cited a report of a
special committee of the NYYC, in 1881, on the Deed and the letters of
George L Schuyler. Rousmaniere's paper was stimulated by the question
as to what a defending club should do when faced with the opportunity
to defend the Cup in a way that 'predictably and by definition would lead
to a mismatch in the defender's favour'.

A mismatch, he said, would arise where a knowledgeable, independent
observer would conclude before the contest that one competitor's
chances of winning are hopeless, which could arise in three situations:

1   where the defender uses a fleet to meet a single challenger;
2   where the defender uses a yacht longer on the waterline than that of
     the challenging yacht;
3   where the defender chooses a yacht of a different and faster type than
     the challenger.

Rousmaniere pointed out that the San Diego Yacht Club chose the third
method in 1988 and sought to justify doing so on the grounds that there
were not, and never were, limitations upon the defending yacht other
than the simple ones of length and rig imposed by the Deed.

He then measured that argument against the historical record and
found that, while the statements of the NYYC about fairness at times
were ambiguous, such as claiming the right to defend with a larger yacht
or any yacht of its choice, its actions always were consistent in meeting
the challenger with a similar yacht.

With the dispute heading back to her court, Judge Ciparick scheduled a conference of all counsel for 12 October 1988. The press got wind of it and began making enquiries about arrangements for their attendance. The judge, however, viewed the conference as a confidential matter between the court and counsel, so she cancelled the conference and ordered the parties, including the New York Yacht Club and the Royal Perth Yacht Club, to submit an agenda of the matters they wished to have considered, after which she would reconvene the conference. Ultimately, the judge set deadlines of 15 November 1988 for the filing of motions in the case and 30 November 1988 for submitting final papers.

George Tompkins' motion on behalf of Mercury Bay was brief and to the point. He asked the court to disqualify the catamaran, declare New Zealand the winner, and direct the San Diego Yacht Club to transfer the Cup to the Mercury Bay Boating Club. This motion triggered a torrent of reaction and it was 28 March 1989 before Judge Ciparick handed down her decision, which said that, when considering the Deed's basic specifications and the challenge notice requirements, the conclusion was inescapable that the donor contemplated the defending vessel to relate in some way to the specifications of the challenger.

The prohibition against the challenger exceeding the stated dimensions indicated the defender would rely upon them and, conversely, if the defender were free and therefore encouraged to build to the absolute specifications of the Deed, without regard to the contents of the challenge, there would be no need for the challenger to reveal the specifications of its craft.

The Deed's use of the terms 'centreboard or sliding keel' in the singular indicated to the court that the donor did not contemplate multihulled vessels, which were in existence at the time of the third Deed. The donor could have provided for their participation by using the plural in reference to centreboard or by specifying dimensions permissible for catamarans. Also, waterline length is of great significance in monohulled races, but loses significance in races between monohulls and multihulls.

The decision concluded: 'Therefore, the nature of the basic vessels set out in the Deed of Gift supports the conclusion that a race limited to monohull vessels was contemplated by the donor.'

Judge Ciparick then stated that 'the most significant sentence of the Deed' is the one setting forth the trust's purpose to promote 'friendly competition between foreign countries'. The emphasis 'is on competition and sportsmanship'. The decision continued:

> *The court finds that the intent of the donor, as expressed in the Deed of Gift, was to exclude a defence of the America's Cup in a multihulled vessel by a defender faced with a monohull challenge. The challenge provision would be rendered meaningless if the defender was provided with the specifications of the challenging vessel and then afforded ten months to produce a vessel with an insurmountable competitive advantage.*
>
> *To sail a multihulled vessel against a monohulled yacht over the type of course contemplated by the donor is, in the opinion of most boating authorities, to create a gross mismatch and, therefore, is violative of the donor's primary purpose of fostering friendly competition.*[8]

The judge then cited Schuyler's own definition of a 'match', and his conviction that no one would cross the ocean to enter a hopeless contest.

The court next found that, while design variations are not precluded, to allow the use of a multihulled vessel would be to countenance more than mere design variations and, against a monohull, it would be to countenance a mismatch ... there was no doubt 'that San Diego's defence of the America's Cup in a catamaran against Mercury Bay's monohull challenge clearly deviated from the intent of the donor'.

The court then reached the following conclusions:

> *Therefore, whether the court limits its inquiry to the trust instrument or accepts extrinsic evidence, it is clear that a catamaran may not defend in America's Cup competition against a monohull. Accordingly, San Diego shall be disqualified in the September 1988 competition. The court is mindful that forfeiture is a drastic remedy in the instance of a competition such as the America's Cup with its large economic significance and prestige. Nonetheless the parties neither seek nor suggest alternative relief upon the disqualification of a competitor, nor is any alternative relief feasible under the circumstances. San Diego was well aware of the risk it ran when it chose to follow the unprecedented course of defending in a catamaran. Barely paying lip service to the significance of the competition, its clear goal was to retain the Cup at all costs so that it*

could host a competition on its own terms. San Diego thus violated the spirit of the Deed.[9]

The court also held that 'the yacht club winning the America's Cup becomes the sole trustee under the Deed of Gift and has an obligation thereunder to insure fair competition'. And that 'San Diego clearly fell short of its obligations as trustee of the Deed of Gift'.

The ruling of the court, then, was that the application by Mercury Bay Boating Club for disqualification of San Diego Yacht Club was granted, and the application of San Diego was denied.

Back in New Zealand, Michael Fay heard the good news during his morning swim at a public pool in Auckland. His initial reaction was:

The judge has come out strongly in support of our beliefs in what the America's Cup means. San Diego didn't want a real race, and even when we offered to delay the race, they didn't want to play the game. Now the judge has stood up for the integrity of the event. This is not a hollow victory. The real issue was the integrity of the Cup and what it stands for. The judge has restated the basic rules of sportsmanship and fair competition, which, for the last 135 years, have been the very essence of the event. The America's Cup is the winner. The Deed works.[10]

SDYC/Sail America, however, were not convinced. Their reactions, for the most part, adopted the theme that the decision was 'inexplicable' in light of the Court's prior rulings, which, they said, were based upon a strict, literal interpretation of the Deed of Gift, whereas now the Court was basing its ruling on an interpretation of what the donor had in mind when he signed the Deed in 1887.

Tom Ehman said: 'We defended the Cup with what we thought was the fastest boat we could design, and now the judge has done a 180-degree turn on us. In reading the Deed and her earlier decisions, we are baffled.'[11]

George Tompkins was moved to observe: 'I don't recall if he [Ehman] was a lawyer but he certainly was a good salesman.'[12]

Malin Burnham rumbled:

I'm not only stunned by this decision, I'm disappointed. I don't know how to analyse it. But I do not like to make emotional decisions. I have a lot of problems with the judicial system in general. While I do not like the decision, I have to decide why it was made, right or wrong. If it is wrong, we will appeal.[13]

Asked if he would like to see an appeal launched, Dennis Conner replied: 'No. I think it is high time the event moved on. I will abide by the umpire's decision. I think the sailors want to get out on the water and race for the Cup on the water. As an American, naturally I'm disappointed in the judge's decision, but as a competitor, I don't like the idea of the America's Cup being in court.'[14]

Not everyone in his organisation agreed with him, however. While Tom Mitchell, an outspoken member of Sail America's public relations department, rekindled the past when he said: 'If we had known she would rule on fairness, we might never have sailed the catamaran. We didn't worry about spirit or intent; we worried about what the Deed said. Now she says spirit was more important.'[15]

Sail America persisted with its now familiar intransigence and, on 14 April 1989, took Ciparick's decisions to the next level of the court system, the Appellate Division of the Supreme Court of New York. The long and wide-ranging dispute was now off on the final legs of its torturous journey.

The five-man panel of the Appellate Division handed down its findings on 19 September 1989. The outcome, reversing Judge Ciparick, was 4–1 in favour of San Diego Yacht Club. The majority decision was written by Presiding Justice Joseph P Sullivan and concurred in by Justices E Leo Milonas and Richard W Wallach. Justice Israel Rubin concurred in a separate opinion, while Justice Bentley Kassal wrote a dissenting opinion.

The *Boston Globe* regarded this turn of events as reducing the America's Cup to ridicule. How four New York justices could get it so wrong, it said, was a source of amazement and it was particularly critical of the quartet's dismissal of the lower court's view that the yachts contesting an America's Cup match should be 'somewhat evenly matched'. The justices said this was 'neither expressed in, nor reasonably inferable from, the language in the Deed of Gift'. To which the *Globe* retorted that if the donors of the Cup had not intended that racing for their trophy should be 'somewhat fair' then the Cup and competition for it should be consigned to history 'because the America's Cup, as a sport, is over'.[16]

The Mercury Bay Boating Club responded on 21 November 1989 with an action in the New York Court of Appeals, in Albany, New York, in support of which San Francisco attorney and yachtsman James Michael independently filed an amicus curiae brief (the Latin expression for a brief by 'friends of the court'). This is a procedure of long standing in English law, whereby a court may be informed by persons, not parties to the particular action, yet nonetheless particularly informed or interested in the outcome.

Michael was a former president of the United States Yacht Racing Union (USYRU), the sport's governing body in America. He had been following the case closely and decided it was time to make the Court of Appeals aware of the concerns shared by so many in the yachting community. In his considered view, the Appellate Division's decision went far beyond merely deciding who had won the September 1988 'match' – the majority of that court had held that considerations of fairness, good sportsmanship and a 'match' on competitive terms were not required by the Deed of Gift, hence they were not affirmative obligations to be observed by the defending club. The majority also said that a defender of the Cup was free to do whatever was not expressly prohibited by the Deed of Gift, even though the result was a hopeless contest in which the challenger had no chance of winning.

Thus the decision, in Michael's opinion, was contrary to fundamental concepts upon which Cup competition and, indeed, the sport of yacht racing existed. Moreover, he discovered he was not alone in these views – there was strong groundswell of belief in the global sailing community that the New York court had failed to recognise that fair play, good sportsmanship and an equal opportunity to win were inherent elements of every amateur sporting event, so much so that it was not necessary that they be reduced to some written caveat. So, the decision, if left standing, not only posed a serious risk of degrading future competition for the America's Cup, but could also become a precedent that could adversely affect many other yacht-racing events.

Ably assisted by Joanne Fishman, former *New York Times* yachting writer (and member of the San Diego Yacht Club's America's Cup

Committee), he set about contacting all the living participants in post-World War II Cup matches (excepting, of course, Dennis Conner). The upshot was an amicus curiae brief signed by 17 legendary Cup figures from the modern era.

Michael observed:

> *There were ten matches for the America's Cup in the thirty-year period 1958–1987. The 'friends of the court', who participated in the amici brief, include every American skipper except two (Briggs Cunningham and Dennis Conner) and every living foreign skipper (except one, Iain Murray) that competed in those matches. Each is a distinguished yachtsman, who has earned worldwide acclaim, both as a sailor and as a true sportsman. Collectively, they represent the real beneficiaries of the charitable trust created by the Deed of Gift to the America's Cup. Their view that principles of fair play and good sportsmanship are implicit and essential parts of the sport of yacht racing and, particularly, races for the America's Cup, is at odds with views of the [New York] Attorney General – the supposed protector of their interests as beneficiaries of the trust. That they are willing to unite together and stand four-square for those principles is an impressive display on behalf of the international yachting community of the concerns created by the Appellate Division's decision.*[17]

The final 17 who joined in the submission of the brief were, in alphabetical order:

Robert N Bavier Jr, skipper of 1964 Cup defender *Constellation* and former president of the United States Yacht Racing Union;

John Bertrand, skipper of 1983 Cup winner *Australia II* and bronze-medal winner in the Finn class at the 1978 Olympics;

Alan Bond, who mounted four successive America's Cup campaigns for Australia, in 1974, 1977, 1980 and, finally, in 1983 when his *Australia II* ended the longest winning streak in sport;

Courageous Sailing Center, a City of Boston youth-oriented sailing programme, and **Dave Vietor**, an officer of the center, who had participated in America's Cup campaigns dating back to 1977;

William P ('Bill') Ficker, skipper of 1970 Cup winner *Intrepid* and the first person to win three of the most coveted trophies in the sport – the America's Cup, the Congressional Cup and the Star World Championships;

Sir James Hardy ('Gentleman Jim'), who was skipper of Australia's challengers *Gretel II* in the 1970 Cup, *Southern Cross* in 1974 and *Australia* in 1980. He was also chairman of the South Australia syndicate in the defenders' trials in 1986–1987;

Frederick E 'Ted' Hood, who skippered 1974 Cup winner *Courageous*, and the defence contenders *Nefertiti* in 1962 and *Independence* in 1977;

Gordon Ingate, who skippered Australia's *Gretel* in the 1967 challenger eliminations, and *Gretel II* in the 1977 trials. A legendary ocean racer, he also represented Australia in the Tempest class at the 1972 Olympics;

Ischoda Yacht Club, founded in 1886, one of the oldest yacht clubs on the Atlantic seaboard (of the USA). Offered to finance, design and build a 90-foot defender for San Diego but was rejected;

Warren Jones, Alan Bond's executive officer in all his Cup campaigns and widely credited with having masterminded the *Australia II* victory in 1983. A student of its Deed of Gift, and an articulate defender of the Cup's traditions;

Arthur Knapp Jr, a legendary figure in sailing, he was part of Harold Vanderbilt's afterguard on the iconic 1937 Cup winner *Ranger* then skippered *Weatherly* in the 1964 defender trials;

Graham Mann, who skippered the British challenger *Sceptre* when Cup competition resumed, now in 12-Metres, in 1958. Rear commodore of the Royal Yacht Squadron, 1994–1999;

Robert W McCullough, who was directly involved in the America's Cup since 1964, as skipper of a contender in defence trials, or serving on, or as chairman of, the NYYC America's Cup committee;

Emil 'Bus' Mosbacher Jr, who skippered *Vim* in the 1958 defender trials and then twice successfully defended the Cup, with *Weatherly*, in 1962, and the iconic *Intrepid*, in 1967. Considered one of the USA's finest helmsmen, he was appointed Chief of Protocol of the United States, 1969–1972;

Noel Robbins, skipper of Alan Bond's beaten challenger *Australia*, in 1977, and executive director of the Royal Perth Yacht Club America's Cup Committee for the 1987 Cup off Fremantle;

Jock Sturrock, skipper of the beaten Australian challenger *Gretel* in the 1962 Cup and of the beaten *Dame Pattie* in 1967. Represented Australia at four Olympics – 1948 in the Star class, 1952 in Dragons, 1956 in 5.5-Metres (bronze-medal winner), and 1960 in 5.5-Metres.

RE 'Ted' Turner, who successfully defended the Cup in 1977 in *Courageous*. He went on to an outstanding ocean-racing career, winning the Annapolis–Newport Race, the Sydney–Hobart classic, the Fastnet Classic and the Southern Ocean Racing Conference and World Ocean Racing Championship in his converted 12-Metre *American Eagle*.

It was an impressive line-up and representation, but it was to no avail. The New York Court of Appeals, on 26 April 1990, by a five-to-two vote, affirmed the decision of the Appellate Division in favour of the San Diego Yacht Club.

The majority opinion was written by Associate Judge Fritz W Alexander and was concurred in by Chief Judge Sol Wachtler, Senior Associate Judge Richard D Simmons, Associate Judge Judith S Kaye, and Associate Justice Joseph W Bellacosa. Chief Judge Wachtler wrote a separate opinion while Associate Judge Stewart F Hancock Jr wrote a dissenting opinion that was concurred in by Associate Judge Vito J Titone.

This majority opinion was so much a repeat of that of the Appellate Division that it smacked of a cut-and-paste job, accepting the arguments of SDYC with little regard to those of the opposing parties. And, again, San Diego's misrepresentations of fact became part of the record. It was almost as though the justices were loath to do their job properly and rule against the USA because, after all, this was only sport.

That impression was reflected in the concurring opinion of Chief Judge Sol Wachtler, who wrote:

This case has little or no significance for the law, but it has caught the public eye like few cases in this court's history. Much of the reason for this attention, apparently, is the supposition that here at stake are grand principles – sportsmanship and tradition – pitted against the greed, commercialism and zealotry that threaten to vulgarise the sport. In the end, however, the outcome of the case is dictated by elemental legal principles.[18]

Wachtler went on to assert that neither the 'unorthodox' challenge by Mercury Bay nor the 'unorthodox' defence by San Diego were prohibited by the Deed of Gift, and the case should end there. This statement ignored all the evidence that Mercury Bay's challenge was not unorthodox. It was precisely what Schuyler envisaged when he constructed his Deed. And, similarly, SDYC/SAF's defence was not, either, unorthodox. It was completely contrary to what Schuyler intended.

Michael Fay; in a telephone interview with Barbara Lloyd of *The New York Times*, said: 'We've always believed we were right. But at the end of the day, the courts found San Diego to be right, and I have to accept that.' Fay added that he planned to send a team to San Diego in 1992 to challenge again for the America's Cup.[19]

The San Diego Yacht Club, of course, was pleased. It recovered the America's Cup from the vault in New York and stepped up its plans to hold the next match commencing in May 1992. Dennis Conner announced that he would go 'full speed ahead' to prepare to defend the Cup, building three new boats for the campaign at a cost of $US4 million apiece.

The reaction of many around the world was one of relief that the legal proceedings were at an end, whether they agreed or disagreed with the decision of the court. John Rousmaniere, in his July 1990 column in *Sailing World*, stepped back and reviewed the decision in his analytical and articulate manner. Noting that the America's Cup controversy 'has forced us to wrestle with the problem of just what constitutes a sport', he observed:

We won't get much guidance from the court decision that finally settled the case in late April. When the New York Court of Appeals ruled for the San Diego Yacht Club in a 5–2 decision, the majority opinion written by Justice Fritz Alexander decided the issue on a narrow legal ground: there was no specific rule prohibiting catamarans.

Using this limited standard, the judges not only dodged forceful historic evidence that the Cup's founders did not anticipate the use of catamarans, but they were able to ignore broad questions about the overriding purpose of the America's Cup and, indeed, any sport.[20]

On 13 March 1992, Judge Stewart Hancock, the author of the Court of Appeal's dissenting opinion, visited the New Zealand Court of Appeal. He carried with him and delivered to Sir Robin Cooke, the president of that court, a letter from Governor Cuomo of New York, which read:

> *On behalf of the citizens of the State of New York, I send greetings and best wishes. Judge Stewart F Hancock Jr who delivers this letter, is one of the Empire State's most distinguished jurists. I had the pleasure of appointing him to our highest court, the Court of Appeals, in 1986. As such, and as a former law clerk at that august institution, you may trust that he has my fullest confidence and support – with one possible minor exception.*
>
> *My advisors have examined the Judge's interpretation of the law of New York trusts as applied to the rule of the seas, and tell me I should treat him as somewhat without compass on the matter. However, this opinion may have less to do with policy than with politics, since one elected [to] public office in the United States is ill-advised to cheer against a boat by the name of 'Stars & Stripes' … and my advisors know that. I expect the good people of New Zealand will understand.*[21]

Sir Robin Cooke, on the occasion of Judge Hancock's visit, remarked that the New York Court of Appeals was a leader among state appellate courts, adding:

> *Its history has gone from the sublime, which was Cardozo, to the catamaran, although it can be said, I suppose, that there was a degree of provocation leading the Court to depart so far from the fairly elementary principles of interpretation. But you, sir, are an honourable dissentient from that decision.'*

Judge Hancock's reply included:

> *What really led to my coming here, as many of you probably know, is the* Law Journal *article which was written in New Zealand by*

Mr Justice Thomas. Needless to say, having made a very competent and fair analysis of the pros and cons of the America's Cup litigation, he came down on the side of New Zealand and his concluding paragraph is really what urged me here. It went something like this: 'And the majority itself? Eventually also, to borrow and distort Lord Atkin's famous dictum in Perrin v Morgan [1943] AC 399, 415, they must confront the ghosts of a dissatisfied George Schuyler and the earlier donors of the Cup waiting on the opposite bank of the Styx to receive them. And there, I suggest, looming spectre-like, but with true judicial bearing behind them, will be Justice Cardozo and the other great jurists of the New York Court of Appeals, their thunderous countenances saying it all.

So that caught my eye and the eye of the Judge who dissented with me, and we decided that it was only fair and proper to have this analysis of the merits of the case brought to the attention of our colleagues. We underlined the last paragraph and called it to their attention particularly. So I wrote back to Mr Justice Thomas and reported on this and said that I had assured my colleagues inasmuch as I am the oldest member of the court and it is highly probable that I shall be on the other side of the Styx first, to do my very best to see that the reception was not quite as chilly as Mr Justice Thomas suggested it might be, upon condition, however, that they did not make the crossing of the Styx in a catamaran.

On 18 March 1992, Sir Robin Cooke replied to Governor Cuomo in a letter:

Judge Stewart F Hancock Jr has delivered to me your letter of 3 March 1992, and we were delighted to welcome to our court a justly famous and honoured Judge of the highest Court of your State.

I cordially agree with everything that you say in your letter, including the implications in the fourth paragraph. It is reassuring to gather that your advisors evidently do not suggest that the Judge's dissenting opinion was wrong, but only that it was impolitic. Not being the holder of elective office, I have no authority to speak for and am not constrained by the possible majority opinion of any electorate; but I am certain that the good wishes of the people of the Empire State are valued and reciprocated to the full by the New Zealand people.[22]

Judge Hancock was one, if not the only, judge in the New York Court of Appeals who was a sailor and could see the issues from the viewpoint of those in the yachting world community. In his dissent, he said:

> The challenge by New Zealand was unquestionably proper in every respect. That San Diego persists in its efforts to cast doubt on the propriety of New Zealand's conduct (a 'suggestion apparently viewed with some favour by the majority'), is surprising in view of the trial court's rulings and the record.
>
> San Diego's attempt to make it appear that, in the late 19th century, catamarans were customarily accepted as competitors in ocean racing is refuted by the record, which demonstrates just the contrary. Catamarans were small, largely experimental and generally not accepted in established yacht races. Only 48 existed in this country between 1820 and 1890. They were never considered in connection with America's Cup races, were too small [to qualify] and not sufficiently seaworthy to make the open ocean voyage required to get to the site of the race.
>
> At the root of this appeal is a fundamental disagreement as to the standards by which San Diego's conduct as trustee should be measured. San Diego applies the standard of 'the marketplace' and assumes it was justified in adopting an 'anything goes' interpretation of the Deed of Gift, as though the case involved a dispute over the meaning of a business contract made between two parties at arm's length. But the standards of 'the marketplace' cannot be the measure of San Diego's conduct as defender and as a trustee under New York law. San Diego and New Zealand are not parties to a dispute over a bargained-for agreement; one is a trustee, the other is not. It is the law of trusts which applies, not the law of contracts.
>
> It is this critical aspect of San Diego's role and its attendant obligations as trustee which both the Attorney General and the majority overlook in their criticism of the trial court for applying a different standard in assessing the propriety of San Diego's defence than it did in evaluating Mercury Bay's challenge. But Judge Ciparick was correct, for only San Diego was a trustee, and it formally accepted the trust and agreed to faithfully and fully comply with its terms.
>
> The concurring opinion of the Chief Judge states the dissent would 'impose a duty on the defender to – well, to do just what?' That critical question, the dissent believes, has been clearly answered. As trustee under

the Deed of Gift, San Diego had the legal duty to meet the 'very high and strict standards' which the law imposed upon it because, in its dual role as competitor and trustee, its interests were in conflict with the interests of the beneficiaries, including the challenger.[23]

In his conclusion, Justice Thomas noted that, notwithstanding Chief Judge Wachtler's concurring claim that the case had 'little significance for the law', he predicted it would attract considerable attention within legal circles, and that: 'It is certain that the majority's decision will not emerge unscathed. Indeed, if I am at all correct in discerning the shallow and flawed reasoning on which it is based, the decision will ultimately be perceived as part of yet a further blemish on the history of a great trophy.'

Many years later, MBBC's New York lawyer, George Tompkins, expressed complete respect for his legal opposition throughout the high-profile dispute: 'They always argued fairly and believed what they were arguing. It was just totally contrary to the purpose of the Deed of Gift and to the concept of the trust that was created.'

Tompkins was not, however, as charitable in his assessment of the conduct of the San Diego Yacht Club and, particularly, of Sail America Foundation, who were instructing their legal representatives:

They never grasped it or, if they grasped it, they masked it. The America's Cup is a challenge competition. The challenger decides what boat shall be used and the deed of trust requires the trustee, the holder of the Cup, to meet the challenge of that boat. You don't do that with a catamaran against a monohull. They manipulated the rules to suit their objective, which was not to have a match with a single challenger.[24]

When it was put to him that, as a result of the full-on, two-year dispute, he was now possibly the world expert on Schuyler's Deed of Gift, he disagreed and deferred to Judge Ciparick:

After all, she got it right, she got it right. I should add that she also made the right decisions every time.

Judge Ciparick made some very brave and bold decisions throughout the history of the case. First she upheld the challenge against a mountain of opposition from San Diego. Then, in a Solomonesque way, when we challenged the use of a catamaran, she said, 'Go and race with it and if you can come back and convince me it was invalid to race, then disqualification may be the end of this case.'

That wasn't a popular decision but it certainly was a wise decision, a bold decision. Disqualifying the catamaran took a lot of courage, a whole lot of courage because, I am sure, she was under a lot more pressure mentally than I was in arguing for that outcome.[25]

It is, perhaps, appropriate that the last word on this highly influential episode of the America's Cup goes to the man who started the whole saga – Andrew Johns – who observed:

It's interesting – the courts [the Appellate Division and the Court of Appeals] took the very narrow view that, because the Deed is silent on the use of catamarans, it, therefore, contemplates their competing.

What the Deed does say is 'Any organized yacht club of a foreign country … shall always be entitled to the right of a sailing match for this Cup, with a yacht or vessel propelled by sails only and constructed in the country to which the challenging Club belongs, against any one yacht or vessel constructed in the country of the Club holding the Cup.'

If you take a similarly narrow view [as the Appellate Division and the Court of Appeals], the Deed spells out that the challenging yacht or vessel has to be powered by sails only but it doesn't make the same specification in terms of the defending yacht or vessel. It is silent. Can that silence in this context, then, be interpreted as the Deed contemplating defending yachts or vessels powered by steam, which were very much in existence in those days? I don't think so!

The further we went up the ladder [of the New York court system], the less comfortable I felt. The decision that came down from the Appellate Division, for instance, was, verbatim, the San Diego brief, apart from the opening sentence, the closing sentence and a couple of verbs in the middle. It was word for word. It didn't have the feel of a considered decision – more like, 'We've awarded to these guys and we don't care'.

At the next level, the last level [The Court of Appeals], the Chief Judge, Sol Wachtler, spent 15 or 20 minutes before the hearing telling the world how important his court was in terms of enforcing law and order and stopping people from committing crimes on the streets. They really didn't have time to waste on a yachting case.

I got the sense, at that level, that our business with the court was treated with a bit of disdain, that the proceedings were impolitic. You could maybe argue that the decision was never right. It certainly, though, was politic the way it came out. Regardless – it was a decision and it ended the matter, and the world carried on.

Looking back, San Diego always wanted to cast us in the light that we had destroyed their regatta – the extravaganza in 12-Metres that they were planning. The reality is that they were handed, on a plate, an opportunity for a regatta, the likes of which had never been seen before.

If you go back and read the news coverage of pre-World War II J-Boat matches, you could walk from one part of Newport, Rhode Island, to the other on top of boats that were all jammed in to watch the races. The coverage, without television, was voluminous. The popularity of the event was enormous, even compared to all subsequent America's Cups with the advent of television. The Mercury Bay challenge provided San Diego with an opportunity on the same scale – a golden opportunity that, sadly, was missed.[26]

09

SOLDIERS OF FORTUNE

It was the biggest smash-and-grab raid in America's Cup history. In February 2000, Italian-born Swiss biotech billionaire Ernesto Bertarelli swanned into Auckland to watch the start of racing in Team New Zealand's first defence of yachting's holy grail.

Bertarelli was a keen sailor and was rumoured to be interested in mounting a Cup challenge of his own. Twenty-four hours later, having waved his cheque book to great effect, he was on his way home again, now the 'owner' of the best yacht-racing talent in the world, including Team New Zealand skipper Russell Coutts and tactician Brad Butterworth, along with the cream of their crew and who knows how much of Team New Zealand's priceless intellectual design and build properties.

When news of this leaked out, the tiny nation of just 3.8 million people, deep in the South Pacific, was stunned. How could it happen? How could it have been allowed to happen?

The country invariably punched well above its weight in international sports, including equestrian, track and field, and cycling, and was a world force in rowing and canoeing. It was also truly a superpower in the increasingly international rugby union and – in sailing.

Here, it excelled in the Olympic classes and had a clutch of medals to prove it. In addition, it ruled the world in international offshore racing, having won every event of note, most several times over, including the globe-girdling Whitbread (now Volvo) Round the World Yacht Race, the Trophée Jules Verne (fastest non-stop around the world) and the daddy of them all, the much-coveted America's Cup, in which it was the first country other than America to win the Cup and then successfully defend it.

It had done pretty much all of this in boats designed and built by Kiwis, with rigs and sails designed and built by Kiwis, and with all-New Zealand crews. Not surprisingly, its support marine industry, on all fronts, was among the most respected and in-demand on the planet.

The jewel in that crown was the all-conquering Team New Zealand, and so it probably wasn't surprising that the reviews of the Swiss raid turned nasty. Coutts and Butterworth, national heroes only weeks earlier, were branded opportunistic mercenaries who had sold their souls, and Team New Zealand's design secrets and campaign know-how, to a Swiss billionaire who wanted to buy the most elusive prize in sport. Bertarelli, in turn, was accused of tearing the heart out of the nation's pride.

However, all was not quite as it seemed and, over time, a more plausible story emerged, one in which the blackguarded Bertarelli simply took full advantage of a golden opportunity that was unexpectedly dropped in his lap, while Coutts and Butterworth were hardly traitors, but rather ambitious – if impatient and sometimes poorly advised – prize talents who wanted to parlay their sailing skills and experience into a lucrative career in the biggest game in town.

The backdrop to Bertarelli's 'opportunity' was a confrontation at the very top of Team New Zealand that had been simmering just below the calm surface of the world's outstanding yacht-racing organisation as it went about its preparations to defend the trophy that it won five years earlier in the waters off San Diego, California.

Team New Zealand's legendary boss, Sir Peter Blake, had made it clear that the 2000 Cup would be his last competitive yachting campaign. He was in talks with the Cousteau Society about taking over the reins of the late Jacques' organisation in order to focus greater attention on the need for better care of the waters of the world. On learning this, Coutts and his followers, more than 12 months out, started working on a structured transfer that would see them being in charge when Blake left. However, Blake and his management team wouldn't have that. They were mindful that, in the much-lauded 1995 San Diego campaign, Coutts had adamantly dismissed anything other than the team's development programme and improving boat performance, tackling the Louis Vuitton Cup qualifiers and then the Cup match one race at a time and taking nothing for granted. Everything else could wait until ultimate victory was achieved.

This strategy worked wondrously well in what, most experts agreed, was the most consummate challenger performance in the history of the event. With Coutts and his crew in superb form, the two *Black Magics* (NZL38 and NZL32) won 41 of the 43 races sailed, including a 5–0 thrashing of Dennis Conner's *Young America* in the best-of-nine Cup match. Blake could see absolutely no reason to change the approach for 2000. Succession could wait until it was all over. He did, however, give Coutts and Butterworth his absolute assurance that they would be the inheritors of what they had helped to create.

Another complicating background factor was the very essence of the America's Cup as a challenge-driven event on a three- or four-year-cycle. Even if you win the Cup, you can only plan three or four years in advance because you may no longer be the trustee and/or the defender after that period of time. This impacts on everything, not least the contracting of commercial and broadcasting rights.

As a consequence, Team New Zealand, which operated under the umbrella of a public charitable trust, was legally structured and operated as a one-campaign entity that was regencrated, starting almost from scratch, if it successfully defended or decided to challenge again at the end of the cycle. To overcome the lack of guaranteed continuity for its commercial partners, its sponsorship contracts included right-of-renewal provisions, at current market rates, should the team successfully defend or challenge again. These provisions helped provide the sponsors with the long-term benefits that they needed in order to undertake medium/long-term marketing strategies.

However, this set-up proved to be unattractive to the would-be inheritors, who viewed America's Cup campaigning in a completely different light to Blake and his team, including his board of directors.

Butterworth accurately summed up the situation when he observed that Blake did not see himself in the America's Cup for the long term. He and Coutts did, and they were not short of options. Enter Ernesto Bertarelli…

In an in-depth interview with the Swiss billionaire, published in England's *Daily Telegraph* on 20 February 2003, Tim Jeffery wrote that, when Bertarelli began to get interested in an America's Cup challenge, he ran into Sir Michael Fay at a charity function in Geneva and asked him if he would ascertain whether Team New Zealand was selling any of its boats. Fay was the merchant banker who mounted New Zealand's first three Cup challenges, in 1987, '88 and '92, so would have been well placed to help.

'It's thanks to him that ultimately Russell gave me a call,' said Bertarelli, who insisted that his original approach was 'simply to buy a boat.'

'It was [however] like putting a message in a bottle and throwing it into the sea. It landed in New Zealand and that's when he [Coutts] called me back. At first I thought he was upset. For me, to have Russell Coutts on the phone was a big thing. He said "You want to buy my boats?" I said "Don't get upset. I'm not trying to raid your team. I'm just wondering … do you guys need money?" He said "That's not going to happen, but on the other hand I am in Europe, why don't we see each other?" It was then I learnt that what seemed a perfect team was not perfect. He was looking for something else.'[1]

Bertarelli, said Jeffery, was well used to sailing with some of the world's top yachtsmen, such as Kiwi Chris Dickson and American Paul Cayard, but the chance to do the Cup with Coutts was irresistible: 'His record is very impressive but [it transpired] he has a very clear vision of a job much wider than that of skipper.'

The two men, similar in age, got on well and Coutts soon outlined his desire to 'build something fresh and new.'

'Which I like,' Bertarelli told Jeffery, 'and his beliefs in the running of the team match mine, with delegation to your peers and a role for everyone. I also think he's the best in this game.'

Bertarelli liked to use mountaineering analogies when telling of his first encounters with Coutts, explaining that if you wanted to climb

Mt Everest you did as Hillary and hired a Tenzing to guide you to the top. Or, if you wanted to climb Mt Blanc, you hired one of the expert guides from Chamonix or from Zermatt for the Matterhorn. When he discovered that Coutts was a gun for hire, Bertarelli had his guide to take him to the top of the America's Cup. Coutts knew the way there.

An article in *The Wall Street Journal Europe* once described Ernesto Bertarelli as the 'crown prince of a Swiss industrial dynasty', a label that could be misinterpreted to infer that he had simply inherited his wealth and place in society, which would be doing him a serious injustice. Born in Rome, on 22 September 1965, Bertarelli completed his education in the USA, graduating from Babson College (near Boston, Massachusetts) in 1989 and earning an MBA at Harvard Business School (also near Boston) in 1993.

His grandfather, Cesare, had founded the pharmaceutical company Serono in 1903. One of its first endeavours had been to extract proteins from egg yolks to produce anaemia treatments, and the company went on in the 1960s to take a pioneering role in infertility treatments.

In 1977, worried about left-wing violence in Italy, Fabio Bertarelli, son of Cesare and the subsequent CEO, moved the company and his family to Geneva. Ernesto, from the age of 10, often accompanied Fabio on business trips and gained increasing knowledge of the ways and working of the company. He succeeded Fabio as the head of Serono in 1996 and, along with his sister Dona, inherited ownership in 1998, on his father's death.

Ernesto changed the company's focus from pharmaceuticals to biotechnology, increasing revenues from $US809 million in 1996 to $US2.8 billion in 2006. The company gained international recognition as a result of its discovery of a natural hormone used in the treatment of female infertility, and for its treatments for multiple sclerosis and growth hormone deficiency. In recognition, Ernesto was awarded the *Légion d'Honneur* by President Jacques Chirac of France.

The Bertarellis sold Serono to Merck KGaA of Germany in January 2007, for a reported $US13.3 billion. Today, Ernesto leads Kedge Capital Group and Ares Life Sciences. Kedge is an investment management group while Ares is a private equity operator. He also chairs Waypoint, a business enterprise for the managers and advisers of the funds and investments associated with the Bertarelli family. The group is active in two areas – life sciences and asset management, including real estate. Headquartered in Geneva, with offices in London, Jersey, Boston and Luxembourg, Waypoint has investments ranging from commercial real estate in London to drug companies. With his sister, Dona, also an ardent sailor, Ernesto co-chairs the Bertarelli Foundation, which focuses on marine conservation and life-sciences research.

He is married to the Decca Records recording artist Kirsty Roper, who was Miss United Kingdom in 1988. The couple live in Gstaad, in south-western Switzerland, with their three children – daughter Chiara, and sons Falco and Alceo. His net worth (in 2017) was estimated (by Forbes) as $US8.9 billion.

The Bertarellis inherited their passion for sailing from their father and Ernesto was first exposed to the history and tradition of the America's Cup when accompanying Fabio on business trips to Plymouth (Massachusetts) and Newport (Rhode Island) – both close to or at the very heart of the New York Yacht Club's 'Cup country'. He became even more of a fan of the event when he was studying at Babson and then at Harvard.

One of the last acts of the Coutts group before they decided to elope to Switzerland was, with the then trustee, the Royal New Zealand Yacht Squadron (RNZYS), to negotiate the protocol for the 2003 America's Cup. Their chosen 'hip pocket' challenger was Italy's Yacht Club Punta Ala, based in a yacht marina development on the coast of Tuscany, some 180 kilometres (112 miles) north-west of Rome's Leonardo da Vinci International Airport.

The key change they made in that protocol was the complete relaxation of the existing nationality requirements for designers and crew. After the win in 1995, Coutts and company wanted to tighten the nationality rules, because New Zealand was producing the best of the sailing and design talents. So this complete about-face could only be viewed, in hindsight, as a way of preparing the ground for the exodus of Team New Zealand personnel that Coutts and Butterworth were soon to lead. In more general terms, it resulted in the progressive removal of nationality from the event altogether and paved the way for matches such as that of 2003, which was billed as New Zealand against Switzerland while, in reality, it was the 'new' Team New Zealand racing the Coutts-led 'old' Team New Zealand masquerading as Swiss. Other similar instances of teams taking advantage of this change of protocol occurred in 2007, when there was only one Swiss national on the Brad Butterworth-skippered *Alinghi* defender (and that was Bertarelli), and in 2013, when *Oracle* Team USA defended the Cup in San Francisco with Coutts running the programme and Australian James Spithill skippering the boat, with only one American in his crew.

The folly of the Cup community in failing to recognise this move for what it was – a self-serving ploy to clear the way for soldiers of fortune to roam randomly through the event, was compounded by the decision to allow the 2003 challenge from Switzerland's Société Nautique de Genève (SNG), Ernesto Bertarelli's home yacht club.

The problem here lay with the wording of The Deed of Gift, which states that: 'Any organized Yacht Club of a foreign country … having for its annual regatta an ocean water course on the sea, or on an arm of the sea, or one which combines both, shall always be entitled to the right of sailing a match for this Cup.'

The NY Supreme Court, in 1984, was asked to rule on the 'arm of the sea' clause in the Deed, when the Chicago Yacht Club, based on Lake Michigan, sought to challenge for the 1987 Cup in Fremantle, Western Australia. The court found that, quite clearly, the Great Lakes were inland seas and therefore the clubs that held annual regattas on those lakes were entitled to challenge for the Cup.

In contrast, Lake Geneva, the biggest of Switzerland's beautiful lakes, could never be considered a sea and is certainly not an arm of the sea. Moreover, while it is 45 miles long, it is only 8.7 miles across at its widest point. So, ignoring any other considerations, it could not, therefore, accommodate the races and courses dictated by the Deed if no mutual consent on such items can be agreed by the defender and challenger. In such circumstances, the Deed specifies that:

'In case the parties cannot mutually agree upon the terms of a match, then three races shall be sailed and the winner of two of such races shall be entitled to the Cup. All such races shall be on ocean courses, free from headlands, as follows: the first race, twenty nautical miles to windward and return; the second race an equilateral triangular race of thirty-nine nautical miles, the first side of which shall be a beat to windward; the third race (if necessary) twenty nautical miles to windward and return.'[2]

It is the 'having for its annual regatta' wording that would ultimately reach out and bring about the downfall of the lake-based Swiss – but not yet.

In the course of its first defence of the Cup, in the year 2000, the Royal New Zealand Yacht Squadron had to address the eligibility of two would-be Swiss challengers – Société Nautique Rolloise and the Club Nautique Morgien – both based on Lake Geneva. The Squadron consulted with the original trustee, the New York Yacht Club, and took legal and other advice before deciding that there was no way a yacht club headquartered on a lake in Switzerland could satisfy the requirements of the Deed of Gift. So, in an earnest endeavour to be inclusive, the RNZYS determined to accept a Swiss challenge if the yacht club making that challenge: a) otherwise complied with the Deed of Gift; and b) made a legally binding undertaking that, should it be successful and win the Cup, it would defend on nominated waters that did comply with the Deed, those waters to be identified in its legally binding undertaking.

One Swiss challenge eventuated, the Fast 2000 campaign of legendary offshore racers Marc Pajot and Pierre Fehlmann, on behalf of the Club Nautique Morgien, which undertook to defend in the Mediterranean, off Hyères, should it be successful. That wasn't to be an issue, however, for Fast 2000 won only two round-robin qualifiers and went home early.

When faced with the same situation in terms of a 2003 challenge from the Société Nautique de Genève, and despite its previous decisions, the RNZYS, incorrectly, referred the matter to the arbitration panel for the event. It was quickly taken to task by SNG's legal adviser in New Zealand, Hamish Ross, who wrote to say: 'Royal New Zealand Yacht Squadron cannot at law, as a Trustee of the America's Cup, delegate its responsibility to accept a challenge to another authority such as the America's Cup Arbitration Panel. The Royal New Zealand Yacht Squadron must make its own determination to accept or reject the challenge.'

Strangely, though, SNG did later accede to the Arbitration Panel deciding on the validity of its challenge and the Panel did, then, deal with the matter, even though a very strong case could have been made that eligibility was outside of its jurisdiction (viz the Hamish Ross letter), because it involved interpretation of the Deed of Gift.

The Panel certainly did that despite interpretation of the Deed being the exclusive domain of the New York Supreme Court. It listened to submissions by SNG counsel on the dictionary definition of the words 'annual' and 'regatta' as used in the Deed and concluded that:

> 'The major issue on whether the SNG's challenge is valid turns on whether it has complied with the "having for its annual regatta an ocean-water course on the sea or on an arm of the sea" requirement of the Deed of Gift ... In the context of the Deed of Gift, the phrase "annual regatta" should be interpreted to mean an organized series of yacht races occurring once a year ... we consider that in judging whether a yacht club has complied with this requirement for the purpose of assessing eligibility, a liberal approach should be adopted.'[3]

Moreover, it found that:

> '... neither the Deed of Gift nor the Protocol have any provision requiring the annual regatta to have been held prior to the lodging of a challenge, nor that the annual regatta must have been held more than once. The only requirement is that the challenging club must be a yacht club "having for its annual regatta an ocean water course on the sea [...]" If it has such a regatta, it is eligible.'[4]

Some six years later, on 2 April 2009, a decision by the New York Court of Appeals revealed the folly of the 2003 Arbitration Panel's findings. The Court considered the same wording in the Deed as the pivotal element in the Golden Gate Yacht Club's petition to have the Société Nautique de Genève's (SNG) challenger of record (for the 2013 Cup), the Club Náutico Español de Vela (CNEV), invalidated (see chapter 10, Bitter Clash of the Titans). It ruled that the word 'having', as in 'having for its annual regatta an ocean water course on the sea, or on an arm of the sea' was 'unambiguous' and that a yacht club did not qualify as a challenger unless it had held at least one annual regatta, on the sea or an arm of the sea, or both, prior to its challenge. As a consequence, the CNEV's challenge was nullified and the SNG was ordered to defend against the next in line, the Golden Gate Yacht Club from San Francisco.

And so the Société Nautique de Genève, represented by Ernesto Bertarelli's Alinghi team, was admitted to the challenger ranks for the

2003 America's Cup, albeit in circumstances that would come back to haunt it and the RNZYS, and the 2000 Cup's Arbitration Panel.

In February 2003, in Auckland, Team New Zealand defended the America's Cup for a second time and, as the fates would have it, the opponent in the best-of-nine match, almost inevitably, was Ernesto Bertarelli. His first-time challenger, *Alinghi*, was skippered by Russell Coutts with his tactician Brad Butterworth and a crew stacked with the cream of his former Team New Zealand crop that had also made the jump to Lake Geneva.

On the water, the 2003 Cup was again a great success, with the races being followed by impressive flotillas of spectator craft and large global television audiences. The Swiss Kiwis defied the odds by beating the unbeatable Real Kiwis 5–0. Ashore, though, the 'Swiss' were constantly reminded that there was still ill-feeling about the defections.

In a 3 January 2003 media release, Alinghi's executive director, Michel Bonnefous, said he had made a complaint to the New Zealand police about threats against the children and family members of the team by a group of patriotic activists who 'spelled out a clear intention to target the children and family of sailors.' Bonnefous added that the team's security advisers and the police were taking the threats 'very seriously', and said: 'Alinghi is an international team. We are open and want to share our passion for sailing. We want the focus to return to sport and to the action on the water. We came here, in New Zealand, to sail, not to have our children threatened.'

In the immediate lead-up to the America's Cup match, after they had disposed of Larry Ellison's *BMW Oracle* 5–1 in the challenger final, Bertarelli, worked hard to focus as much attention as he could on what he saw as unfair public perceptions of his team, particularly the 'BlackHeart' advertising and PR campaign mounted by disgruntled Kiwi elements, which sought to use the 'betrayal', by Coutts and Butterworth in particular, to engender loyalty to Team New Zealand.

An editorial in the 1 February 2003 *New Zealand Herald* newspaper put a stop to that when it revealed:

'As the Herald-DigiPoll survey shows, Mr Bertarelli is boxing at shadows. Fully three-quarters of those polled reject the notion that his key sailors, Russell Coutts and Brad Butterworth, betrayed New Zealand. A majority

endorse their right to sail for Mr Bertarelli's millions. At the presentation of the [Louis Vuitton] challenger cup two weeks ago, a sizable crowd gave the 15-nation Swiss team generous, polite recognition of their victory. The very failure last month of the BlackHeart campaign to achieve a critical mass of public opinion against those men and Alinghi further undermines Mr Bertarelli's imagined "campaign of aggression".

A vocal minority probably does feel aggrieved by the defections. A growing number, though, is tired of his [Bertarelli's] attempts to use that criticism to sermonise about fair play and to paint New Zealanders and their sense of sportsmanship in a poor light beyond these shores. It has also been unfortunate that the police cannot rule out the growing public suspicion that threatening letters targeting Alinghi members might have emanated from close to the syndicate itself.'[5]

The New Zealand police did thoroughly investigate the complaint but no further action was taken.

There were no such concerns on the water, though. The Swiss campaign, not surprisingly, very much resembled those of Team New Zealand in 1995 and 2000, with the daunting combination of Coutts and Butterworth at the top of their game and nigh-unbeatable in the all-important start skirmishes. What was surprising, though, was the catastrophic performance of the once-invincible Kiwis. The team that wrote the book on successful campaigning seemed to have lost its copy, while Coutts and company followed it chapter and verse.

The Swiss pursued an evolutionary approach to boat design and development, with a managed programme that had, with some embellishments, 'Team New Zealand '95' stamped all over it. Team New Zealand, in contrast, adopted a revolutionary approach and its designer-led programme hit the corners of the design rule, striving for more and more speed. Weight savings were sought everywhere and, in the process, reliability was sacrificed as weight savings were sought everywhere. As a result, in the build-up the Kiwis broke, beyond ready repair, one of their two race yachts and looked to go perilously close to losing the other when, in the fresh winds of race one (of the best-of-nine match), it shipped water at an alarming rate into the low-freeboard cockpit. The weight of the incoming flood loaded the boat up to the degree that gear failures were inevitable and skipper Dean Barker was forced to retire.

The Kiwis regrouped and took it to the Swiss in races two and three, but Coutts handled the pressure and helmed *Alinghi* to a 3–0 lead with hard-fought wins by 7 seconds and 23 seconds. The New Zealanders certainly weren't lacking boat speed but their would-be revival was betrayed in race four when, again in willing conditions, the boat's mast snapped on the second upwind leg and Barker was forced to withdraw for a second time. Coutts finally put the dejected and embarrassed home team out of its misery, winning race five by 44 seconds, more gear failures again hampering the defender.

In his first attempt, the 37-year-old Ernesto Bertarelli had become (to date) the Cup's only first-time winner, and its youngest. He was also taking the contest for the oldest trophy in sport back to Europe for the first time since 1851.

Coutts, though, was in familiar territory. He had now won the Cup three times – twice as a challenger (for New Zealand in 1995 and now Switzerland in 2003) and once as a defender (for New Zealand in 2000) – equalling the record of the Scotsman Charlie Barr, who had migrated to America and helmed the successful defenders *Columbia* (in 1899 and 1901) and *Reliance* (in 1903). Coutts had now gone undefeated in 15 races straight, in three different Cup matches spread over eight years, and the same impressive claim could be made by five of his crew (tactician Butterworth, trimmers Warwick Fleury and Simon Daubney, mastman Murray Jones and bowman Dean Phipps).

In between all this, in June 2000, Coutts received one of his country's highest honours when he was made a Distinguished Companion of the New Zealand Order of Merit for his services to New Zealand yachting (an honour that he parlayed into a knighthood when, in 2009, the restored National Government readopted the most prestigious of British honours).

Bertarelli and his team were welcomed home to Geneva as sporting heroes and basked in the warm glow of a job exceedingly well done, but it wasn't long before Bertarelli was exposed to a darker side of the man he had hired to take him to the top of his sailing Everest – and the resultant falling-out and parting of ways were like a re-run of Team New Zealand's experience.

As Bertarelli set about the task of organising a major sporting event as well as a defence of the oldest trophy in sport, he came to the realisation that his main man Coutts wasn't on the same page as his boss. What started out as variances of opinion, on organisational matters and on a venue (on the sea or an arm of the sea), soon became irrevocable differences and, in July 2004, Bertarelli and Coutts parted company.

The first outward signs of trouble surfaced a month earlier when Alinghi was scheduled to race in the UBS Trophy regatta in Newport, Rhode Island. Coutts declined to sail. Taken aback, Bertarelli told the *Daily Telegraph*'s Tim Jeffery (22 June 2004): 'For me to find that he doesn't want to jump on an Alinghi boat is a bit of a surprise given that what I basically hired him for was helming. If the guy doesn't want to do his basic task, we have a bit of problem.'[6]

Bertarelli couldn't explain what was behind Coutts's decision [not to sail] but, according to Jeffery, he believed it had nothing to do with their relationship, money or Coutts's position in the decision-making hierarchy: 'It's not a question of relationships. For me, it's very clear. We won the cup. We rolled in to 2003 and signed all the necessary contracts and we agreed all the financial terms and everything was to happen as planned. Then, suddenly, he is dissatisfied.'

Bertarelli, though, was well wide of the mark. The situation between the pair was deteriorating for all of those reasons and was a major factor in the eventual complete breakdown of their relationship.

By this stage, it had already been announced that Valencia was Bertarelli's choice of venue for the Swiss defence of the Cup in 2007. Coutts was known to strongly favour the waters off Cascais in Portugal and observers viewed this as a telling example of his reduced influence in Geneva. Bertarelli's only comment (to Jeffery) was: 'He contributed, he was briefed but, at the end of the day I have to take some decisions. We can't change roles here.'

As it eventuated, it appears that the venue selection and the procedures followed were the final straw, certainly for Coutts.

Because the Société Nautique de Genève obviously couldn't defend in its home waters, Lake Geneva, Bertarelli and his newly formed America's Cup Management (ACM), run by his right-hand man Michel Bonnefous, started the search for an alternative venue that did comply with the requirements of the Deed.

Initially, Coutts was prominent in the process and it was no secret that his venue preference was Cascais, 30 kilometres (19 miles) to the west of Lisbon on the Estoril coast of Portugal, also known as the Portuguese Riviera.

According to his Portuguese friend and contact, Patrick de Barros, Coutts, with Bonnefous, visited Cascais even before the team went to Auckland for the 2003 Cup and de Barros took his schooner *Seljm* to New Zealand, to follow the action first-hand while continuing to investigate bringing the event to Portugal should the Swiss succeed and become the defender.[7]

The then 58-year-old Patrick Monteiro de Barros was one of Portugal's richest men – a highly successful business entrepreneur and a sailing world champion in his own right. Born in France, to a French mother and Portuguese father, he spent his childhood and adolescence in Portugal, where he attended the Colégio Francês, before earning his degree in economics and business management in France. He spoke fluent Portuguese, French, Italian, German, English and Spanish and had been handling, very successfully, his family's finances since he was 18, when his father had died.

De Barros was an achiever who moved quickly and had the ear of the Portuguese government. When, armed with the Cup, Team Alinghi returned to Europe and called for tenders for venue rights to its first defence, de Barros was appointed to chair and organise an official Portuguese bid for those rights, on behalf of Lisbon/Cascais. The Portuguese government funded the endeavour and de Barros had a team of 30 people working for him, out of offices in Cascais.

There were, however, other declarations of interest in those rights – from Barcelona, Elba, Marseilles, Naples, Palma, Porto Cervo and Valencia – and the Bertarelli team had some work to do in order to arrive at a more manageable line-up of contenders. The list was eventually reduced to five – Cascais, Marseilles, Naples, Palma and Valencia – and then four when Palma withdrew.

The Portuguese bid was submitted in July 2003 and, according to de Barros, involved the complete transformation of an old fishing-boat harbour near the entrance to the Lisbon estuary and the construction of a €600–€700-million real-estate project nearby that would feature a five-star hotel and a range of residential and commercial options. The racing would take place off Cascais, 16 kilometres (10 miles) away. The bid also provided all the onshore facilities, including syndicate bases for the regatta and important tax exemptions for competing teams and personnel.

By October 2003, it was clear, de Barros said, that ACM was talking seriously with Cascais and Valencia only. Early in November, he received a phone call from Michel Bonnefous, asking for a meeting 'at the very highest level' – ie with the Portuguese prime minister – and, because Bertarelli did not see it as proper to be going to either Cascais or Valencia at such a late stage in the bid process (the decision was due to be announced at noon on 27 November 2003), could the meeting be in Geneva?

The Portuguese PM was, anyway, going to be in Geneva on 10 November 2003 to receive an award, so de Barros was able to set up the requested meeting, which was attended by the PM, his chief of staff and de Barros for the Portuguese, and Ernesto Bertarelli and Michel Bonnefous for the Swiss. The main topic of conversation at the meeting, said de Barros, was how the Swiss (Bertarelli), independent of the tender itself, could be involved in the real-estate development opportunity in Lisbon.

Five or six days later, de Barros received another telephone call from Bonnefous, who said: 'We want to come to Portugal but we want more money.' De Barros asked, 'How much more?' and the reply represented a 'substantial increase' on the €55 million that the Portuguese already had on the table (in cash and on top of all the other elements in its bid papers). The 'substantial increase' was in the region of another €50 million.

De Barros realised that the Portuguese government wouldn't agree to that so he proposed a different formula – in lieu of more money, offer the Swiss an attractive share of the proposed real-estate development. The Swiss went for it and, that afternoon, Bonnefous flew to Lisbon to start on the legalities and the paperwork. Interestingly, said de Barros, he brought with him a different lawyer to the one who had been involved so far. This one reported directly to Bertarelli as opposed to ACM or the SNG, even though all the documentation confirming Cascais–Lisbon as the venue stated clearly that everything was subject to final sign-off by SNG.

The day before the decision on the venue was to be announced, de Barros telephoned Bonnefous to ensure that everything was on track. The ACM chief told him that all was fine. So, the next day (27 November 2003) de Barros, his lawyer, and some of his bid team members flew to Geneva, arriving at 8.30am.

At 10.30am, in his Geneva hotel suite, de Barros met with Betarelli's lawyer and handed over a supplementary report from the Portugal Television Network stating that it would cover the next America's Cup off Cascais in 2007 at a price acceptable to ACM. The lawyer confirmed that everything was in order but was still subject to the approval of SNG, and the clock was ticking.

Given that ACM already had a man in Lisbon starting on arrangements for the formal Portuguese unveiling of Cascais as the 2007 Cup venue, de Barros was confident this was a mere formality and he assumed that all was well for a Portuguese event in 2007.

When he arrived at the Geneva announcement venue, however, he immediately realised that Bertarelli and Coutts were absent. Strange. He made eye contact with Butterworth, who was present and had 'a kind of look on his face'.

Then the commodore of SNG stepped up to the microphone and announced: 'And the winner is – Valencia.' De Barros was completely stunned. It was now obvious that the meeting with the lawyer earlier that morning had been a ploy. No SNG confirmation of the award to Cascais was required because the decision had already been made to stage the event at Valencia.

Later, de Barros said, he confronted Bonnefous: 'I thought we had shaken hands.' Bonnefous just looked at him and replied: '*C'est la vie.*'

Graciously, de Barros insisted that this was not his worst experience in business dealings. He was, however, sad that it had all come down to money. Cascais was a better sailing venue for the Cup, and Coutts recognised that, but sailing conditions were a subordinate consideration in the final bid process and, by this time, Coutts was already on his way out of the door.

De Barros lamented: 'I'm from a different generation – when you shake hands you shake hands. I have sailed for many years and I don't mind to lose. But not like this, not like this.'

When de Barros ultimately caught up with Coutts, the former Alinghi supremo was 'very upset – and can't hide it'. He (de Barros) thought that Coutts' contract and deal with Bertarelli included a major say in the venue for the defence. But that was not how it worked out.

'He [Coutts] always saw the attraction of Cascais as a fantastic place to sail the America's Cup, all year around,' said de Barros, 'and, with the objective of establishing a European circuit in catamarans, Cascais was seen as a natural hub, with appropriate permanent facilities. Russell's situation quickly deteriorated, however, and I think we got caught up in the middle of all of that.'[8]

'All of that' gained momentum through the spring and early summer months of 2004 until, on 6 July, the *Daily Telegraph*'s Tim Jeffery wrote that Bertarelli and Coutts were locked in negotiations 'as they seek to go their separate ways.' Jeffery quoted Coutts, saying: 'We've been in mediation for several months. I've got fundamental concerns and differences of opinion on the management direction of Alinghi. I advised him [Bertarelli] at the beginning of May that I would not be available to sail.'

Then, on 27 July 2004, Jeffery reported that:

'The schism has become a sacking: Last night the Swiss America's Cup holders, Alinghi, fired Russell Coutts, the New Zealander who led them to victory 16 months ago. Coutts was fired for "repeated violations of his duties" by Ernesto Bertarelli, the Swiss biotech billionaire who had hired him away from Team New Zealand in May 2000 after a comparable disenchantment with the directors behind the Kiwi Cup defenders.

The New Zealander has never fully explained the root cause of his disaffection with Bertarelli, a man with whom he appeared to have forged a deep friendship. But a source familiar with Coutts' contract said that helming was a minor responsibility of his duties.'[9]

The Alinghi media statement on the firing stated:

'Also particularly damaging was Russell Coutts' undisclosed involvement in the planning and development of a new race series, a commitment incompatible with his responsibilities and duties (see chapter 11, Troubled Waters). In his capacity as a member of the board of Alinghi Holdings, Russell Coutts manoeuvred himself into an inextricable conflict of interest.'[10]

Then, on 28 July 2004, Jeffery wrote:

'Forget Swiss neutrality and peacekeeping, it is all-out war between billionaire Ernesto Bertarelli and Russell Coutts, the New Zealander instrumental in making Team Alinghi the first European winner of the America's Cup.

On Monday, Alinghi sacked Coutts as skipper and team leader for Switzerland's 2007 defence of the Cup. Yesterday Coutts said of the dismissal: "It's an attack, that's for sure … I have not wanted to comment in any detail up until now because Ernesto and I were in legal mediation. But now I am. I had clear commitments and understandings in my contract about my role and responsibilities and there has been a series of breaches."[11]

In turn, Bertarelli said: 'It's not about money. I think, as people have found out, he is a difficult guy to motivate. I'm not the first one facing this issue.'

Bertarelli was not, either, about to fold his tent. He told Jeffery:

'I think you've got to use people where they are best at, and I couldn't see Michel Bonnefous helming the boat and Russell being in the office, drafting contracts. I thought the logical approach was to use Russell leading the team and yet contributing to overall construction and Michel drafting the contracts. Which basically is what they did with Alinghi in 2003.'[12]

On 28 July 2004 the *New Zealand Herald* reported Coutts saying that he had been unhappy with the team's management style and direction for some time:

'I found the role he [Bertarelli] increasingly insisted I occupy in the syndicate was at considerable variance with the one we had discussed at length during and since the last America's Cup campaign. This and other issues were clear breaches of the contract I had entered into with him.'[13]

Then, on 8 September 2004, The *New Zealand Herald*'s Julie Ash reported that Bertarelli had claimed that Coutts' salary ranked with those of the greatest footballers. Ash said:

'In an interview with the Swiss newspaper l'Hebdo, Bertarelli said he had remained silent until now because he did not want to engage in a "ping pong" match with someone who had been his friend. Russell Coutts' salary ranks among the top 20 in Switzerland. He is as well paid as the greatest

football stars of today. I cannot divulge the terms of the contract but you'd be shocked. His salary does not lag behind that of the main Swiss CEOs.'[14]

Bertarelli told the paper:

'It was clear from the beginning that if we were to win the cup, we would create two operational companies: Team Alinghi that would be in charge of the team, reporting to Russell, and America's Cup Management headed by Michel Bonnefous, which would be in charge of managing the event. It was Russell himself who defended this idea, which is why his subsequent about-face puzzles me.'[15]

Ash wrote that Bertarelli, according to *l'Hebdo*, said it had been clear by February that Coutts was no longer committed to Alinghi:

'He came to my office and told me, "I am not motivated any more. I won the cup three times. I have other projects. I would like to quit." He gave me his resignation, but I refused to accept it. He had total control on Alinghi. He was the one who decided to forgo the operational aspects.'[16]

Coutts said he had not seen the *l'Hebdo* article in question so declined to comment other than to say he had never resigned and was surprised that Bertarelli had discussed his salary. Two days later he told the authoritative American online sailing newsletter *Scuttlebutt* that Bertarelli's claims and statements were outrageous and untrue:

'I am looking at all my legal options. But I have to make it clear that I am astounded at the tone of the accusations and absolutely reject these claims. I am frankly appalled at the way Ernesto is attempting to rewrite history. I originally entered into this campaign with Alinghi with a very high level of commitment. Contrary to his latest suggestions, our differences resulted from Ernesto's management style and his failure to honour our contractual commitments. After our success in 2003, I had expected to continue to play a central role in team leadership and be fully informed and involved in all key decisions but this was denied me. We mutually agreed my salary a long time ago which was similar to the amount agreed for our successful 2003

campaign. It is totally ridiculous to suggest that my salary was in any way comparable with those of top soccer stars.

What's not widely understood is the fact that when Ernesto Bertarelli illegally terminated my employment, the restraint provisions in my contract ceased to apply. This explains why he instigated a new rule in the America's Cup Protocol excluding me from participating in the competition only 10 days before he dismissed me. I object to being excluded and believe the new rule is unsportsmanlike, and, although clearly aimed at me, bad for sailing in general.

The facts are that I love the America's Cup. I worked hard for Alinghi and I am proud of what we achieved as a team. I am trying to maintain a sense of appropriate behaviour, and avoid this sort of messy public exchange. However, this latest outburst by Ernesto is a deliberate attempt to damage my reputation and I will continue to respond to such false claims in order to protect myself.'[17]

Both sides having vented their spleen, all then went comparatively quiet until 24 March 2005, when a remarkably terse media statement was issued by Margrethe van der Stroom Holdener, Alinghi's head of communications. It read:

'Please find below the information on the settlement between Russell Coutts and Ernesto Bertarelli. As you will note, the parties have agreed that no further comments will be made on this matter and that this is all the information available to us. Therefore, we are not in a position to assist you with any further information. We wish you a nice Easter break.'[18]

Van der Stroom's 'information' stated:

'Ernesto Bertarelli, Alinghi Holdings and Russell Coutts announced today that they have amicably settled their past disagreements. As part of this settlement, Russell Coutts shall not sail for another team in the 32nd America's Cup. Ernesto Bertarelli and Russell Coutts both expressed their deep satisfaction with this positive outcome. Both parties have agreed to make no further comments.'[19]

10

BITTER CLASH OF THE TITANS

The 2007 America's Cup, sailed off Valencia in June and July of that year, was mostly everything that Ernesto Bertarelli claimed it to be, with 11 challengers from nine different countries – including first-timers China, Germany and South Africa.

The challenger eliminations produced some real upsets – none greater than Larry Ellison's fancied *BMW Oracle* losing by 3 minutes 15 seconds to the greenhorn Chinese in round robin two – and they continued into the challenger semi-finals. On one side of the draw, Emirates Team New Zealand's *NZL92* comfortably beat Spain's Desafío Español 5–2. But in the other semi, Ellison and *BMW Oracle* found themselves in trouble again, 1–4 down to the Prada-sponsored *Luna Rossa*. One more defeat, and they were gone.

In one last desperate play, Ellison, a hands-on owner and highly proficient yachtsman himself, rang the changes – sacking his New Zealand skipper Chris Dickson (replacing him with another Kiwi, Gavin

Brady), bringing in Denmark's Sten Muhr as principal helmsman, and promoting himself to the afterguard. It was, however, too little, too late. *BMW Oracle* lost race six by 33 seconds and was sent packing with Ellison an unhappy man.

The highly competitive computer-software tycoon and the hugely talented yachtsman Dickson enjoyed a rollercoaster relationship. With Dickson as his skipper and tactician, Ellison had achieved outstanding success in his 78-foot Bruce Farr-designed ocean-racer *Sayonara*, winning four successive maxi-class World Championships in a run of 25 victories in 27 starts. Notable among those wins were line honours and her division in the 1995, and then the storm-lashed 1998 Sydney–Hobart classics.

The latter was, for Ellison, a 'life-changing experience'. Little wonder, since the event saw the Hobart fleet being caught in 70-knot (hurricane-force) winds in the notorious Bass Strait. Six sailors lost their lives, another 55 were winched to safety by helicopters, and five yachts were sunk. Of the 115 starters, only 44 made it to the finish line in Hobart. An understandably shaken Ellison told the Brisbane *Courier Mail* that he didn't actually 'win' but just happened to be the first to survive, and vowed that he would never do the 628-mile race again, even if he lived for another 1,000 years.

When Ellison, in 2000, after his fourth successive world maxi title in *Sayonara*, made the decision to challenge for the 2003 America's Cup, unsurprisingly he took the backbone of his ocean-racing team with him, including his skipper/tactician Dickson, who, at age 39, already had a wealth of Cup experience. He had exploded on to the Cup scene in 1987 as the 26-year-old skipper of New Zealand's KZ7 'Kiwi Magic' in Fremantle, and was 37–1 on the scoresheet before going down 1–4 to Dennis Conner's *Stars & Stripes* in the challenger final. In 1992, he was skipper for the Nippon Challenge campaign in San Diego, and then in 1995 – again in San Diego – mounted his own challenge for the Cup (on behalf of the Tutukaka South Pacific Yacht Club) in the Bruce Farr-designed *TAG Heuer*.

Ellison displayed admirable loyalty to the tempestuous Kiwi yachtie who invariably seemed to be at odds with his team. There was never any question about Dickson's sailing ability – he was absolutely world class – but his people skills, or lack of them, repeatedly caught him out, especially in the close-knit, high-pressure environment of an America's Cup campaign.

Ellison did his best to watch the back of his favourite skipper/ tactician, frequently reminding the Kiwi's detractors that he was the best sailor on the boat, but there were occasions when even Ellison couldn't wallpaper over the anti-Dickson cracks in the Oracle ranks. Consequently, he had to remove Dickson from the Oracle crew at the business end of the 2003 event in Auckland, and then reinstated him to lead the 2007 Oracle campaign in Valencia, only to again have to remove him from the boat when Oracle was 1–4 down (to Italy's *Luna Rossa*) in the challenger semi-finals (she lost 1–5).

After that Valencia defeat Ellison, asked by a journalist whether it was worth spending $US100 million to win the America's Cup, replied: 'I don't know, I have never won the America's Cup. But I can tell you this – it certainly isn't worth a hundred million dollars to lose the America's Cup.'

Lawrence Joseph 'Larry' Ellison, the American businessman, entrepreneur and philanthropist, who is co-founder of Oracle Corporation, was born in the Bronx, New York, on 17 August 1944, to a 19-year-old, unwed Jewish mother and an Italian/American father who was a pilot in the United States Army Air Corps.

At the age of nine months, the infant Ellison contracted pneumonia and, unable to cope, his mother gave him up for adoption to her aunt and uncle who lived on Chicago's south side. His adoptive father, Lou, was a Russian Jew who had come to the USA in 1905 and changed his difficult Russian name to Ellison on arriving at the Ellis Island immigration gateway in Upper New York Bay. Larry Ellison did not know he was adopted until he was 12 and did not meet his biological mother again until he was 48.

From an early age, Ellison showed a real aptitude for maths and science, and was named science student of the year at the University of Illinois. During the final exams in his second year, however, Ellison's adoptive mother died and he dropped out of school. The following autumn, he enrolled at the University of Chicago but dropped out again after the first semester.

By now, Lou Ellison was convinced that his adopted son would never make anything of himself, but the seemingly aimless young man had in fact already learned the rudiments of computer programming in Chicago and took this skill with him to Berkeley, California, where he was able to start a new life. He spent the next eight years bouncing from job to job (mostly computer-related) and, while employed as a programmer at Amdahl Corporation, he participated in building the first IBM-compatible mainframe system.

In 1977, Ellison and two of his Amdahl colleagues, Robert Miner and Ed Oates, founded their own company, Software Development Laboratories (SDL), with Ellison serving as chief executive officer. Here, he realised the commercial potential of the concept of a Structured Query Language (SQL) that he had come across, while still working at Amdahl, in a paper called 'A Relational Model of Data for Large Shared Data Banks', written by Edgar F ('Ted') Codd, which the author had developed at IBM.

Ellison and his partners in SDL took the idea and ran with it, winning a two-year contract to build a relational database management system (RDBMS) for the CIA, the code name for which was 'Oracle'. They finished the project a year ahead of schedule and used the time at their disposal to develop their system, which they also named Oracle, for commercial applications. Larry Ellison was on the launch pad to become one of the world's most successful, and wealthy, individuals.

In 1980, SDL had only eight employees and a revenue of less than $US1 million, but the following year, IBM itself adopted Oracle for its mainframe systems and SDL's sales doubled, annually, for the next seven years. Ellison renamed the company Oracle Corporation, after its bestselling product.

Oracle Corporation went public in 1986, raising $US31.5 million with its initial public offering, but some 'accounting issues' helped to wipe out the majority of the company's market capitalisation and, in 1990, Oracle Corp posted its first losses. Its market capitalisation subsequently fell by 80 per cent and the fledgling Ellison empire appeared at this time to be on the verge of bankruptcy.

Accepting the need for drastic change, Ellison replaced most of the original senior staff with more experienced managers, and delegated the running of the business to these professionals while he channelled his own energies into product development. A new version of the database program, Oracle 7, released in 1992, swept the field and made Oracle the industry leader in database management software so that, in only two years, the company's stock regained much of its previous value. Success continued and, as Ellison was Oracle's largest shareholder, he became one of the wealthiest people in the world.

Ellison now set his sights on growth through acquisitions, and over the next several years he gobbled up several companies, including PeopleSoft, Siebel CRM Systems and Sun Microsystems, all of which helped Oracle reach a market cap of roughly $US185 billion with some 130,000 employees by 2014.

For the company's first 37 years, Ellison was Oracle's only CEO. In 2014, he relinquished that role, entrusting the post to two long-time associates and adopted the position of executive chairman while continuing to serve as chief technology officer.

In May 2017, *Forbes Magazine* estimated Ellison's net worth to be $US52.2 billion – seventh in a list of the world's wealthiest that was headed by Microsoft's Bill Gates, who was worth an estimated $US86 billion (151st in the same list was Ellison's arch sailing rival Ernesto Bertarelli, estimated to be worth $US8.6 billion).

Although he also owns a raft of other properties, including the island of Lanai, in Hawaii, Ellison's principal home is in Woodside, California. He has been married four times – to Adda Quinn (1967–1974), Nancy Wheeler (1977–1978), Barbara Booth (1983–1986) and Melanie Craft (2003–2010) – and has two adult offspring (David and Megan), to his third wife, Barbara Booth.

While Ellison was lamenting the failure of his 2007 Cup campaign, the Louis Vuitton Cup challenger final that he missed out on saw *Luna Rossa* suffer a 5–0 clean sweep by Emirates Team New Zealand, now being run by Grant Dalton, another of his country's Whitbread Round the World Yacht Race veterans, although it was a lot closer than the scoreline indicates. With the exception of race three, which it won by 1 minute 38 seconds, Emirates Team New Zealand's victories were achieved with a margin of less than a minute.

The best-of-nine America's Cup match, then, was a re-run of the 2003 edition – Team New Zealand against Alinghi – but on this occasion the roles were reversed: the Kiwis were the challengers while the Swiss, representing the Société Nautique de Genève, were the defenders. To call them 'Swiss' was, though, once more, something of a stretch. *Alinghi*'s

17-man crew comprised six New Zealanders (including the now-skipper Brad Butterworth), three Americans, two Australians and two Italians, plus one each from Canada, Holland, Spain – oh, and Switzerland (Ernesto Bertarelli was again the only Swiss national on the boat).

It was a sensationally close series, the two big yachts, never more than 40 seconds apart, swapping fortunes and the lead from start to finish. *Alinghi* won race one by 35 seconds but went down in races two and three, by margins of 28 seconds and 25 seconds, to trail 1–2. She then bounced back with three straight wins, by 30 seconds, 19 seconds and 28 seconds, to reach match point going into race seven. That decisive race, on 3 July 2007, came down to *Emirates Team New Zealand* having to complete a penalty turn right on the finish line. The Kiwis mistimed that turn ever so slightly and *Alinghi* squeezed across the finish line – just 1 second ahead. The drama had been surreal, the television images fantastic and, as a result, yachting had finally made it, and big time, on the small (but so commercially important) television screen.

The picture was just as rosy on the event side of the equation. When all the accounts were finalised, the 32nd America's Cup made a profit of more than €30 million ($US53 million) that was shared by the 12 participating teams – 50 per cent to Alinghi and the other 50 per cent divided between the rest, with those who went the furthest in the regatta getting the most (Team New Zealand's 'take' as the beaten challenger was rumoured to be in excess of $US10 million).

Michel Bonnefous, the CEO of America's Cup Management, said in a media release:

> *This is a significant step forward in allowing Cup teams from this cycle to be on a solid financial footing for the next Cup. The 32nd America's Cup has been the largest, most open and widely accessible America's Cup in 156 years of history. Over 6 million people have visited its venues, and its television footage has reached 4 billion viewers (in more than 150 countries). I think all of us can be proud of what has been achieved here in Valencia over the last four years. This first America's Cup in Europe has been a big step forward for the oldest and most prestigious sporting prize … we have worked collectively with the teams, sponsors, host city and the media to evolve the America's Cup so that it reflects the times we live in, while remaining true to its heritage.*[1]

As *Alinghi* crossed the finish line in that final race, the Société Nautique de Genève accepted a pre-organised 'hip pocket' challenge from Club Náutico Español de Vela (CNEV), which was immediately the Challenger of Record for the next edition of the Cup and, on 5 July 2007, SNG and CNEV released a protocol for the next America's Cup in 2010. It was a draconian document that immediately had would-be challengers in revolt and threatening boycott, blasting away, in a storm of challenger protest, all the warm and fuzzies generated by the success of the 2007 regatta.

Supposedly negotiated with CNEV, but in fact dictated by Bertarelli's advisers, the terms and conditions for the next edition of the Cup blatantly vested control of everything in the defender, right down to the exclusive powers to appoint all event authorities and officials, including race juries and umpires. Additionally, SNG allowed itself until 31 December 2007 to advise challengers of the 'when, where and in what' of the next event, giving itself a huge advantage in the design stakes.

When the protocol storm broke, nobody in the Swiss ranks wanted to take ownership of the dreaded document that was causing so much trouble and Cup followers were left wondering about the parts that Bertarelli and Butterworth played in it, for they must have signed it off.

Larry Ellison didn't wait around to find out. He went for the jugular to expose what he saw as an audacious Bertarelli power play to gain complete control of the Cup. He moved quickly and decisively, dispatching one of his private jets from California to Valencia to pick up his rules man, Tom Ehman, and legal support and then fly them on to Geneva where, on 11 July 2007, Ehman, with a Swiss notary bearing witness, personally presented to SNG's secretary a one-on-one Deed of Gift (DOG) challenge in the name of the Golden Gate Yacht Club (GGYC). GGYC made it clear in a follow-up media release (dated 12 July 2007) that the draconian SNG protocol had caused it to take this approach – 'It [the Protocol] alters the very nature of the competition, giving unprecedented and unfair advantages to the Defender ... [it] provides no opportunity for a fair and equitable competition.'

GGYC also emphasised its charge that the Club Náutico Español de Vela (CNEV) was an illegitimate challenger that did not comply with the 'annual regatta' requirements of the Deed of Gift – a brand-new yacht club specifically created for this challenge, which had never conducted a regatta of any kind. As more details emerged, it transpired that CNEV had no boats, no clubhouse and only four members – all vice-presidents of the Spanish sailing federation.

The other would-be challengers quickly moved in behind the initiative, six of them co-signing, with Oracle, a letter to the Société Nautique de Genève and Club Náutico Español de Vela expressing their strong opposition to the thrust of the protocol and its offensive content. The list of signatories comprised Areva Challenge (France), Emirates Team New Zealand, Luna Rossa (Italy), Mascalzone Latino (Italy), United Internet Team Germany and Victory Challenge (UK), and the letter, known as Exhibit 2, stated:

'In our collective role as past Challengers and prospective Challengers, our opinion is that this Protocol is the worst text in the history of the America's Cup and, more fundamentally, it lacks precisely the mutual consent items which are required.

Some of the essential features of the Protocol are as follows:

- *The obligation which previously required the Event Organiser (ACM) and all Regatta Officials to be neutral has been erased*
- *Any Challenger that disputes the Protocol may be disqualified from the competition by the Defender*
- *There is a prohibition for the Challenger of Record to act in the interest of other Challengers*
- *ACM has powers and rights which significantly exceed the position of any Defender in any other Protocol in history*
- *The Defender, through ACM, is given the power "unilaterally" to establish the rules for all the events, including the Challenger Selection Series, giving the Defender a crucial and unfettered role in determining the Challenger for the America's Cup. This is without precedent and is absolutely contrary to the Deed of Gift*
- *The essential rules of the event will be imposed by ACM and changed at any time without even consultation with the Challengers*
- *There is absolutely no certainty on the format, schedule or venue of the competition, qualifying regattas, defender series or scoring*
- *For the first time in history, the Defender is designing the Class of boat in secret with no contribution by the Challengers*

- *You have granted the Defender rights never before granted in a Protocol, such as having more boats than the Challengers or participating in the Challenger Selection Series, except the Challenger Final*

The essential consequences of your signature of the Protocol for the Challengers are as follows:

- *The asset value of the current AC boats is almost zero*
- *The Protocol makes it impossible to close a budget, now or in the near future, for any team or to seriously talk to sponsors for the next AC*
- *The Protocol harms the competitive position of the Challengers*
- *The Protocol lacks all the neutral management provisions that guarantee a fair contest*
- *The Protocol eliminates the powers of the Challenger Commission and greatly reduces those of the Challenger of Record*
- *The most important Sailing Rules will be known only 60 days before racing (in the previous AC they were known years ahead or several months); this implies that it is impossible to train for Match Racing and that the Defender will have an incredible advantage on the water*
- *Sport justice has gone back to before 1960s*
- *The essential elements of the competition have changed, taking all the balances and guarantees from the Challengers and vesting them in ACM and the Defender*
- *This is overall a radical change in the America's Cup, which jeopardises the participation and survival of the event*

You are well aware that serious questions have been raised about the legitimacy of the newly created and purely instrumental entity called "Club Náutico Español" to advance a Challenge under the provisions of the Deed of Gift. In the sincerest hope that the America's Cup competition will not have to endure the turmoil associated with litigating that issue, but will rather move forward with the balanced and fair procedures and protocols that have historically characterized this competition, we ask you to dissolve "Club Náutico Español" and withdraw your Challenge within the month of July 2007.'[2]

That deadline passed without progress and Ellison, reading the signs, took matters into his own hands. On 20 July 2007, he initiated proceedings in the New York Supreme Court to have CNEV declared an invalid challenger and, next in line, Golden Gate Yacht Club installed as the new Challenger of Record. The Cup was back where everyone said they did not want it to be, and the ensuing legal and media exchanges were even nastier than they had been during the three-year vitriolic spat between San Diego Yacht Club and Mercury Bay Boating Club when they trod the same torturous path in 1987–1990. The journey, though, was remarkably similar and, this time, it would be more than two years before all legal options had been exhausted and the New York Court of Appeals handed down a final opinion.

In tennis parlance, it was another three-setter with enough tie-breakers along the way to keep the accounts department of any large law firm happy. Golden Gate won the first set 6–0 when, on 27 November 2007, the lower court ruled CNEV to be an invalid challenger and declared Golden Gate to be the legitimate Challenger of Record for the next edition of the Cup.

It went to a tie-breaker in the second set when SNG appealed and the Appellate Division (of the New York Supreme Court), on 29 July 2008, voted 3–2 to overturn the lower court decision and reinstate CNEV as the Challenger of Record.

Then it was game, set and match, 6–0 in the third, when, on 2 April 2009, the Court of Appeals ruled unanimously to reverse the Appellate Division and the CNEV was again knocked out, replaced by the Golden Gate Yacht Club and its challenge in a yacht or vessel that would be 90ft on the waterline with a 90ft beam. And this time there was no way back. The match referee had ruled and SNG had to defend as challenged by GGYC or forfeit the Cup.

The court-ordered upshot of all that, off Valencia in February 2010, was an America's Cup match that truly was a clash of the titans – a one-on-one grudge duel between two extremely wealthy businessmen/entrepreneurs that, in its own way, was almost as bizarre as the dog vs cat 'match' in 1988. This time, though, the combatants, at least, were both multihulls, albeit (as befitted the occasion) the two largest and most outrageously hi-tech multihulls the sailing world has ever seen – Alinghi's a 90ft waterline, soft-sail catamaran and Oracle's a 90ft waterline, wing-sailed trimaran.

There were several ironies in all of this. In the dash to be first in with a DOG challenge, Tom Ehman dug into his files and had no qualms about borrowing the documentation of the Mercury Bay Boating Club challenge that he had previously so maligned. In his haste, however, he appears to have copied that documentation chapter and verse and so mistakenly nominated a 90ft waterline keel yacht rather than the intended 90ft waterline multihull.

SNG pounced on this and sought to have the GGYC challenge invalidated because of the error, but Judge J Leland DeGrasse of the Appellate Division ruled on 29 July 2008 that:

> 'SNG takes issue with GGYC's description of the challenging vessel in the certificate as a "keel yacht" while specifying dimensions suggestive of a multihulled vessel, such as a catamaran … it is clear, however, that even if the certificate contained a possible ambiguity, SNG was not at any time actually confused or misled by the Certificate, as the record indicates that SNG fully understood that GGYC was going to race a catamaran.'[3]

A very close shave indeed for our friend Tom, for one can only imagine what Mr Ellison's reaction would have been if all his efforts and expense had come to naught because of a simple copying oversight.

Then there was the fact that Bertarelli and SNG were tripped up by the very wording in the Deed that should have made invalid Bertarelli's original challenge for the Cup, in 2003. The Court of Appeals decision of 2 April 2009 ruled that the word 'having', as in 'having for its annual regatta an ocean-water course on the sea, or on an arm of the sea', is 'unambiguous' and that a yacht club does not qualify as a challenger unless it has held at least one annual regatta, on the sea or an arm of the sea, or both, prior to its challenge.

Moreover, that far-reaching 2 April 2009 decision invalidating the CNEV as a challenger was written by none other than Carmen Beauchamp Ciparick. One by one, the judge – now on the Court of Appeals' bench – and the New York Supreme Court system were dealing with all the big-ticket items in Schuyler's Deed of Gift that might be seen, by a less than scrupulous challenger or defender, to provide opportunity.

Judge Ciparick recalled:

> 'We interpreted the Deed to mean that a challenger has to have had at least one regatta on the open seas before they make their challenge. CNEV

hasn't, so we invalidate them. It is unanimous, everybody agrees with my interpretation … So, once again, I am part of America's Cup history. I've been sitting on the Court of Appeals since 1994 … all seven of us sit on every case. This time it was a different portion of the Deed of Gift that we had to interpret – the qualifications of the challenger. I drew the writing [of the decision] quite randomly – it was sheer coincidence. But I remember thinking at the time: "No one's going to believe this."[4]

While the Swiss were still getting their heads around the full implications of Ellison's DOG challenge, the Oracle powerhouse lobbed another grenade over Bertarelli's wall when he unveiled to the sailing world that he had signed Russell Coutts as his campaign boss and skipper and, in the process, had cleaned out just about everything and everyone that had gone before, including Coutts' Kiwi contemporary, Chris Dickson.

Nobody but Ellison and Coutts knew the details but apparently Coutts' financial terms for taking over were expensive enough to make even the billionaire gulp, and the legendary skipper wanted full control. Ellison, though, did the deal and Coutts was back in the America's Cup, on his terms. Straight away, he would be going head-to-head with his former boss, Ernesto Bertarelli, and his old mate Brad Butterworth.

The duo – Coutts and Butterworth – were contemporaries in that they had both emerged from the production line of New Zealand sailing talent in the 1970s, but they reached the very top of their profession by quite different routes before combining to be the most formidable skipper/tactician duo in the long history of their sport's prestige event.

Russell Coutts was born in Wellington, New Zealand, on 1 March 1962, but grew up in Dunedin, a harbour city in the lower half of the country's South Island. He first came to sailing prominence when, in 1978, he won the Tanner Cup in the ubiquitous 7ft P-Class trainer – almost a prerequisite for New Zealand's future champion skippers (Chris Dickson won the same trophy a year earlier).

Coutts subsequently targeted the world youth championship in one-person dinghies, finishing third in 1979 in Italy, sixth in 1980 in the USA, and first in 1981 in Portugal. He then switched to the single-handed, one-design Laser, with an eye on graduating into a Finn for a tilt at the sailing Olympics and, off Long Beach, in 1984, he won the Finn gold medal at the Los Angeles games – the first New Zealand yachtie to win a single-handed class at the Olympics.

Coutts completed a Bachelor of Engineering degree at Auckland University, in 1986, but there weren't many good engineering jobs going so he decided to try to make a career out of sailing, bringing to the table in all of his ensuing campaigns his invaluable engineering background, along with his natural skills, powers of concentration and fierce competitiveness.

His list of titles and achievements in and through sailing is almost too long to contemplate but he became a national hero in his home country when he skippered *NZL32 (Black Magic)* to a stunning 5–0 victory in the 1995 America's Cup, off San Diego, and then successfully defended it with another clean-sweep victory in the 2000 match in Auckland. The hero became villain, however, when he led an exodus of Team New Zealand personnel to Ernesto Bertarelli's Alinghi, and then brought them back to Auckland to beat Team New Zealand in the 2003 match.

In the process of all this, Coutts was named World Sailor of the Year in 1995 and in 2003, and was skipper of four America's Cup winners (for three different countries): *NZL32* and *NZL60* for New Zealand (in 1995 and 2000); *Alinghi* for Switzerland (in 2003); and Larry Ellison's trimaran, *USA 17*, for America (in 2010). In June 2000, Coutts was made a Distinguished Companion of the New Zealand Order of Merit for his services to New Zealand yachting, and converted that to a knighthood in 2009.

Brad Butterworth, OBE, was born in April 1959, in the farming community township of Te Awamutu in the Waikato district of New Zealand's North Island. His introduction to sailing – his father building a boat in the backyard – was quintessential New Zealand, as was his progress through the junior ranks in the P-Class and the Starling trainers. He started out in keel boats as a bowman, while working as an apprentice sailmaker with North Sails in Auckland, but he soon built a reputation as a helmsman and was given his first big break by Peter Blake, to be the specialist driver on the chartered Bénéteau 46 *Lady B* in the 1983 Admiral's Cup in England.

From there, it was onwards and upwards in offshore racing, his achievements included being: one of two specialist helmsmen (Peter

Lester was the other) on the Farr-designed *Propaganda*, which led New Zealand to Admiral's Cup victory in 1987; tactician on the *KZ7 'Kiwi Magic'* for New Zealand's inaugural America's Cup challenge in 1987 (in Fremantle); specialist helmsman on Peter Blake's all-conquering *Steinlager 2*, in the 1989–1990 Whitbread Round the World Yacht Race; tactician on *NZL20* for New Zealand's 1992 America's Cup challenge in San Diego; tactician on *NZL32* for New Zealand's historic 1995 America's Cup win in San Diego; tactician on *NZL60* for New Zealand's successful defence of the Cup in Auckland in 2000; tactician for Switzerland's *Alinghi* when she won the America's Cup in 2003 in Auckland; skipper and tactician for *Alinghi* when she successfully defended the Cup off Valencia in 2007; and skipper of the giant Swiss catamaran *Alinghi* that lost the Cup to Larry Ellison's equally giant trimaran in the 2010 Deed of Gift match, off Valencia; and so on.

He first teamed up with Russell Coutts when the pair were in charge of the back-up boat for Sir Michael Fay's unsuccessful 1992 challenge, in San Diego, slipping readily into the support role that led to him and skipper Coutts becoming the most successful pairing in America's Cup history – both of them having been on the winning boat no less than four times (Coutts in 1995, 2000, 2003 and 2010 and Butterworth in 1995, 2000, 2003 and 2007). Butterworth, in 1995, was made an Officer of the Order of the British Empire (OBE) for services to yachting.

Being on opposite sides in the 'clash of the titans' put a severe strain on even the very close friendship of the two Kiwi yachties. Coutts tried in vain to unravel some of the damage done by the draconian SNG/ CNEV protocol but Butterworth steadfastly toed the Bertarelli party line by insisting that Ellison was taking the 'back door' route in his bid to win the Cup (in court) only because he viewed Alinghi as being too strong to defeat on the water.

He told *Agence France-Presse* on 15 July 2009: 'They just want to go to court, they think they can win it in court,' adding that he was 'very disappointed' by the legal move taken by Oracle, which accused Alinghi of trying to change the rules for their multihull duel. 'We are just constantly going back to court,' he said. 'Really our motivation is just to get these races down on the water. We just want to get sailing.'[5]

In a deteriorating environment of lawsuits and counter suits, accusative media conferences and increasingly barbed press releases, it took several more trips to court before the terms for a match were finally sorted, and one of those was to determine where the races should be staged.

In August 2009, SNG announced that Ras al-Khaimah, of the United Arab Emirates, would be the venue. It was, from the outset, a provocative and controversial proposal – to stage an event of such international stature in such a remote (and light-wind) location, at a venue that also was very near Iran (with which Ras al-Khaimah had an ongoing border and waterway dispute, not to mention the USA's ongoing challenges in that troublesome part of the world). SNG claimed that the proposal was in the interests of introducing the event to new players and audiences, but most observers saw it for what it really was – in the interests of Bertarelli's business ambitions while making life as difficult as possible for his arch-rival Ellison.

GGYC promptly filed a motion requesting 'that the Court issue an Order directing that the 33rd America's Cup be held in Valencia, Spain, in February 2010, unless the parties mutually consent otherwise'. According to GGYC, Valencia was mentioned in the 2 April 2009 court order (ejecting CNEV) as a venue that both parties had indicated they agreed to and, on 27 October 2009, Justice Shirley Kornreich ruled that Ras al-Khaimah was not a Deed-legal venue and that the race must take place either in Valencia or in the southern hemisphere (it was rumoured that she was very leery of ordering an American team to race in potentially hostile waters).

Ultimately, it was agreed that Alinghi and BMW Oracle would go head to head off Valencia, in February 2010, in a best-of-three match over the courses stipulated in the Deed, absent mutual consent.

Alinghi built a catamaran that was 90ft on the waterline with a bowsprit that made it 'about' 120ft overall, with 70ft beam. Controversially (of course), it used a generator to power its essential hydraulics systems, for trimming and making rig and equipment adjustments. It was a more conventional approach that probably reflected the catamaran culture of racing on Switzerland's big lakes, but it also flirted with the boundaries in design and construction. On 8 July 2009, the giant cat and its 164ft mast were airlifted, by a Mil Mi-26 helicopter, from Villeneuve, at the south-eastern end of Lake Geneva, where it was built, to its launch ceremony off the waterfront of Geneva itself.

BMW Oracle Racing went for a 90ft trimaran that had a footprint the size of two basketball courts. It was subjected to 14 months of development off San Diego before it was shipped to Valencia. The most dramatic modification made was the switch to a rigid wing sail that was 190ft tall and some 80 per cent larger than the wing of a Boeing 747 airplane. The structure was very high aspect ratio (very tall and narrow) and comprised two main elements separated by a vertical slot through which air could flow. The rear element was made up of several separate sections, the angle of attack of which could be adjusted separately (much like the flaps on an airplane's wing). Thus the lift of the sail could be controlled very finely, both overall, and for each section.

It was a brilliantly designed and engineered development, achieved under the direction of *BMW Oracle*'s racing design director, former Team New Zealand structural designer Mike Drummond, and proved a game changer. In early testing, the big tri hit boat speeds of 28 knots in 10 knots of wind. She later proved capable of sailing upwind at more than two-and-half times the wind speed.

This wasn't the first time a wing sail had been used on a multihull in the America's Cup. Dennis Conner's catamaran for the controversial 1988 defence against Michael Fay's 90ft waterline monohull featured a wing, produced by a team that included famed aerospace designer Bert Rutan, who would later engineer Virgin Galactic's commercial spaceliners. However, the *BMW Oracle* wing was twice as tall as the one on Conner's *Stars & Stripes* and couldn't be operated by manned ropes and lines alone. So, hydraulic motors powered the rotation of the rig, the camber of the main flap area, and the individual trim of the eight separate control flaps on the trailing edge of the wing. As with the Alinghi catamaran, the power for the hydraulics was provided by an auxiliary generator.

While the design, engineering and construction of this incredible boat and rig were major feats in themselves, the logistics of where and how to store the giant wing structure, how to transport it and how to fix it vertically on to the boat were almost as impressive.

Constructional engineer Mike Drummond cut his teeth in the America's Cup as part of Michael Fay's campaigns in 1987 (*KZ7*), 1988 (*KZ1* – 'The Big Boat') and 1992 (*NZL20*). Next, he was structural designer for Team New Zealand when it won the Cup in 1995 (*NZL32*), successfully defended it in 2000 (*NZL60*), and then lost it in 2003 (*NZL82*). He then switched to Alinghi for the 2007 Cup (*SUI100*). The Swiss syndicate wanted to renew his contract at the end of the 2007 campaign in Valencia but he got a call from Russell Coutts offering him the plum role of design coordinator with Oracle.

This was in August/September 2007 when the GGYC vs SNG court case was in its infancy and everyone was hoping that Alinghi would yet see the writing on the wall and withdraw or amend its draconian protocol. So, at that stage, the next event was going to be in monohulls and, accordingly, Drummond put together a programme that would see BMW Oracle start building in mid-January 2008. In the interim, though, Coutts was covering all bases, pending a decision from the New York Supreme Court, and had the French design firm Van Peteghem Lauriot-Prévost (VPLP), world leaders in multihull design, working away on a maximum-size Deed of Gift boat.

In a last-ditch bid to hammer out a more acceptable compromise protocol, Coutts flew to Geneva on 17 December 2007 for one-on-one discussions with Butterworth, but he was badly stood up. Butterworth, apparently under instructions from higher up, was in London instead, and there were no further negotiations. That was enough for the American syndicate. The Oracle hierarchy immediately made the decision to stop wasting time and money on a monohull and, instead, to concentrate all resources on a DOG multihull. It would be a trimaran, because the French experience was that trimarans were quicker all-round propositions than catamarans, except in a certain narrow set of circumstances. The original French work pointed to a tri with three soft-sail rigs – 125ft, 138ft and 150ft. Then Alinghi introduced light-airs Ras al-Khaimah as its proposed venue for the match, and the rigs were all increased in size, the tallest to 175.5ft and then 176.8ft.

Drummond, meanwhile, was running a special project within his overall programme, looking at a wing-sail rig alternative and, by early 2009, the data coming out of that project was promising enough to prompt them to get serious about the set-up. In April 2009, the decision was made to go with the wing and it was built in time for sailing trials in San Diego in November that year, before everything was shipped to Valencia, which had finally been confirmed as the venue for the one-on-one DOG match in February 2010.

Drummond recalled that the space-age tri was 'always a work in progress' with improvements continuously introduced. For example, in May 2009 there were new outer hulls. Then, in September 2009, work began on a 25ft extension to the wing, to make it 223ft tall, along with major alterations to the main hull, including the removal of the keel that had been fitted originally, leaving new daggerboards and rudder only. This last change was a risk in that there was no certainty they would be able to tack the boat without a keel. However, the Velocity Prediction Program (VPP) numbers promised that the new daggerboards, allied to the no-keel-configuration, would result in a 45-minute gain around a DOG course. It was, then, a no-brainer.

Although nothing had leaked out, the Oracle trimaran, Drummond said, was not quick to begin with but gradually they got to the vessel's real potential through the raft of changes that were brought on stream. The ultimate version of the huge wing sail, with its nine adjustable control flaps, was the *pièce de résistance*. The trimaran that went to the America's Cup start line in Valencia, then, was 90ft on the waterline by 90ft beam, with a rigid wing mast that towered 223ft above the deck. Michael Fay's 'Big Boat' apart, nothing remotely like it had been seen in any yachting event since the leviathans, such as the 144ft *Reliance* and the *Shamrocks* of the Sir Thomas Lipton era in Cup history (the 1800s and early 1900s).

The February 2010 clash between the two giants had Cup aficionados jetting in from all over the world. This was a match not to be missed and, after all the bitter courtroom wrangling, there were some lighter moments before racing finally got underway. One of these occurred when Sir Michael Fay and his former campaign legal adviser, Andrew Johns, were walking along the road to the syndicate bases in Valencia and a large BMW limousine pulled up alongside them. Out leaped Oracle rules man Tom Ehman, clearly enjoying the benefits of having a luxury car manufacturer as a main sponsor. Quick as a flash, Sir Michael quipped: 'G'day, Tom – who are you driving for today?' Unabashed, Ehman bear-hugged his former adversary and proclaimed: 'Michael, we're all standing on your shoulders. None of this would have been possible without your endeavours [with the Big Boat challenge].' The group then piled into the limo and headed for the Oracle compound where Coutts provided a VIP tour of the challenger tri.

The much-anticipated match was scheduled to start on 8 February and the large, international media contingent assembled for the traditional pre-race press conferences. There were two of these instead of the usual one because, it was rumoured, the hostile protagonists declined to appear together.

An upbeat Ellison, who had been dubbed 'The Prince of Darkness', quipped: 'The tension between the two teams certainly has helped to create interest. It's like a heavyweight championship fight where the fighters don't like each other.' Conversely, Bertarelli was clearly angry about everything that had taken place, and stated: 'A fantastic event [the America's Cup] does not need this kind of – excuse the expression – bullshit!'

Fickle light winds delayed proceedings and racing was postponed until 10 February. Rough seas then forced a further postponement until 12 February, when, at last, principal race officer Harold Bennett, from New Zealand, was satisfied that conditions across the course area were fair and ordered a start in 5 knots of wind. The Deed of Gift course was 20 miles to windward and return.

Alinghi was penalised for a foul in the entry to the start box and then both boats were above the line in a dial-up. The Swiss defender wriggled clear but *BMW Oracle* was in irons and was 650 yards astern by the time she got underway. In a match race between two 'normal' yachts that would have been game, set and match right there, but these weren't 'normal' yachts. With the breeze building to 8–10 knots, the wing-sail trimaran sailed higher and faster, and was 3 minutes 21 seconds (1,530 yards) ahead at the turn.

If the tri was surprisingly fast upwind, she was sensationally so on the return downwind leg, hitting speeds in excess of 28 knots in just 8 knots of wind. She crossed the finish line more than 10 minutes ahead and that became 15 minutes, 28 seconds by the time *Alinghi* had completed her penalty turn for the pre-start infringement.

BMW Oracle's Aussie skipper, James Spithill, wasn't surprised by the tri's upwind performance: 'I always thought if we were able to fly a hull we'd be faster upwind, but – I was genuinely amazed downwind. We did a great job on the entry. We were able to get a piece of them and force a penalty.'

Alinghi's Kiwi skipper, Butterworth, was irritated by persistent post-race press conference questions belabouring his rival's recovery on leg one, retorting: 'What do you want me to say? They sailed from behind us to in front of us. That's pure speed.'

The American challenger's 10-man crew for the race comprised three Kiwis, two Australians and two Italians, and one each from the USA, Holland and France. With light winds forecast, Ellison opted to watch the race from a support boat with his campaign boss Coutts. Ernesto Bertarelli fared better and was in the 14-man crew for his catamaran, on which the line-up comprised six Kiwis, three Swiss, two French and one each from Canada, Spain and Holland.

Two days later, principal race officer Bennett patiently waited all day for the wind to settle enough for him to order a second start. The scheduled course was an equilateral triangle with 13-mile legs (39 miles in total). It was very late in the day, and only 30 minutes before the start deadline, when a light breeze settled in right across the course area and Bennett immediately prepared to initiate the start sequence. However, he was faced with a mutiny. The crew on his official start boat, provided by Bertarelli's America's Cup Management, refused to obey his instructions, claiming there was too much swell for the race to be held.

On a video of the incident, shot by one of the team on board, Bennett can be seen pointing to the flag mast and yelling at one of his mutinous Swiss 'helpers': 'Get out there.' The Swiss assistant remains seated and Bennett yells again: 'Signals please.' With barely a minute to the start gun, Bennett exclaims: 'Aaah – we are fucked, we can't do this. These guys have just fucked us!' However, help was at hand and two non-mutineers – including Oracle's rules man Ehman – leaped into action. The flags were flown in the correct sequences and the start gun was fired – right on schedule.

Astonishingly, *Alinghi* again copped a pre-start penalty, this time for not being outside the designated start box at the race warning signal as she rushed to claim the starboard end of the line. *BMW Oracle* lined up for the port end, got a good jump at the gun and grabbed an early 250-yard advantage. In the shifty conditions, she stretched that lead to 875 yards before *Alinghi* started to claw her way back to lead by 76 yards at the first cross. The next time they met, the gap was down to 55 yards and it was a real match race, but not for long. *Alinghi* tacked again and it was a slow one. *BMW Oracle* rolled over her rival and was 28 seconds ahead starting into the first reaching leg. She bore away and accelerated to a 492-yard lead that grew steadily to 820 yards, then 1,093 yards and on out to nearly 1,640 yards. It was all over. *Alinghi* continued the fight and closed the gap, but not by enough. The American trimaran was still 5 minutes, 28 seconds ahead at the finish line and the Cup was on its way back across the Atlantic – this time to San Francisco.

Ellison was one of two Americans on board for that decisive race, and the software tycoon had clearly enjoyed the experience, gushing to the press: 'It's absolutely awesome. Valencia, *muchas gracias*. I am so proud of this team, proud to be a part of this team and I'm proud to bring the America's Cup, after a long absence, back to the USA.'

Quick to put some stakes in the ground, Ellison claimed:

'I haven't made any decisions at all [on a venue for GGYC's defence of the Cup]. We have to talk to the city of San Francisco. This requires a lot of support, lots of support from the city to do America's Cup bases … We do [however] have a Challenger of Record, and one thing I'd like to assure everybody about the 34th America's Cup is that there will be a completely independent jury, there will be completely independent umpires and it will be an independent group that manages the next America's Cup. It will be a level playing field for all competitors.'[6]

Harold Bennett's problems in starting the race hadn't gone unnoticed and ISAF (the international sailing body) announced that it would investigate the whole affair. A vastly experienced and respected PRO, Bennett had been shrewd enough to discern the potential for problems because of the Swiss-only complement on board his start/finish boat, including SNG Vice-Commodore Fred Meyer. In the interests of fairness and balance, therefore, he had invited aboard Oracle's Ehman who, in addition to being a rules' authority, was a long-time race official and sailing judge. Commodore Meyer was less than happy but Bennett held his ground.

He recalled:

'I conferred with both teams, with Russell and Brad, and we agreed on a number of points that I would follow before starting a race. Primarily, there would be no crapshoots. There would be wind, and it would be

consistent right across the course. We followed the agreed procedures for race one and everybody judged it to be pretty good. Race two, though, was a bit more difficult. We sat out there all day waiting for conditions to settle and I wasn't that far away from having to call it off for the day. I had until about 4.30pm to get a race started. At around 4pm all of the wind indicators [across the course] lined up with a similar breeze. It was only around 7 to 8 knots but it was pretty close to all being in the same direction, and everything was as per my agreement with Russell and Brad. So I said: "OK, let's go."

We called the boats and they both acknowledged that they were good to race, and I was about to authorise the flag sequence that would signal the start when the people from the Swiss yacht club [SNG] that were assisting me decided they were not going to help me any further. They didn't believe the conditions were right [to race] – for whatever reason, they didn't want to race. We did have a bit of a swell but it wouldn't have been a metre and, in my view, everything was fine for racing. We were going to sail.

I was pissed off but there was no time to mess around, so I co-opted Tom [Ehman] and a Spanish chase-boat driver – a former race official – to man the flags, while I did the timing. It was close but we got it done and the race was finally underway. I knew I had made the right call … there was no question about that – and, later on, ISAF backed me fully.'[7]

While all of this, court case and all, had been going on in New York and Spain, the mainstream Cup community had been sitting on its hands for more than three years awaiting the outcome of the lengthy spat between the two billionaires, and the sailing world was now eagerly anticipating a speedy return to the norm of a multinational America's Cup regatta, hopefully in a new class of high-performance keel yachts, on San Francisco Bay. These expectations were based on the premises that the Cup winner defends the trophy in its home waters, and the best close-quarters match racing is delivered by monohulls, not multihulls.

Coutts, however, had other ideas. Nobody knows what deal he had with the new Challenger of Record, Club Nautico di Roma, or, for that matter, with the new trustee of the Cup, the Golden Gate Yacht Club, but in the weeks after GGYC's victory he was busy around the world selling his and, apparently, Ellison's vision of the ultimate, television-friendly Cup, investigating all sorts of initiatives, not least mounting the next defence in Europe and doing so in multihulls. There was no sign of any input from the Club Nautico di Roma – on its own account or on behalf of would-be challengers, with whom it was not communicating. And those would-be challengers were starting to get nervous, even sniffing some Alinghi-like skulduggery, despite Ellison's post-victory promises.

Coutts, of course, had recent history involving multihulls. In February 2007, while beached by Ernesto Bertarelli, he and leading American sailor Paul Cayard, with Patrick de Barros, had announced they had teamed up with Portuguese sports promoter João Lagos, of Lagos Sports, to fund the creation of a new World Sailing League (WSL), which would race identical, state-of-the-art 70ft catamarans on a global circuit, with the winner of the league, each year, receiving a cheque for $US2 million. Events in venues in the Mediterranean, Northern Europe, the Middle East, Asia, North America and South America were anticipated and both Cayard, who had been beached by Larry Ellison early in the 2007 America's Cup, and Coutts were committed to skippering teams in the league.[8]

This proposal had been hatched in 2006, in the Cascais residence of Coutts' influential Portuguese friend de Barros (he who was duped in the negotiations for 2007 AC venue rights). De Barros brought Lagos Sports to the table, as a partner in the venture, and persuaded the then Portuguese government to resurrect the shelved redevelopment of the Lisbon fishing-boat harbour, now to cater for a World Sailing League event as opposed to the America's Cup.

On the back of all this, French naval architects Marc Van Peteghem and Lauriot Prévost were commissioned to design a new 70ft catamaran for the League. De Barros revealed that Cayard had wanted a large, lightweight monohull but Coutts insisted on a state-of-the-art catamaran so that racing could be staged close to the shore, in order to optimise spectator potential. The plan was to build 14 of the new one-design cats in 2008 and be ready to launch the series during 2009.[9]

De Barros also outlined that construction of the prototype of the new cat had already started when Portugal voted in a socialist government

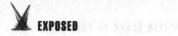

and any redevelopment of the fishing-boat harbour was promptly cancelled. Then, Lagos Sports went bankrupt when terrorist threats caused the cancellation of the 2008 Paris–Dakar rally in which Lagos was a major stakeholder. There was no other funding in prospect and the proposed World Sailing League died on the vine.

From Coutts' perspective, the exercise was not, however, all a waste of time and effort – he now had the iconic America's Cup brand at his disposal and that would soon change everything. According to de Barros, the America's Cup World Series in 45ft catamarans that Coutts made an integral part of the 2013 and 2017 editions of the Cup was a direct descendant of the failed WSL.

As for the possibility of the Cup holder GGYC defending at a venue other than its own home waters … this outrageous prospect raised its ugly head for the first time after Dennis Conner's *Stars & Stripes*, in 1987, trashed Iain Murray's *Kookaburra III* off Fremantle. Conner and his business mentor, Malin Burnham, were lead players in the campaign entity Sail America Foundation, which had a deal with San Diego Yacht Club, under which, if *Stars & Stripes* won off Fremantle, Sail America would become the manager of the club's defence of the trophy. In Sail America's view, that agreement covered the right to decide the venue.

The yacht club naturally assumed that any defence of the Cup in its name would be staged in its home waters off Point Loma. This was precisely what George Schuyler had in mind. But Sail America had a completely different agenda and, immediately following the win in Western Australia, started touting venue rights to other potential locations such as Hawaii, Long Beach (California), Atlantic City (New Jersey) and even Fremantle. It did so under the guise of seeking a venue with more wind than light-airs San Diego, but many Cup followers saw it for what it was – an opportunity to sell the venue rights for considerable profit. Later versions of Sail America Foundation, notably from Geneva and San Francisco, would turn that process into an art form.

Although there are many who deem themselves authorities on the America's Cup Deed of Gift, in this author's experience, there are, or have been in recent times, only four people with the credentials to genuinely make that claim: former New York Supreme Court Judge Carmen Beauchamp Ciparick; yachting historian and author John Rousmaniere; Sir Michael Fay's Cup legal adviser Andrew Johns; and former member of the New York Yacht Club's America's Cup Committee, the late James Michael. First reserve would be Mercury Bay Boating Club's American attorney, George Tompkins.

Ciparick was the first New York Supreme Court judge in the Cup's long history to have to make rulings on contested legal interpretations of George Schuyler's wording of the Deed and, probably more importantly, the intentions behind his wording. She had no previous exposure to the Deed or the Cup but, in the hugely influential Mercury Bay vs San Diego case, clearly came to understand what Schuyler wrote and what he intended and, accordingly, came down with some very correct and brave decisions – correct because they were eminently logical, and brave because, thankfully for the Cup and justice, she had the integrity to rule against an American team and for a foreign entity, even though she was an American judge in an American court.

The judge displayed the same logic and understanding when, in April 2009, she handed down the decision of the New York Court of Appeals that ruled invalid the challenge for the Cup by Ernesto Bertarelli's convenience Club Náutico Español de Vela (CNEV), because it did not meet the 'annual regatta' requirements of the Deed.

Rousmaniere is the New York Yacht Club's historian and chair of its Library Committee. He is an erudite and enthusiastic authority on Schuyler, the Deed of Gift and the America's Cup and a noted author, on the Cup and things maritime. He and Andrew Johns have remained good friends since the latter went to New York in 1987 to undertake the research of the Deed that led to Mercury Bay's 1988 challenge with a 90ft waterline monohull, and the pair regularly exchange views on the Cup and the Deed.

Although Johns' original exposure to the Deed was on behalf of the law firm that he worked for, his deep interest in the Deed, like Rousmaniere's, is founded on a passion for the Cup and the core values that it is supposed to represent, not on any vested interest.

The same could be said of the late James Michael, whose original exposure to Schuyler and the Deed were as a qualified attorney and highly capable sailor on the New York Yacht Club's America's Cup Committee. In those capacities, he was regularly called on to give opinions when disputes or questions arose regarding the Deed or measurement and/or rules issues. As a result, like Andrew Johns, he carried out extensive research in the New York Yacht Club library and archives.

Before his death, in 1998, Michael wrote an opinion on where Schuyler intended a club to defend should it win the Cup. It reads:

> 'On the question of venue, nothing in the Deed expressly or impliedly authorizes the defender to change the venue from its home waters, unless, and only if, it is done with the mutual consent of the challenger…
>
> The current Deed still retains the provision, first added in the 1882 Deed, that to qualify as a challenger, a yacht club must have "for its annual regatta an ocean water course on the sea, or on an arm of the sea". The purpose of this requirement, patently, is to make certain that, when a challenger wins the Cup, and then becomes the defender in the next match, its home waters will provide the "ocean courses" which must be used when mutual consent is lacking … the donors incorporated the reference to the "usual course for the annual regatta" of the defending club as a protection to the challenger, when the parties could not agree.
>
> The deletion of those words in the 1887 Deed was not intended to destroy that protection to the challenger, nor to give power to the defender to name whatever venue would give it the greatest advantage and put the challenger to the greatest disadvantage. Such an interpretation would be in direct conflict with the donor's purposes to assure a fair and sportsmanlike match, conducted in accordance with the cardinal principle of the challenger and defender contending "on equal terms".
>
> It would also ignore the fact that George L Schuyler deleted the words in question to enhance the protection of the challenger. In the matches up to 1887, many of the races were sailed on the New York Yacht Club's "inside course", which included the waters from Hoboken to Southwest Spit. These confined waters and the currents, shifting winds and heavy traffic of New York Harbor made this course, in the words of Lawson's History of the America's Cup,

a "bad course at best, and a source of hot anger and fierce discontent to British skippers".

When rewriting the Deed in 1887, George L Schuyler recognized that "annual courses", such as the Royal Yacht Squadron's "around the Isle of Wight" and the New York Yacht Club's "inside course", did not guarantee a fair match; thus he deleted the reference to them. Nothing in the history, however, suggests that he intended to permit the venue to leave the defending club's home waters, and as already observed, the continuation of the qualifications required for a club to challenge suggest the contrary.

In a letter by George L Schuyler to the New York Yacht Club in July 1890, he comments on the reasons for the change in the definition of the courses, as follows: "The matter which I thought of greatest importance, when the new Deed was drawn up, was that of courses. I wanted it so arranged that in case of a disagreement as to the conditions of the races, the boats would race in the sea without time allowance, and thus avoid the possibility of a challenger being left to the mercy of a club course where she would not have an equal chance to win."

It would be abhorrent to any fair-minded person to convert a change in the Deed, which Schuyler made to better the challenger's protection, into one which would truly put the challenger at the mercy of the defending club.

… if the issue of venue should ever come squarely before the [New York Supreme] Court, it is submitted the ruling will be that the defending club must hold the match in its home waters, unless the challenger mutually agrees to move it elsewhere."[9]

The question of where the holder of the Cup should defend was not an issue in terms of the 1988 (San Diego Yacht Club vs Mercury Bay) match because Sail America finally tidied up some of its differences with SDYC and agreed with MBBC that the 1988 'match' should be raced off San Diego, and shifting the venue was never a consideration in terms of SDYC's second and third defences, in 1992 and 1995.

Similarly, there was no debate about venue in terms of the Royal New Zealand Yacht Squadron's defences, in 2000 and 2003, when the Cup regattas were only ever going to be raced in the Squadron's home waters off Auckland.

It was only in 2003, when Ernesto Bertarelli's *Alinghi* won the Cup on behalf of the Société Nautique de Genève, that Cup waters became murky, with 'convenience' challengers making their debut in order to circumvent Schuyler's Deed and enable the pursuit of private agendas. In that process, Schuyler's insistence that: 'It is distinctly understood that the Cup is to be the property of the Club [holding the Cup] subject to the provisions of this Deed, and not the property of the owner or owners of any vessel winning a match' went out of the window.

11

TROUBLED WATERS

The spring months – March through May – are reputedly the most inviting time to visit San Francisco. The days are characteristically cloudless and mild, and Thursday 9 May 2013 was one out of the box as two big racing catamarans – one from America, the other from Sweden – went head to head in training for the famed America's Cup regatta, the start of which was now only a couple of months away.

With the Golden Gate Bridge and Alcatraz Island as backdrops, *Artemis*, from the Royal Swedish Yacht Club, and *Oracle* Team USA, representing the home town Golden Gate Yacht Club, were readying for another joust in their workout. Both were state-of-the-art 72-footers, designed and built especially for the 34th edition of the Cup. With towering aerofoil wings instead of traditional soft mainsails, the new class of 'boats' were immensely powerful and capable of speeds in excess of 40 knots.

Some would translate 'powerful' into 'potentially dangerous', but there were no signs of trouble as *Artemis* turned downwind in 18–20 knots of breeze to position herself for the start of the next match-up with *Oracle*. The manoeuvre was standard routine in most sailboats but in these sailing machines, which accelerate so quickly as the wind transitions from ahead to aft, the vessel can become a runaway.

In the blink of an eye, that's exactly what happened to the Swede. *Artemis* charged off like a spooked thoroughbred and, before anything could be done to prevent it, buried her slender bows into the wave ahead and pitchpoled. This caused the front beam that connects the forward sections of the two hulls to break up and the port hull to part company with the structure, while the 131ft-tall aerofoil wing crashed down on to the wreckage of what had been the forward beam and the still-attached starboard hull.

The *Artemis* crew of 11 were jerked overboard by the violent halt but help was close at hand in the form of four rigid inflatable chase boats that had been involved in the workout. They rushed to pick up the swimmers while emergency services ashore were alerted to what was, for the moment, a capsize (albeit, a serious one). However, capsize became catastrophe when a head count came up one short. Someone was still in the water, but who and where? The first answer wasn't long coming. The missing crewman was the eternally jovial Andrew 'Bart' Simpson, *Artemis*'s strategist and jib trimmer. But where the heck was he? Finally, rescue divers from one of the chase boats found him, apparently trapped under and hidden by some of the larger pieces of the wrecked carbon-fibre beam and aerofoil.

One report says that 'crew members could see him [Simpson] fighting for his life and dived beneath the water to try and set him free. They handed [him] emergency oxygen bottles – which hold about ten breaths each – in a bid to keep him alive in the hope rescue crews would arrive in time.' Quick as the response was, it was all in vain. By the time the unconscious Simpson was freed, he'd been underwater for around 10 minutes and the determined efforts of his own crew and police rescuers failed to revive him.

Nobody was quite sure about the sequence of the events that became a disaster. Did the boat disintegrate because of the nose dive or were structural failures the cause of it all? Regardless, for the moment, the America's Cup in San Francisco went into survival mode while the rest of the sailing world rushed to pay tribute to one of its luminaries.

On 21 May 2014, an inquest in Bournemouth, England, found that Simpson died 'as a result of an accident'. Richard Middleton, the assistant coroner for Dorset, said: 'I have heard how he sustained injuries, predominantly to his head and neck', adding that Simpson's death should be recorded as 'blunt trauma with drowning'.

The funeral for Simpson was held at Sherborne Abbey in Dorset, England, on 31 May 2013. The church was packed with 500 or 600 people, as well as media, and the pall-bearers included his old rivals and close friends Iain Percy and Sir Ben Ainslie, both of whom gave readings.

The San Francisco medical examiner's report into the death was finally released on 16 October 2013, held up by the need for a toxicology report (which found that the only drug in Simpson's system at the time of his death was caffeine). The report said that blows to the head, body and limbs contributed to death by drowning and that blunt trauma also contributed (the report didn't specify how). Simpson was wearing a helmet, wetsuit, flotation device and shoes when he died.

Four chase boats had assisted the other 10 crew members off the crippled sailboat, the report said: 'But the subject remained trapped for approximately ten minutes [and] was then located, floating in the waters of the bay, unconscious.'

Andrew James Simpson MBE was born on 17 December 1976 in land-locked Chertsey, in southern England. He caught the sailing bug while, as a young boy, visiting his grandparents in Christchurch, Dorset (on the English Channel coast).

Simpson started his competitive sailing career in the Laser class, before switching to the heavier Finn class, in which he won the bronze medal at the 2003 ISAF Sailing World Championships, in Cádiz. His training partner was Ben Ainslie, who won the gold. He then moved to the two-man Star class, partnering lifelong friend Iain Percy. The pair won a bronze medal at the 2007 ISAF Sailing World Championships in Cascais, qualifying for the 2008 Summer Olympics in Beijing where they won Star gold. In 2010, he and Percy won the Star World Championships in Rio de Janeiro and then, in 2012, the silver medal in the 2012 Olympics in England. After the Star class was removed from the Olympic sailing disciplines, Simpson turned his attention to the America's Cup, joining his former skipper, Percy, who was running the Artemis sailing programme for the 2013 challenge in San Francisco.

It was said that while Ainslie and Percy were at the top of their age group coming through the ranks in British sailing, Simpson was third but he was always first in size and strength – and comic relief. Hence the nickname Bart. The news of his death prompted tributes from all around the world, most of them lauding his sunny nature and the strong team ethic that he brought to whichever campaign he was involved in.

'Bart' Simpson left behind a wife, Leah, and young sons, Freddie and Hamish.

The tragedy sent the already troubled event into a tailspin. While it was the first loss of life, it was the second time in seven months that an AC72 had pitchpoled and disintegrated while undertaking the same bear-away manoeuvre in San Francisco's fresh conditions (*Oracle* Team USA met the same fate on 17 October 2012).

Amid rumours that the event could be cancelled because of safety concerns, civil and regatta authorities moved quickly to establish what had happened. Two investigations were launched – one by the San Francisco Police Department (a normal procedure in the event of loss of life) and the second by America's Cup Race Management (ACRM), led by its head, Iain Murray.

In a media conference call, Murray said that establishing the sequence of events would be crucial in ascertaining precisely what had led to the fatal capsize and, while structural failure had been suggested as the cause, there was, at that point in time, no evidence to suggest whether a structural failure caused the capsize or whether it happened as a result of *Artemis* burying her bows during the bear away. Murray observed: 'There is all sorts of speculation as to what happened and there appears to be a difference of opinion as to what came first. At this stage, we don't know.' As to whether the event would proceed, Murray said: 'We have had an excellent relationship with the US Coast Guard who issued the [event] permits. We have a great trust in each other and I believe that they see the actions that we are taking as the right actions. There has been no discussion of withdrawing permits or of stopping racing.'

Just weeks away from the beginning of the challenger elimination series, for the Louis Vuitton Cup, the event that had been billed as the most ambitious step in the modern America's Cup was in deep trouble. There were only a disappointing three challengers anyway, and the future of one of those, the Swedish entry *Artemis*, had to be doubtful indeed. Then, the *Luna Rossa* campaign, from Italy, was considering whether it should go home – which would leave only *Emirates* Team New Zealand to carry on with the 34th challenge for the Auld Mug.

It would all get a lot worse before the regatta graph plunge showed any sign of bottoming out.

Murray's biggest headache appeared to be that, despite claims to the contrary, the Cup regatta had not yet been issued with an event permit by the US Coast Guard, which had final jurisdiction over what does or doesn't happen on the waters of San Francisco Bay. And how was that bureaucracy, in the most bureaucratic city in the most bureaucratic state in the union, going to react to a catastrophic crash and death in its waters that had made headlines all around the world – for all the wrong reasons?

Murray strove manfully to resolve the multitude of issues he now faced and, after conducting his own investigation, on 22 May 2013 he issued to the contestants – challengers and defender – a list of 37 Safety Recommendations 'that should be implemented immediately'. The list was clearly intended to pacify the police and US Coast Guard and addressed all aspects of racing an AC72 catamaran in San Francisco, including structural testing of the vessels and their equipment, crew safety and emergency gear, and regatta procedures.

The most obvious safety measures were the personal equipment that everyone would have to wear/carry, including buoyancy aids (with quick-release mechanism), body armour (incorporating protection for spine and against puncture and impact wounds), an electronic head-count system, underwater crew-locator devices, underwater breathing apparatus (capable of hands-free operation), and helmets (of high-visibility colours and exacting specifications).

The additional on-the-water support equipment that would be required included: two rescue boats attending each AC72 yacht while sailing; rescue divers and rescue swimmers, ready to enter the water immediately; a minimum of one paramedic (or an appropriate medical practitioner) on one of the rescue boats; a defibrillator to be carried on the rescue boat carrying the paramedic; and recovery nets.

All this – for a sailboat race?

Surprisingly (or maybe not), the spooked Cup syndicates went for it all, even as far as the sharing of what would normally be regarded as sensitive structural information with the not-so-advanced among them. Until, that is, Emirates Team New Zealand (ETNZ) and Luna Rossa got to grips with a subsequent amendment issued by Murray, which said:

> 'The Regatta Director has been advised by the Competitors and organizers that they agree to all of the Supplementary Recommendations No.2 with the exception of:
>
> • An additional 100 kilograms being added to the maximum weight of an AC72 Yacht for safety purposes
> • Rudder elevators being permitted to extend beyond maximum beam; and
> • A 150 millimeter reduction in the required clearance of rudders relative to the sternplane
>
> Regardless, as Regatta Director I feel strongly that the foregoing three recommendations, though not unanimously agreed, must remain in force … Supplementary Recommendations No 2 will be submitted to the US Coast Guard to form part of the Regatta Safety Plan.'[1]

This is where the until now compliant ETNZ and Luna Rossa parted ways with the Regatta Director who, they asserted, had 'exceeded his jurisdiction' by trying to impose changes to the AC72 Class Rule without, as required, the unanimous support of all affected. Moreover, they made it abundantly clear that they considered that Murray's rudder elevator proposals were not safety issues at all but were performance driven and would benefit the defender, *Oracle* Team USA, and its Challenger of Record, *Artemis*.

With the clock ticking, the regatta's International Jury was asked to mediate the confrontation and appointed two of its members to attempt that solution. It was, however, to no avail, leaving ETNZ and Luna Rossa to formally apply for a jury ruling 'that the Regatta Director has exceeded his jurisdiction in seeking to introduce amendments to the AC72 Class Rule without obtaining the unanimous consent of the Competitors, as required by Clause 4 of the Class Rule, and that any such amendments are invalid and of no effect.'

In support of its application, ETNZ submitted that amendment procedures needed to be followed, particularly in respect of the Class Rules, because competitors had relied on them in respect of their design programmes: 'Competitors undertook their design programs knowing that the Regatta would be sailed in AC72s in San Francisco, a known windy venue, between July and September 2013 with an upper wind limit for starting racing of 33 knots.'

The Kiwis claimed that they 'always believed that this upper limit was unrealistic' but 'knew that the Defender's design brief for the drafting of the Class Rule was that the design had to be capable of sailing in anything, as the intention of the GGYC and the Challenger of Record was that the event was intended to be a TV spectacle where there were no postponements of racing due to wind conditions.'[2]

The New Zealanders made it clear that they applauded and supported the recommended changes relative to crew safety and protection but the ultimate responsibility for safety of the yacht's design rested with competitors, not with the regatta director or the various event authorities. Moreover, they pointed out that while the Class Rule did not itself regulate safety,

> '… it does allow a safe yacht to be designed within the parameters of the rule – as our design's 120-day track record demonstrates. [It] has proved it is possible to design a safe yacht under the AC72 Class rule suitable for sailing in San Francisco conditions, but it does come with performance sacrifices, more noticeable in light winds.'[3]

What the New Zealanders were saying is that, while they fully supported the recommendations that addressed the safety issues highlighted by Bart Simpson's tragic death, there was something else going on here. Under the guise of safety, lower wind limits and the freeing up of certain design constraints were being railroaded through, and these moves, if allowed, would favour two of the four teams in the regatta. As ETNZ had the full support of Luna Rossa in its objections, that left only the defender *Oracle* Team USA and the injured *Artemis*.

And therein was the root cause of the stand-off in terms of Murray's proposed rudder elevator amendments. It was no secret that *Oracle* Team USA and, particularly *Artemis*, had been completely outflanked by New Zealand's development of foiling systems, which enabled their AC72 to skim some 5ft above the water, riding on its minimal-drag 'stilts' at speeds in excess of 40 knots. As if that wasn't alarming enough for the defender, the ingenious men from the far side of the world were showing that, downwind, they could change direction (gybe) without coming down off the foils and, even more worryingly, were also showing signs of being able to do it all upwind as well. Playing catch-up, *Oracle* Team USA was now able to ride its foils but not reliably and certainly not as efficiently as the Kiwis.

The straight-shooting Max Sirena, skipper of *Luna Rossa*, made his view of proceedings absolutely clear in an interview with the Italian daily newspaper *La Repubblica*: 'Oracle and Artemis are doing something shameful, and they are doing it by exploiting the death of "Bart" Simpson, a sailor, a friend. And I am fed up of accepting everything in silence.'

Luna Rossa and Team New Zealand, he said, had succeeded, in three years of work, to make their catamarans 'fly' (ie 'sail' on foils above the water) and it was much faster. Oracle Team USA and Artemis were scampering desperately to catch up. He didn't mind that but he objected strongly to this latest twist in how they were seeking to do so, and observed:

> *'Now Oracle is able to "fly" but not in a stable manner, and they need to change the rudders in order to stabilize. The only problem is that you cannot do that. To modify rudders as they want, you have to change the measurement rules. It's like we were made to build a car with engine capacity 2000cc and now, a week before the race, they want to run with a 2200cc. But the worst thing is that they want to pass this regulatory modification as a decision for reasons of safety. It is not for safety. It is only for performance.*

They tell us that we are unsporting [for opposing the relevant changes to the Class Rule] when actually, it is them who are exploiting the incident of Artemis to obtain advantages in water. There is a safety issue – of course it exists and, it was right [of Murray] to intervene [with the safety recommendations]. He proposed 37 points to improve security. Thirty-five we all agreed with but, the other two only helped Oracle and Artemis to regain lost ground.

With New Zealand, we proposed: "Let's agree now to the 35 while we think about the other two … And we manage to have the 35 points passed. But then comes the follow-up notice from Murray, against which we protest.'[4]

Murray, meanwhile, contributed to *Scuttlebutt Europe* to provide, from his perspective, some clarification:

'I issued 37 safety recommendations to ensure our racing this summer will be as safe as possible. Of the 37 recommendations, all have been strongly supported by the teams except for the one dealing with rudder elevators. Currently, there is a lot of misinformation about what this recommendation is and what it means.

In simple terms, rudder elevators are winglets on the rudder blade which act as control surfaces. The elevators are horizontal and control the pitch of the yacht. As with any rudder, a large surface area provides better control but comes with a drag cost. My safety recommendations increase the span of the rudders to a minimum of 2.1 metres and stipulate a minimum size of the elevators at .32 square metres, attached to the bottom of the rudder in the most submerged position possible. The aim is to minimise the chance of a pitchpole (when the bow of the boat submerges and the stern rises out of the water). The AC72s need control at all times as they are travelling in excess of 40 knots and the hydrodynamic loads when turning the rudders/ elevators at speed is substantial.

The current rule forces each competitor to fix the angle of the elevators each morning by 8.00am, when the boat is measured. But different angles of attack on the elevators are necessary for different wind strengths. Under

*my safety recommendation, the teams can adjust the angle of attack on
the elevators up until five minutes before the race start, allowing for more
control in the conditions they are likely to encounter in that race. Under
the current rule and under my proposal, the elevators cannot be adjusted
while racing.*

*I have yet to hear a convincing argument from any team that my
recommendation will not enhance control and thus safety during racing.
What I have heard is that this recommendation will make the boats easier
to control and more stable.*

*This is a safety issue, pure and simple. Deeper, submerged rudders, with
bigger elevators and control surfaces fixed at the most appropriate angle of
attack for the conditions, simply make the boats safer.'*[5]

Oracle boss Russell Coutts, on the New Zealand radio station Newstalk
1ZB, chipped in with the assertion that Team New Zealand was
dreaming up conspiracy theories and that the changes recommended
by Murray would not ultimately impact on who won the regatta: 'They
thought that we had some sort of adjustable trim tab on there and
they thought we were gaining some sort of advantage out of this. We
support Iain Murray. We think he's done a good job for making the
boats safer.'

Artemis chief Paul Cayard, meanwhile, gave a very strange
interview to the *San Francisco Chronicle*'s Tom Fitzgerald, in which he
branded the AC72 as 'too big, too powerful and too dangerous'. He
explained that his home town, San Francisco, was one of the windiest
venues in the world: 'That's a good thing if you've got the right tool
for it. It's a horrible thing if you've got the wrong tool [and] right now,
we've got the wrong tool. We've got a boat that's made for San Diego
[where the winds are much lighter], and we're trying to race it in San
Francisco.'

Cayard continued with the claim that all the teams knew that racing
in the shadow of the Golden Gate Bridge was going to be dangerous
but: 'We probably never really, as an event, grabbed that reality enough
and did something about it. So *Oracle* capsizes and [that] opened
everybody's eyes: even the 72-footers can tip over. Fortunately, nobody
was hurt there, but the boat was destroyed completely, and then ours
was probably the straw that broke the camel's back.'

In the meantime, he added, the elements to have the best America's Cup ever were:

'… all right around us. We can touch them. If we'd just had the AC45s [the smaller cats used in the build-up AC World Series for two years], we'd be beating the teams off with a stick. We'd have more entries than the place could hold, and we'd have all their markets. Maybe the Cup wouldn't have the on-the-edge, peak-of-the-sport appeal it needs if mere 45-footers were used, but the worldwide impact of the event would make up for that. If China was racing, we'd have Chinese media, Chinese internet. South Korea, France would be in it. Great Britain would be in it. Germany – every country would be racing in it. My guess is they'd have to limit [the field] to 12. What San Francisco was now left with in 2013 was a very exclusive competition that might or might not capture the non-sailing public's fancy. It's just too expensive a competition.'[6]

That all smacked very much of someone lamenting that his team had designed and built the wrong boat for conditions with which he should/would have been more familiar than anyone else in the fleet.

Then, just before the International Jury was to convene to review the matter, regatta director Murray added a new twist to proceedings by threatening to scuttle the event unless his safety recommendations were upheld. This stand seemed to ignore the fact that the only issues still to be sorted were those that would allow different rudder elevators.

In the *San Francisco Chronicle* (again), Tom Fitzgerald reported Murray as saying that, if the jury agreed with Emirates Team New Zealand and Luna Rossa, he would go back to the US Coast Guard and say he didn't think the racing would be safe. In that case, the Coast Guard would almost certainly withdraw the event's permit and, 'without a permit to race on San Francisco Bay, there will be no regatta.'

Although he was speaking in the context of safety, this reported statement served only to fuel the conspiracy theories that the rudder-elevator changes that Murray was seeking were not, in fact, safety driven. But Murray refused to take that lying down.

Sail World reported on 4 July 2013 that he [Murray] had met with the media on Wednesday 3 July to address issues raised in the protests filed by Emirates Team New Zealand and Luna Rossa Challenge [against his proposed 37 changes to the Safety Rules]. He described as 'baseless' claims that his proposals were:

> 'changing the game one week before the regatta: "I made these recommendations to the teams on May 22, over six weeks before the first race of the Louis Vuitton Cup," he said. "At that meeting, all of the teams agreed to all 37 of the safety recommendations." Disappointingly, for competitive reasons, two of the teams are now protesting over some of these safety recommendations. But I don't believe you can pick and choose. These safety recommendations are a package and together they increase safety for our sailors and they are now Rules of the event.'[7]

ETNZ boss Grant Dalton countered with the assertion that the larger elevators recommended by Murray were not 'necessary or safe at all'. If allowed, the elevators would extend beyond the beam (or width) of the boat and, if a crew member fell over the side, with the 7.5-ton machine charging at 50mph, the elevator could cut him in half.

If, to the outside world, all this squabbling seemed bizarre, the regatta itself, due to start in just a few days' time, turned ridiculous when Luna Rossa declined to race in the Louis Vuitton Cup round robins until the International Jury had handed down its verdict on whether Murray was exceeding his authority. They would only rejoin the fray if the verdict was in favour of itself and ETNZ.

Artemis's back-up boat would not be ready to race for some weeks, even though the team was working around the clock, so Team New Zealand, the last man standing, would have to sail alone if it wanted the points available. And that's what happened: on race day one (7 July 2013), *Luna Rossa* were a no-show. Instead, with the television cameras and crowds on the San Francisco waterfront bearing witness, was a black, foiling 72ft catamaran travelling effortlessly at sensational speeds around San Francisco Bay and, yes, gybing on the foils downwind and, yes, looking suspiciously like she was also foiling upwind too. It was impressive to say the least, but it wasn't racing – it was a demonstration by a challenger going through the motions in order to collect the single point up for grabs.

Race day two (9 July 2013) was the same, only this time the no-show, for obvious reasons, was *Artemis*. Race day three (11 July 2013), too, was no different, except that this time it was *Luna Rossa*'s turn to 'fly' solo in the absence of the Swedes, the Italians having joined the action at this point after the International Jury handed down its findings regarding Murray's amendments – in favour of ETNZ and Luna Rossa. The jury had also ordered the regatta director to withdraw his requirements in terms of rudder elevators and to make the views of all the competitors known to the US Coast Guard with regard to the Marine Event Permit. In other words, Regatta Director Murray exceeded his authority and the additional changes (to the original 37) that he sought to impose were nullified.

The farce on the water continued for the next 20 days until the woeful sham of the Louis Vuitton Cup round robins was over, with ETNZ unbeaten on 9 points (from four race wins and five forfeits) in the races it chose to contest. *Luna Rossa* was second with four forfeit 'wins' (it lost four on the water to ETNZ).

The next scandal wasn't long in coming.

On 26 July 2013, boatbuilders who were preparing the AC45 yachts to be used for the Youth America's Cup, a side feature of the main event, had reported some suspicious changes to the strictly controlled class set-up of at least one of the yachts owned by Oracle Team USA. The regatta Measurement Committee had followed up on the report and found evidence of illicit tampering.

The International Jury was called in to investigate further and took until 3 September 2013 to hand down its findings and decisions. In its preamble to those, it said:

> 'On 4 August 2013, the Jury received a report from Richard Slater of Oracle Team USA (OTUSA) concerning a contravention of the AC45 Class Rule C15 (a) and Racing Rules of Sailing. The report was in respect of yachts Oracle Racing Team Spithill, Oracle Racing Team Coutts, and yacht BAR [chartered to Ben Ainslie Racing by Oracle Racing Team] during certain regattas.'[8]

The jury had followed up the report and interviewed 18 members of OTUSA and five employees of America's Cup Race Management (ACRM) and decided there was cause for a jury hearing to determine whether OTUSA had breached Article 60.1 of the Protocol (which deals with the protection of 'The Reputation of the America's Cup' – in other words, with anything that brings the America's Cup and the sport of sailing into disrepute).

The jury's investigations, with input from the regatta's Measurement Committee (MC), found the three strict one-design yachts in question had been tampered with in ways that could only be judged to be in pursuit of performance gains – there was 'clear evidence' of rule infringements.

In plain language, it appeared that someone in the organisation of the defender of the America's Cup, Larry Ellison's powerful Oracle Team USA, led by knight-of-the-realm Sir Russell Coutts, had been cheating.

In submissions to the jury, OTUSA contended that the tampering discovered was not 'performance enhancing' while Emirates Team New Zealand insisted that it was, and Nick Nicholson, chairman of the Measurement Committee, observed to the jury: 'I have never known a sailor to make a change [to his boat] that would make the boat slower.' He added that, with limited resources, the MC had relied on a level of trust from the competitors. When asked how he felt when he found unauthorised modifications, he replied: 'I felt old, and used, and stupid.'

The jury was of the view that:

> 'Each of the modifications were made in the belief that they would enhance performance; whether they would actually enhance performance is not directly relevant. The performance enhancement would likely be small, but making many small enhancements is the nature of winning races at the top level of the sport, particularly in a one-design class with a "closed" rule.'[9]

The jury also observed: 'It seems inconceivable that boat riggers initiated these changes without the knowledge of managers, or the direction of sailors, if not skippers (as is claimed by OTUSA).'

As a consequence of it all, OTUSA was penalised 'one point for each of the first two races of the Match in which they would otherwise score a point' and ordered to pay a fine of $US250,000 ($US125,000 to the Andrew Simpson Sailing Foundation and $US125,000 to a charitable organisation selected by the Mayor of San Francisco, to provide support to at-risk youth in the San Francisco Bay area).

The jury said it had 'no intention to impose a penalty that will determine the outcome of the [America's Cup] Match, which should best be determined on the water and not in the jury room' but said the penalty would have been heavier but for the cooperation it had received from OTUSA.

In the middle of it all, Ben Ainslie Racing (BAR) withdrew from the America's Cup World Series events that were implicated (the AC45s were used for that series) and Ainslie sent an email to say: 'As skipper … I had no knowledge whatsoever that the boat was being raced out of measurement. I am deeply disappointed by this incident and will do all I can to assist the relevant parties in any further investigations.' OTUSA followed suit and the jury ordered the regatta director to re-score the series for the two years affected by the 'modifications'. OTUSA and BAR were given 14 days to return all prizes, awards and trophies.

Concurrent with releasing the above findings and decisions, the International Jury on the same day (3 September) also released its conclusions in a separate Rule 69 case involving allegations of gross misconduct on the part of five OTUSA shore crew and sailors. The allegations were a result of the jury's investigations into tampering with the AC45s. Three of the five were banned from any further involvement in the 2013 America's Cup while a fourth was banned from sailing in the event until after four races had been completed.

OTUSA chief Russell Coutts described the decisions as 'outrageous' and was reported by the *San Francisco Chronicle* saying: 'I'm astounded, to be honest with you, that they penalised the whole team for this. Imagine an Olympic team and one member infringes a rule. Does that mean the whole team gets penalised?'

By this stage, the Louis Vuitton Cup elimination racing was over and done with. Predictably, *Emirates* Team New Zealand and *Luna Rossa* summarily dismissed a hapless *Artemis* in the semi-finals and then ETNZ, just as readily, disposed of the Italians, 7–1 in the challenger final (the Kiwis' one loss – a race two disqualification – was because its chase boat had to render 'outside assistance' when the race boat suffered a hydraulics failure and couldn't control its wing sail and/or daggerboards).

Now it was the 34th match for the America's Cup with the defender, *Oracle* Team USA, taking on the challenger, *Emirates* Team New Zealand, in a best-of-17 match, and there was no love lost between the two combatants. The contest was very one-sided as ETNZ raced to an 8–1 lead and needed just one more win to take the Cup back to Auckland. OTUSA, starting with a 2-point deficit, was no match for the polished New Zealanders who were handling their big cat with rare skill and nailing the tactical calls on a racecourse that could be a minefield of strong currents and shifty winds.

Then, overnight, the picture changed dramatically with the OTUSA boat suddenly looking like it was on rails when foiling. Skipper James Spithall backed his media-conference swagger with new-found dominance on the water, helped in no small way by the tactical nous of his tactician, Britain's Sir Ben Ainslie.

As OTUSA clawed her way, one win at a time, back into the game, there were growing rumours that the Americans had used the lay day after race day 11 to install a secret piece of equipment that had been adapted, at great expense, from Boeing 747 technology developed to smooth out the jumbo jet's flight. Nicknamed 'Herbie', only billionaire Larry Ellison could afford it. It all seemed credible because it was now OTUSA that looked unassailable while the New Zealanders, under real pressure, were making costly mistakes, and the seismic shift in fortunes became one of the greatest sporting comebacks of all time with OTUSA wrapping up the match 9–8.

Long after the dust had settled, former Team New Zealand, Alinghi and Oracle design guru Mike Drummond revealed the reality of the overnight turnaround. OTUSA's supposedly space-age foiling assist system, he told the *New Zealand Herald* newspaper, was a simple mechanical feedback loop and not, as speculated, an electronic system driven by a computer. The 'magic' button that helmsman Spithill had been seen to press when the OTUSA boat started to foil was, he said: 'Very similar to turning on a light switch. It just sends some fairly dumb current or voltage down the line, which at the end of the wire opens up a hydraulic valve. The foil moves and, when it has moved half a degree, it closes the valve again.' The major gain over the manual system used by Team New Zealand was the accuracy provided by the half-degree presets, which eliminated the variations in hydraulic pressure that came from their grinders and smoothed out the ride.

Why, then, was OTUSA so far off the pace earlier in the regatta?

In Drummond's view, it was due to a lack of coordination between replacement wing trimmer Kyle Langford and Spithill, following Dutchman Dirk de Ridder's suspension from the event (he was one of the two OTUSA sailors banned as a result of the AC45 tampering case). The relationship between helmsman and wing trimmer was, he said, similar to two people attempting to drive a car around a corner at high speed:

> 'You've got the steering wheel and I've got the accelerator. As the car drifts outside the corner with a bit of understeer, I could let the accelerator off or you could turn the wheel or we could both do a bit. I'm sure after a year's practice we'd be pretty good at it, but after a day's practice we'd be lousy.'

Oracle didn't sail their boat as well to begin with. Their wing was needing to be trimmed a lot more and, tactically, they made some mistakes. They didn't start as well. There were a whole bunch of things but I don't think foiling was to blame for their performance in the first half of the regatta. It was almost every other aspect of their sailing, and when they eliminated their mistakes and the coordination between the wing trimmer and the helmsman improved markedly, and when they developed their upwind foiling quite rapidly, finally the potential of the boat came through. Their programme was at fault for not preparing them well enough for the Cup but they were good enough to improve during the Cup to pull off a miracle, really.'[10]

That 'miracle' – the most unlikely of comebacks – was dramatic stuff and, allied to the impressive television and still photographic images of the incredibly powerful AC72s tearing around the waters of San Francisco Bay at better than 40 knots, saved the event from being totally written off as one of the worst in Cup history.

But, where to now, with the AC72s consigned to the scrapheap and the whole event downsized to smaller catamarans in, of all places, the British territory of Bermuda and the American defender ignoring Schuyler's clear intent that the holder of the Cup should defend in that Club's home waters?

12

FOILED?

It would prove to be the most dramatic day in the 2017 America's Cup – Tuesday 6 June on Bermuda's Great Sound – and the events that unfolded almost changed the course of Cup history.

The wind was already gusting to the regatta maximum of 24 knots when Emirates Team New Zealand's 50ft catamaran *Aotearoa* left the dock, on schedule to meet Sir Ben Ainslie's *Land Rover BAR* in race three of the challenger semi-finals. Very quickly, she was back, with a damaged lower flap on her huge wing sail.

With the clock ticking down to the race start, the ETNZ shore crew set about hauling the 78ft wing out of the boat and replacing it with the team's back-up rig. In just 55 minutes *Aotearoa* was again on her way to the start area where Ainslie, one of the greatest yachtsmen ever, was waiting to resume his quest to end Britain's 166-year wait to regain the trophy lost to the New York schooner *America* in 1851.

The Kiwis made the start with just minutes to spare but, in the gusty winds sweeping the Great Sound, both crews were wary of engaging in the usually aggressive pre-start manoeuvring. The New Zealanders, in particular, couldn't risk any more damage.

Ainslie was in the controlling position at the gun and was clear ahead as he bore away into the short reach to the first mark with the Kiwis in hot pursuit. ETNZ helmsman Peter Burling and his skipper Glenn Ashby were content to keep the race close until, on the second leg to windward, they engineered the opportunity to pass their rival and sailed away to win by 2 minutes and 10 seconds, going 3–0 up in the first-to-five series.

It was all beginning to look very familiar – Burling and Ashby happy enough with a conservative start and then using *Aotearoa*'s speed and superior stability to close in and pounce on any opportunity to take over the lead. It made for exciting viewing for the folks back home, glued to their television sets at 5 o'clock in the morning, and there was a lot more to come before this day was done.

The two semi-finalists were soon at it again in the preliminaries to race four. Both boats copped fouls in the pre-start, so they cancelled themselves out, before Ainslie peeled away with a clear lead as he crossed the line.

As *Aotearoa* turned downwind for a high-speed chase to the first mark, she launched frighteningly into an out-of-control nosedive, her bows digging into the wake of the fleeing *Land Rover BAR,* her rudders and elevators high in the air and the top of her 78ft wing sail in the water ahead of her as the twin hulls and joining platform tipped past the vertical. Three of the six-man crew were hurled overboard while the other three, including Burling, were left clinging to precarious positions, still in their work places inside the starboard hull. It was a sudden, scary accident that had rescue boats, including the support RIBs of both syndicates, racing to render assistance.

Those in the water were quickly recovered and, as soon as everyone was accounted for, the ETNZ support team set about the tricky task of getting the catamaran back on its feet and under tow to her base ashore. The British picked up a race win but nobody, least of all Ainslie, was happy about the outcome.

The big question now, though, was whether the ETNZ campaign was over. Their one operational wing sail had suffered a lot of damage in the pitchpole and looked in very poor shape, while the Kiwis' only other sail was already in the boat shed awaiting repair after the harm suffered when heading to the start area earlier in the day. Additionally, the twin hulls and joining platform of *Aotearoa*, with all their sensitive electronics and hydraulics systems, had been subjected to a severe dunking in salt water that would not have done them any good at all.

Could the Kiwis, renowned for their resilience and innovation, salvage their campaign and get back out on the race course before 2pm the next day for two more jousts with the British? They had something like 19 hours and that didn't seem nearly enough.

That evening, at about 5pm, team boss Grant Dalton called a meeting of his 85-strong team at which his right-hand man Kevin Shoebridge briefed everyone on the plan of attack that had been hatched with the team's boatbuilders and engineers. The target, Shoebridge explained, would not be a hasty repair in order to race the next day but a more substantial reparation that would see *Aotearoa* back out there again in two days' time, in much better shape to tackle whatever was still to come. It would mean forfeiting two races and handing points to the Brits but it was the more prudent solution.

The whole situation cast more scrutiny on why, supposedly in the interests of cost saving, the challengers (but not the defender) had been limited to constructing just one new race boat for their campaigns. The common belief was that syndicates usually built multiple boats to enable two-boat testing as an essential part of their R&D programmes. Some of that was true. However, the bottom-line reason for building more than one race boat was to provide insurance in case of a complete catastrophe like that experienced in 1995 when the Australians sank while racing Team New Zealand in the semi-finals of the challenger eliminations in AC29. On that unforgettable day, *OneAustralia,* in willing conditions off San Diego's Point Loma, broke nearly in half and slipped into the Pacific depths with alarming rapidity. It looked like it was 'game over' for the Aussies, but they had a trial horse back-up boat and, within a couple of days, were completely operational again, even taking a race off the seemingly unstoppable Kiwis before going down 1–5.

On this occasion though, ETNZ didn't have the same luxury. Its one race boat was damaged with its only operational wing sail in tatters. If they could not deliver the almost-impossible in the repair shop then their campaign might be over.

It was an all-hands, around-the-clock effort as the syndicate's boatbuilders and the engineers set about putting Humpty back together again. The bottom flap from rig two was salvaged and fitted to rig one, while sensitive electronic and hydraulic systems were fully checked out and restored. As a bonus, it was then that the wind gods decided that enough was enough – the lone-wolf Kiwis deserved a break. It was blowing above the regatta maximums the next day and racing was postponed, giving ETNZ the extra 24 hours they needed in which to complete their more thorough rehabilitation without gifting any points to the opposition.

Fingers were pointed at regatta boss Iain Murray for allowing racing on the fateful day since all four remaining challengers had suffered damage. However, Dalton directed his anger at the defender, Oracle Team USA which, he said, had been directly instrumental in establishing and preserving upper wind limits for the regatta that were unrealistic.

The ETNZ boss, on 8 June 2017, told *Newstalk ZB*'s breakfast-show host Mike Hosking:

'I've read and heard quite a bit of criticism of the race director but he was playing it by the book. There's a much bigger or deeper issue in play here that's gone on for a number of years, as a lot of things do with the America's Cup. The event authority [ACEA] would not allow the [maximum] wind speed to be dropped from what was 25 knots. Iain Murray, on behalf of the teams, negotiated it down to 24 knots. That's about as much as he thought he could get away with. I've had the view for a number of years that these boats would be unsailable in those conditions and that someone would crash. It just happened to be us. Criticism of Iain Murray is unfounded. The bigger issue is the pressure that he is subjected to.'[1]

Dalton told Hosking that the carnage inflicted on the challenger fleet played right into Oracle's hands.

'That's the game,' he said. 'That's why they didn't want the wind limit dropped. Later in June, there will be less wind and off to the races go Oracle. This is exactly the game that they want to play. If the opposition was basically destroyed and a weaker team could get through to challenge, cobbled back together, that's exactly what they want.'[2]

Dalton described most of the damage to the Team NZ boat and wing sail as 'superficial', but admitted that ETNZ was vulnerable to any more wing harm in the racing ahead:

'In San Francisco, we only ever had one wing and this time we've only used one [when working up] in New Zealand – our second one came on stream when we got here. So, it's not unusual for us to have one wing but you certainly feel a bit safer if you've got two that are fully operational.'[3]

His bigger concern, though, was the possible psychological impact of the pitchpole experience on the crew:

'As Kiwis, you sometimes don't think that's a big deal, when it is. With the calibre of these guys, they crash and burn in their dinghies quite a bit, but the possible psychological consequences of what they've been through here are real and we've got to be conscious of that. We need a good day tomorrow, get out there, try to put the semi-final away and regroup on Friday [local time], before we go to the final. The forecast tomorrow is not fresh to frightening, but it's still pretty well up there. One clean day and all this will be nothing more than a memory.'[4]

When racing resumed two days later, the New Zealanders were determined to finish the job on the Brits as quickly as possible. In race one, on what would prove the last day of the series, they struck gremlins in the prestart when the foot control that Burling used to raise and/or lower the port daggerboard would not activate properly and the board would not stay down. As a result, *Aotearoa* trailed *Land Rover BAR* by nearly half a minute crossing the start line. There was no panic. Although highly conscious of the tender state of their boat, the Kiwis set out after their rival and clawed back the deficit until, two-thirds of the way up the second beat *Land Rover BAR* slipped down off her foils and briefly had both hulls in the water. That was the opening that Burling had been working for. *Aotearoa* instantly hit the front and went on to win by 20 seconds.

The Kiwis, at 4–1, were on match point but, despite the extreme pressure, Ainslie wasn't about to fold. He won the start of the second race of the day and turned in a masterly performance, leading all the way and denying ETNZ any passing opportunities. That made it 4–2 to the Kiwis who were still on match point with one more race to go that afternoon.

It was now Burling's time to show what he was made of and the youngest skipper in the regatta came out swinging with his most clinical performance so far. He cleaned out Ainslie at the start and raced away to win by more than 500 yards with *Land Rover BAR* left far behind on a course to the regatta exit. Game, set and match to ETNZ, 5–2.

While Burling heaped praise on the New Zealand shore crew for their non-stop labours to get the ETNZ campaign back on track and keep it there, a bitterly disappointed Ainslie was typically gracious in defeat. Of the New Zealand performance, he said: 'They've really been very aggressive with their design – from the cyclors to the daggerboards, how they've set up their boat, the trim of their boat. Hats off to Team New Zealand and Kiwi ingenuity.'[5]

There was to be an unexpected sequel to the ETNZ pitchpole saga, which only surfaced later when team principal Matteo de Nora gave a rare interview to *New Zealand Herald* feature writer Jane Phare (*NZ Herald*, 8 July 2017).

De Nora is a Swiss-Italian billionaire businessman who has become a very close friend of ETNZ boss Grant Dalton and has backed his Cup endeavours for the last 14 years. According to Phare, de Nora's Italian father was a professor of physics and chemistry while his mother was Swiss. Their extensive travels resulted in de Nora being born in the USA and becoming a Canadian citizen. The family business, founded in the 1920s, was in the electrochemical industry and had now expanded and diversified throughout the world.

A resident of Monaco, de Nora maintained that New Zealand was his second home. Here, his contributions to ETNZ and his other philanthropy were recognised in 2011 when he was made a Companion of the New Zealand Order of Merit (CNZM). De Nora funds tinnitus research in New Zealand and supports the neurology research unit at the University of Auckland and, in 2016, received a Friend of New Zealand Award at the KEA World Class New Zealand Awards.

In the Phare interview, he took a swipe at the French who, he claimed, turned their back on ETNZ in its hour of need after the pitchpole incident.[6]

De Nora asserted that, within two hours of the pitchpole, Team New Zealand asked the French for help with equipment and parts. At first, the French refused but then said they would consider providing the assistance requested for a fee of €300,000 ($NZ468,500). In turn, that offer was abruptly withdrawn, 'most likely', de Nora says, 'once Oracle got wind of it.'[7]

Three days later, on 11 July 2017, Groupama Team France took to the columns of the American online newsletter *Scuttlebutt* to refute the reported de Nora claims. In a team statement, the French said:

'Relevant facts:

• Team New Zealand capsized in Bermuda on June 6th during the semifinals opposing them to the candidate in contention.

• Following that event, the French challenger, who was by that time eliminated, has been contacted to help Team New Zealand.

Our answer to Team New Zealand was as follows:

The official request was made by Kevin Shoebridge not Grant Dalton, as stated in the article, our answer was negative. Two reasons mainly explain our decision:

1) We were still sailing after being eliminated to pursue our training and fulfil sponsoring opportunities for the 36th America's cup. Therefore, having no spare parts on site, this would have compromised our plans.

2) By agreement with our sponsor, who owns our material and our boat, we did not want to favour Team New Zealand over Land Rover BAR in the semi-finals. Team New Zealand expressed their opposition to the other teams' vision for a certain stability towards AC36. Team France being 100% commercially funded and without private investors, this strategy was vital in order to protect the potential future of the team.

For your information Team France never requested any financial compensation.

Finally, regarding the allegations of interference from defender Oracle Team USA, we wish to clarify that it is of course false and unfounded. We are disappointed that such information has been released without checking with the concerned teams first.

Our team continues to work on the future and is looking forward to reading the 36th America's Cup Protocol.'[8]

The normally assertive Dalton had been unusually quiet and subdued throughout the second half of the ETNZ campaign. That was partly because of the 'Dalton Clause', breaches of which could have resulted in punitive financial penalties (a mandatory $US25,000 fine for a first offence, $US100,000 for a second and an eye-watering $US250,000 for any subsequent breaches). But it was also a deliberately implemented policy to keep Dalton out of trouble and the team focussed on the job at hand.

So, who is this (now) 60-year-old who, in 2003, agreed to take the remains of the once-proud Team New Zealand, brought to its knees by defections of its top sailing and design talent, and rebuilt it in its former image?

Born on 1 July 1957 in Auckland, Dalton is a spectacular fusion of driving ambition, fierce determination and in-your-face attitude. He is known throughout the sailing world as Dalts, and what you see is what you get.

Grant Stanley Dalton, OBE, is first and foremost an offshore sailor. He has raced around the world seven times, beginning with line-honours on the Frers maxi *Flyer* in the 1981–1982 Whitbread race (after failing to make the cut for Peter Blake's crew for the Farr-designed *Ceramco New Zealand*).

He then raced with the legendary Blake as a watch captain on the Holland-designed *Lion New Zealand* in the 1985–1986 Whitbread before, as a 32-year-old, mounting his own campaign in the Farr-designed *Fisher & Paykel* in the 1989–1990 Whitbread.

That was the year of the all-dominant New Zealand maxi ketches when the masthead *F&P* went head to head with Blake's fractional rig *Steinlager 2* (both Bruce Farr designs) in a nine-month match race that captured global attention. Blake won all six legs of that race, on line and handicap, to wrap up overall honours in a fabulous, clean-sweep show of force. But Dalton, in *F&P*, was snapping at his heels for the entire journey.

While Blake moved on to the America's Cup, Dalton did a further Whitbread campaign, in the 1993–1994 maxi *New Zealand Endeavour* and then two more circuits of the globe in the now-Volvo Ocean Race – in the Volvo 60s *Merit Cup* (1997–1998) and then *Amer Sports One* (2001–02). He then skippered the maxi catamaran *Club Med* to victory in the non-stop Le Race around the world.

Ironically, this former 18ft-skiff sailor achieved all of this, and more, while disliking the environment in which he'd chosen to make his mark, and that only underlines the dogged determination that would later drive him on to win the America's Cup.

The reality is that Dalton lived in Blake's considerable shadow for much of his early career, and he didn't enjoy it. The two legendary New Zealand yachtsmen trod remarkably similar paths to international success but they could not have been more different in terms of physical presence and personality.

While Blake was tall – 1.93m (6ft 4in) – and reserved with an unmistakeable air of authority about him, Dalton was shortish and brash, and seemingly always the underdog. Both, however, were amply endowed with ambition, commitment and resolve, if in different ways.

In 2002, after Blake had been shot and killed while on an environmental expedition in the Amazon, I interviewed Dalts for Sir Peter's biography and, with typical frankness, he observed:

'We were chalk and cheese really. Pete was a seaman. I've never been a seaman in my life. Pete could navigate and was extremely good at it. I can't navigate. He was a complete yachtsman in that respect. I have never been one at all.

Pete was interested in and could identify birds and sea life. I couldn't give a shit. Birds have got wings and whales are things that you'll run into if you're not careful. They'll bugger your race.

Pete loved the sea. I don't. It's cold and wet and you can't get much sleep. It just happens to be my chosen arena for competition. That was true of Peter too, but he was much more at peace in that environment. I just want to get in there and out of there as quickly as I can.

Pete loved cruising. I hate cruising – haven't been cruising in my life, wouldn't buy a boat if it was the last vehicle on the planet.

So, we differed completely in our philosophies. He was a much more rounded person, his whole personality was more complete, and I admired him for it. Having said all that, put us both in a one-man Laser dinghy and I reckon I'd kick his arse.'[9]

Until the epic *Steinlager 2* v *Fisher & Paykel* confrontation, the aggressive, younger Dalton did not fully respect his former skipper: 'I had learned a lot from him but at that stage I didn't have respect for him because I thought that he didn't push hard enough. I was 26 and probably was pushing too hard. Pete said later he wasn't sure that I knew when to button off, which maybe was true, up to a point.'[10]

That view changed completely during the 1989–1990 Whitbread race, when Dalton came to admire and respect his arch rival and even sought his advice.

Again, with typical Dalton bluntness, he recalled in interview with me:

'Although F&P was second, we weren't even in the hunt. He [Blake] dicked us good in what was arguably the best Whitbread race ever. People talk about it being a close race. It wasn't because, after the first leg, he was gone. After that it was really good stuff. Coming across the Great Australian Bight, for instance, when he was surfing right up our arse – wow! But, basically, he just gave us a lesson. The final margins may not have looked much but, in actual fact, there was a chasm between the two campaigns. So, from then on, I employed what I'd learned from Pete – the way he set up and ran the Steinlager campaign and the way he went about sponsorship. Hell, he wrote the book on sponsorship. All we've done is follow the chapters and adapt them to our own ends.'[11]

Blake, at that point in time, was approaching the zenith of his leadership, management and communication skills while Dalton was, really, just setting out on the same journey.

It took the latter another 26 years to close the gap, battling against new commercial and competitive realities that Blake never had to surmount but, on the evidence of his 2017 campaign in Bermuda, he had learned his lessons well.

One of his smartest moves, at the very start of the 2017 campaign when still haunted by ETNZ surrendering what looked an unassailable lead in the 2013 match, was to recognise that his sailing team had to be changed and fresh new blood had to be introduced. That meant that the popular incumbent skipper Dean Barker had to go. And go he did, to make way for the then 24-year-old rising Olympic star and world champion skiff sailor Peter Burling. And with Burling came his equally youthful forward hand Blair Tuke.

This wasn't a popular move with the New Zealand media or public and Dalton, of course, bore the brunt of the displeasure.

However, in his July 2017 *New Zealand Herald* interview, Matteo de Nora shed more light on those events revealing that, after San Francisco in 2013, and up against the Oracle/Russell Coutts culture and team, they [ETNZ] knew 'normal' wouldn't work for the 2017 campaign: 'We knew we had to be 20 per cent better in every area and every department, otherwise they [Oracle] would find a way to do us over…'[12]

That meant that ETNZ had to make a series of decisions that were bold and, in some cases, brutal. Replacing Barker was one of the 'brutal' decisions, but it was only made after an intense review. Barker was offered the different role of sailing coach and performance manager, but he declined.

Peter Burling, MNZM (Member of the New Zealand Order of Merit) was born on 1 January 1991, in the Bay of Plenty port township of Tauranga, the second son of a doctor mother (Heather) and a teacher father (Richard). A quiet and sometimes shy boy, Burling spent his early summers on the water – in the family runabout on the Rotorua lakes, or outside his grandparents' home in the Bay of Islands when, unknowingly, he was straight across the Kerikeri inlet from an equally young fellow by the name of Blair Tuke, with whom he would one day share an Olympic gold medal and race alongside in the America's Cup.

Burling was a somewhat reluctant debutant in sailboats. When he was a six year old, his father bought, for the older Burling brother Scott, a well-worn wooden Optimist dinghy called *Jellytip*, for the princely sum of $NZ200. Dad Richard took the boys out on Tauranga's Welcome Bay estuary where they got just as much joy from swimming under *Jellytip* as they did sailing on her.

A couple of years later, the two Burling boys joined the Tauranga Yacht and Power Boat Club (TY&PBC) and were introduced to sailboat racing. Young Peter's world changed completely and his life would never be the same.

In a 16 June 2017 feature on Burling for New Zealand Newsroom, Suzanne McFadden, former yachting writer for the *New Zealand Herald*, wrote that 'the club's old salts recognised straight away that there was something special about the eight-year-old blonde kid that had just joined their ranks' and former club commodore Gary Smith had told her: 'Pete always had the X factor. He could look at the same patch of water as the rest of us and see something different about it.'[13]

Burling was also an outstanding academic, sitting university papers a year before his time and then studying for a degree in mechanical engineering at the University of Auckland. So, not only did he love to sail boats, he also loved to understand how they worked. He was just 23 when he was signed up to introduce new blood to ETNZ for its latest challenge for the Cup, in Bermuda, and 24 when he was named to replace the departing Dean Barker at the helm.

'Burling', McFadden wrote, 'has an instinctive feel for a boat, which plays a major role in his ability to eke out more speed: "Feel is a big part of it. Being able to feel if the loads are increasing or decreasing, how the boat is moving forward and knowing what to change."'[14]

When the boat pitchpoled on that wild June afternoon on the Great Sound, 'a wrung-out and bruised Burling' publicly shouldered the blame for one ruinous manoeuvre. Those who know him well say that, although he had made errors in Bermuda, as he got to grips with the new class of foiling cat and with the nuances of match racing, he 'owned' his mistakes and learned quickly from them. To emphasise this point, McFadden quoted former TY&PBC commodore Smith, saying: 'He [Burling] makes good decisions quickly. He has better decision-making skills than your average sailor, and maybe that's because of the speed with which he makes those decisions.'[15]

McFadden quoted Olympic representative Finn sailor and two-time America's Cup winner (with Team New Zealand) Craig Monk saying:

'Burling's sailing résumé is second-to-none. He's ahead of where Ben Ainslie (the four-time Olympic gold medallist and British America's Cup skipper) was at his age and he's certainly well ahead of anyone we've seen in New Zealand before. He's highly intuitive and a leader among the new generation of sailors who have mastered apparent wind sailing (boats sailing so fast they create their own wind). He's cut from just the right cloth for this kind of "flying" America's Cup – short, focused racing, mostly up on the foils – where you can't afford to make a mistake. He is a fighter pilot and he looks the most relaxed when he's holding the wheel doing 48 knots.'[16]

Burling proved to be an inspired (if fairly obvious) replacement as ETNZ's helmsman, with all the natural attributes to tame and turn loose the new breed of foiling catamaran that evolved from the controversial downsizing of the boats to be used in Bermuda.

The 'AC 50' was 49ft 2in (15m) long with 27ft 9in (8.45m) beam and sported a 79ft (24m) tall, 1087sq ft (101sq m) wing sail with a small jib headsail. Its projected top speed was 50 knots.

According to Oracle Team USA tactician Tom Slingsby, gold medallist for Australia in Lasers at the 2012 Olympics in England, the newcomer came about as a result of the early challengers for Bermuda sailing foiling versions of the AC 45 cats used in the build-up world series events.

In interview with Matt Sheahan for the 2 April 2015 edition of *Yachting World*, Slingsby said:

> '*I think all of the teams who have been sailing the so-called AC45 "turbo" boats over the past few months have been surprised by the performance they've seen, which is partly what inspired the idea of a new, smaller class [for the 2017 America's Cup in Bermuda]. In our boat, we were doing roughly the same speed as the 72s [used in the 2013 Cup in San Francisco] when the breeze was up, and we were maybe a little faster than the 72s in lighter winds. We hit close to 46 knots of speed in 16 knots of wind, and I think there is a lot more to be gained still.*'[17]

He added that, given the rapid development along with the constant underlying pressure to reduce the cost of Cup campaigns, there seemed little reason not to change.[18]

Slingsby's analysis, more than two years out from the Cup regatta, would prove to be remarkably accurate but, for now, the focus and attention was on the 2017 Louis Vuitton challengers' final between ETNZ and Artemis Racing, from Sweden, that had come from behind with three wins to edge out Softbank Team Japan 5–3 in the other semi-final.

The Swedish hope was skippered by Burling's great 49er class rival, the 31-year-old Australian Nathan Outteridge. The two had dominated the exciting two-man Olympic-class 49er for nearly a decade – Outteridge with forward hand Iain Jensen and Burling with Blair Tuke. The Aussies had won the 49er world championship in 2008, 2009, 2011 and 2012, before the Kiwis took full control with world title wins in 2013, 2014, 2015 and 2016. In the midst of all that, Outteridge had pipped Burling to the 49er Olympic gold medal in England in 2012, before Burling reversed the order at the 2016 Olympics in Brazil.

It was a match-up to savour. *Artemis* was viewed to be one of the fastest yachts in the regatta, particularly in breezes towards the top half of the 6–24-knot regatta range. *Aotearoa*, however, looked to have a greater performance range and was super-quick in breezes at the lighter end of the scale. The difference between the two might come down to Outteridge's better record in the starts, if he then had the ability to hold out against the best come-from-behind team in the event. And so it proved.

On day one, in 8–13 knots of breeze, Outteridge got the better of all three starts but only managed to convert one into a win. The Kiwis again looked content with being conservative off the line and then relying on superior all-round speed and boat handling to catch up. In a first-to-five series, ETNZ was 2–1 up and they'd almost literally run their opponent down.

Under a heading that read 'Artemis Skipper Takes A Dive, Avoids Disaster,' the *New Zealand Herald*, on 11 June, recounted how Outteridge feared for his safety when he was almost run over by Team New Zealand during race three on the opening day. The Aussie helmsman had raced across the aft end of the boat to swap sides in a tack and finished the dash with a baseball-type slide towards his helming position. He slightly miscalculated his approach, however, and careered straight over the side of the boat and into the water.

As he surfaced, his first sight was of the chasing Kiwi boat charging straight at him.

Outteridge confessed that he panicked, mindful of the rudder elevators under the stern of the New Zealand boat: 'I thought Pete [Burling] was going to run me over … he was aiming straight for me. Eventually [though], we made eye contact and he missed me by about a boat width.'[19]

He added: 'It's not the first time it's happened to myself or to many people on these boats, and it probably won't be the last either. I was just looking for something to grab onto. These boats are pretty aero, so there wasn't really much there ... I tried to grab some net or a bit of the boat but just missed everything and ended up in the water.'[20]

One who was all too aware of the danger in going over the side from these new generation catamarans with T-shaped elevators (wings) at the bottom of their rudders was Team France skipper Franck Cammas, who nearly lost his right foot in a training accident on Quiberon Bay, Brittany, in November 2015.

On that day, Cammas went over the port side of his work-up 32-footer and was struck by the horizontal stabiliser. He suffered a compound fracture of both the tibia and fibula of his right leg and his surgeon at the University Hospital in Nantes said the foot had almost been torn off by the impact. The accident ended Cammas' hopes of qualifying for the 2016 Olympics in Rio de Janeiro, and it also caused him to miss the opening events in the America's Cup 2017 world series of build-up events.

The breeze was up a touch for day two of the ETNZ v Artemis clash – blowing 11–15 knots. Was this the big opportunity for the Swedes? To begin with, the answer looked to be 'yes'. With shorter, high-speed foils than the day before, Outteridge again won the start – it was closer this time though – and powered over the top of his rival, reaching speeds of 45 knots to keep the Kiwis at bay all around the course. The score was now 2–2.

The second race of the day was sailed in fractionally less breeze and the New Zealander minimised the Swede's foil advantage on the reach to the first mark and then settled down to the chase proper. Faster and higher on the first upwind leg, Burling squeezed his rival off his hip two-thirds the way up the beat, led through the windward gate by 100 metres (100 yards) and extended that margin all the way to the finish to go 3–2 up.

The breeze was back to 12–15 knots for race three and Burling was now proving a tougher proposition in the pre-start, but Outteridge again used his faster mode on the reach to lead at the first turn. It was an arm-wrestle downwind but ETNZ again sailed higher and faster upwind to open up a 300-metre (300-yard) advantage. It looked to be done and dusted until Burling botched his approach to the bottom gate and ended up crawling with both hulls in the water while the Swedes came roaring in for the kill. However, pedal power saved the day, and the blushes, for the Kiwis as their cyclors frantically generated enough 'oil' into the hydraulics system for Burling to get *Aotearoa* back on her foils and sneak home and win by just one second. ETNZ was now on match point at 4–2.

There was no respite in the schedule and the two rivals were out there and ready to go again the following day with New Zealand needing just one more win to wrap it all up. Burling set Kiwi pulses racing when, in light airs, he finally won a start, but,the breeze soon died completely and the proceedings were abandoned.

After a lengthy delay, the breeze finally filled in again, to around 8–9 knots, and into action the pair again went. *Aotearoa* once more edged the start at the port end of the line but *Artemis* was on her hip to windward and straining to blast over the top of her rival on the short reach to the first turn. Burling hung on, though, and a nicely timed luff on final approach removed the *Artemis* threat so that *Aotearoa* could ease was away to a 200-metre (200-yard) lead going through the leeward gate and starting into the first beat. Now it was the same old story – *Aotearoa* higher and faster upwind and nothing the opposition could do about it. Downwind – the New Zealanders picked their way expertly through the shifts and scorched through the finish line doing 37 knots, more than 400 metres (437 yards) ahead of the Swedish opposition. The score was 5–2, game over, and redemption against *Oracle Team USA* and James Spithill beckoned.

While the two challenger finalists were settling their differences, the defender Oracle Team USA was taking advantage of its close collaboration with Softbank Team Japan to engage in some realistic race practice that would give it an accurate gauge on performance in the final preparations for the Cup match. This was another major departure from normal practice and it had Cup followers completely puzzled.

ETNZ's counter was to bring on stream more of its very latest generation of performance enhancers. These were refinements as opposed to game changers but, at this stage of the proceedings, every little bit helped and it would be surprising if it was any different in the Oracle camp. If the Americans had significant extra speed up their sleeve, they would be bringing it on line now. For ETNZ, there was also the opportunity for performance coaches Murray Jones and Ray Davies to work some more with the fast-improving Burling on his starts, an area in which Oracle's Spithill was expected to be particularly aggressive.

The big day – Saturday 17 June – and the breeze at the early afternoon start time for race one of the much-anticipated Cup match was a puffy 9–11 knots. The two adversaries entered the start box on time and, when the traditional jousting for the best starting position had been done, Spithill led the way to the line with Burling pushing him hard from just astern. With the breeze dying, Spithill was in trouble and, almost unbelievably, he nudged *Oracle*'s bows over the line early to cop a premature start penalty. Burling fed his rival a parting luff to slow him further and then peeled away to build up a race-winning lead. It looked like it'd be an emphatic win – until *Aotearoa* ran into a hole in the breeze at the leeward gate for the last time and, as the Kiwis sank down off their foils, the defender came charging in with an unexpected victory now a strong possibility. In the nick of time, though, the challenger's cyclors answered the call and powered vital 'oil' into the trim and control systems for *Aotearoa* to slowly regain her foiling composure and cross the line a much-reduced 30 seconds ahead.

That win made the match score 1–1, because the defender had started a point ahead thanks to some more strange rule making.

Craig Leweck, editor of the San Diego-based online sailing newsletter *Scuttlebutt* had been prompted to observe (in the 14 June 2017 letter):

> '… *in forming the rules for the 35th edition [of the America's Cup], the Defender has pushed this championship structure to extremes not previously seen (or imagined?).*
>
> *We've had:*
> - *A team pocketing points before the Challenger Series began*
> - *The Defender racing in the Challenger Series*
> - *A team pocketing points before the America's Cup Match begins.*
>
> … *Good luck to the broadcasters explaining this one … But, the Challengers signed up for this gig, so no use now debating the rules. Rules are rules. If you want to play the game, you accept the rules and play up to their absolute limit. All games are the same.*
>
> *As for the impassioned fans, however, that's another story. Kiwi Tom Weaver [crew boss for the Italian syndicate Mascalzone Latino in the 2003 and 2007 Cups] couldn't contain himself when considering the*

structure of this America's Cup. He wrote in to say: "This 2017 edition of the America's Cup has to be the most crooked contest in an event historically famous for being stacked in the defender's favour. This latest edition makes the New York Yacht Club's shenanigans over a period of 130 years look like kindergarten compared to the Oracle Team USA idea of fair play in 2017."[21]

Leweck was right, though. The challengers had, much earlier, accepted the rules for this event so there was no point in bleating now. Just get on with the job at hand and be the first to a net seven wins.

Race two that first day, in the same puffy light winds, was more of the same. Burling again won the start and powered away with *Aotearoa* significantly quicker and higher on the upwind lags. The course was a minefield though and *Oracle* played the shifts well on the second beat to be neck and neck with her rival starting the final downwind leg. The starboard boundary on the downwind leg came up fast and ETNZ was the first to gybe. The tricky manoeuvre was executed brilliantly but *Oracle* blew hers and dropped down off the foils. Race over. *Aotearoa* zoomed away to a lead of almost 500 metres (547 yards) and crossed the finish line 1 minute 28 seconds ahead.

It had been a testing day for both crews and *ETNZ* skipper Glen Ashby was quick to praise the work of his cyclors: 'It was a massive effort on the hydro. The shifty, puffy conditions meant huge movements of the daggerboards and wing. We never stopped trimming and the boys got an absolute flogging.'

Regardless of how you looked at it, *ETNZ* had started the day on minus one and finished it on plus one leaving a bottom line that read: 'Six more wins to go.'

The breeze was up a touch for day two of the match, raising the hopes of *Oracle* supporters. The Defender moded its boat differently to take full advantage, but it made little difference. *ETNZ* sailed to two more comfortable wins to go three clear heading into a five-day break before racing resumed the following weekend.

Skipper Spithill told the post-race press conference that night: 'They will be a very important five days. We must use them wisely. We've got to get faster. That's pretty obvious.' Everything, he said, was 'back on the table' and the team would be working 24-hour shifts, using all their resources to find more speed. And he warned: 'We have been here before. It's not over' – clearly reminding everyone, not least Peter Burling who was on the media stage alongside him, of *Oracle*'s dramatic comeback from 1–8 down in the 2013 America's Cup match.

Burling's calm response was: 'We've also got a massive list of things that we want to work on. We sailed better today but we also made a lot of mistakes and we are a long way from where we want to be. And, we know if we step back, they will catch us.'

Spithill's bravado made for good media coverage and sound bites but the reality of his predicament was somewhat different.

There was no denying that the Aussie skipper and his team had achieved minor miracles in their AC34 recovery, from a lot further back than they were now, and five days seemed a luxurious amount of time compared with the 48 hours they had had in San Francisco. However, the challenge in Bermuda was quite different and there was not nearly as much that they could do to turn their defence around.

Ironically, that was because of the sweeping changes that were made, midway through the 2017 Cup cycle, to introduce the smaller, 50ft catamaran. Those changes brought in more one-design elements than were in the Class Rule for the original 62-footer and would now severely restrict what Oracle Team USA could change. The wing and daggerboards, for instance, were no-go areas. Oracle could change foil tips and might have been able to build a new set of rudder elevators in a week, but there would be no time left for testing, making such an approach very risky. So, another miracle comeback through dramatic change was extremely unlikely. Oracle's best chance of significant improvement lay in better manoeuvring and crew work.

As for ETNZ, it was more a case of 'steady as she goes'. The Kiwis seemed to have remedied their biggest cause for concern – their starts. Burling had now won three of the four so far, and shared the other. There was, however, still room for smarter covering of the opposition when ahead. So, for both teams, the improvements they would be chasing meant more time on the water than in the boat shed.

And that was the way it went down. After just two days in the shed, Oracle Team USA was back out on the Great Sound and it looked as though any changes made were minor, not major. A day later, they were joined – albeit not in the same stretch of water – by ETNZ, who had enjoyed a day off before getting stuck into the fine tuning that they still wanted to achieve. This left the media corps to seek other sources of copy and they turned their attention to what they saw as a very real possibility of major changes at the back of the Oracle boat, with tactician Tom Slingsby, an Olympic gold medallist in Lasers, taking over the helm from Spithill.

At the media conference the evening before racing was scheduled to resume (on 24 June), Bernie Wilson, from Associated Press, asked Spithill directly – would he be on the wheel tomorrow? Spithill dodged the question adroitly, replying that 'everything is on the table' and that included people, too.

There was, however, no change in the afterguard on *Oracle* when she entered the start box for race five of the contest. Spithill was on the wheel with Slingsby in his usual place alongside him, and the aficionados were expecting fireworks from the Australians. Spithill had been uncharacteristically subdued thus far but now, with his back to the wall and Burling all over him in the pre-starts, he was fully expected to come out with guns blazing.

If you were an Oracle fan, the forecast for the resumption of the regatta held little hope of salvation – similar conditions to the previous weekend, with light but raceable breezes that would be absolutely to the liking of the challenger.

Burling picked up where he'd left off and edged his rival in the start but *Oracle* showed new-found pace on the first upwind leg and led, briefly, for the first time in the Match. However, the Kiwis soon restored previous order. Aided by a port-starboard penalty for Oracle, they raced away to win by 2 minutes 4 seconds. Under the pressure, Spithill and his team were now making costly mistakes and, in a trade-off for more speed, they had sacrificed stability, which had cost them dearly when they splashed down off the foils towards the end of race five.

It was, however, ETNZ that made the big mistake in race six, getting the second windward leg all wrong and leaving the door open for Oracle to snatch an invaluable, if unexpected, first win by 11 seconds. With the score at 4–1 to ETNZ, there would be no more breaks in racing from here on – the pair would keep at it until the Match was decided but, as it eventuated, that would not take long.

ETNZ sailed superbly to win races seven and eight and reach match point in short order. The New Zealand boat handling was its best yet while Burling and Ashby rose to a new level of course management, covering carefully and allowing the opposition precisely nothing in the way of opportunity.

And so to what would prove the final day of the regatta – Monday 26 June 2017. It was blowing a touch over 8 knots at the start with a mix of 6–12 knots forecast for the race – again, right in New Zealand's sweet spot. The start was shared but *Oracle* was on *Aotearoa*'s starboard hip coming off the line and managed to nudge ahead on the power reach to the first turn where the Defender led by just three seconds. The Kiwis, however, made a better fist of the gybe at the starboard boundary line and led by 5 seconds going into the leeward gate.

The two boats split tacks at the start of the first windward leg – ETNZ heading to the left of the course, Oracle to the right. When they came back together again, ETNZ was 130 metres (142 yards) in front. The gap continued to grow, even though Burling and Ashby were trading some of it in order to cover what the opposition was doing. *Aoteraoa* rounded the top mark with a 230-metre (252-yard) lead. This became 300 metres (328 yards) at the leeward gate and stayed that way for the rest of the journey with *Aotearoa* a very comfortable 55 seconds clear as she crossed the finish line.

While the New Zealanders finally let their hair down and began to celebrate a consummate 7–1 victory, the feisty Spithill, who had almost made a career out of taunting the New Zealand media (not to mention, on occasion, Kiwi skippers) was impressively humble in what was obviously a devastating defeat that he hadn't seen coming. Close to tears, he told the Cup media:

'We're disappointed right now, but full credit to Team New Zealand. Man, what a series … they made fewer mistakes and they fully deserve victory. They took a different path to all the other challenging and defending teams, and that unknown element may have been a factor in the outcome. They were down there [in New Zealand] training on their own, and you've really got to give credit to them for the incredible job they've done.'[22]

It was all over – mission accomplished by Emirates Team New Zealand. The Auld Mug would soon be in its special Louis Vuitton travelling case flying first class to Auckland where, at the Royal New Zealand Yacht Squadron, the custom-made security display case that had been built for it in the early 2000s had been a temporary home for one of Team New Zealand's several Louis Vuitton Cups (in the absence of the real thing). Travelling with it, after one of the most controversial editions in the Cup's controversial history, would be the hopes of many that the Kiwis would act assertively to restore to the event the history, tradition and prestige that had made the Auld Mug one of the most sought-after trophies in sport.

13

BACK TO THE FUTURE

The first hints that New Zealand would take immediate steps to restore many traditional strongpoints and traditions to the America's Cup came on 26 June 2017, the very day the Kiwis won back the trophy by completing a 7–1 rout of the 35th defender, Oracle Team USA on Bermuda's Great Sound.

On *Newstalk ZB* that morning (in Auckland), Emirates Team New Zealand boss Grant Dalton told breakfast show host Mike Hosking that New Zealand would respect the history and tradition of the Cup and how it should be run, making it a fair event for all.

He emphasised:

'… This is a key message that we want to relay going forward, that it's a privilege to hold the America's Cup, not a right. That was embodied in the way Team New Zealand was under Sir Peter Blake - we'll try very hard to be good enough to keep it [the Cup] but, if you are good enough to take it from us then, you will, and we won't [play with the rules to] make sure you can't.'[1]

Then, on 18 July 2017, the Cup's new trustee and defender, the Royal New Zealand Yacht Squadron (RNZYS), and its Challenger of Record, Circolo della Vela Sicilia, gave a first hint of the content in the protocol for AC36, to be released in September 2017, that would embody just how they planned to do that.

In a brief media release, they stated that they were considering staging the challenger eliminations and the 36th America's Cup Match in the waters off Auckland in the New Zealand summer months of 2021.

The release continued: 'In recognition of the fundamental condition of the Deed of Gift that the Cup be preserved as a perpetual Challenge Cup for friendly competition between foreign countries, the Protocol will contain a "constructed in country" requirement for competing yachts and a nationality requirement for competing crew members.'

If you allied that up-front declaration of intent to further statements made by the team's patron Matteo de Nora, and one of its directors, Sir Stephen Tindall, and joined the dots, the next Cup was going to be raced in Auckland's Hauraki Gulf through the months of January–March 2021. This would occur in boats that, to a large extent, had been built in the country of the yacht club defending and/ or challenging. Moreover, crews would have to meet much stricter nationality requirements than those used in Bermuda, when the US defender had 10 Australians in its 14-strong sailing team and only one American, grinder Cooper Dressler, who made it on board for just three of the nine races sailing.

In terms of the basic essentials that would-be challengers would want to know – the when, where, who and in what of the next event – that left only the class of boat to be used in 2021.

One very logical argument was that New Zealand would want to continue with the 50ft foiling catamaran class in which it had out-designed and out-sailed everyone else in Bermuda. To walk away from such obvious superiority would, the argument went, be negligent. That was countered, however, by the informed view that Prada boss Patrizio Bertelli – head of Circolo della Vela Sicilia's challenge syndicate Luna Rossa and a declared traditionalist – very much wanted a return to monohulls. Given his long-term good relationship with ETNZ, the odds then appeared to favour the choice of a new class of modern, high-performance monohulls almost certainly longer that 70ft overall and sailed by large crews.

There was, though, one other outstanding and highly contentious item from AC35, certainly from the ETNZ and Luna Rossa perspective: that of the defender in Bermuda racing in the challenger eliminations and taking a bonus point on into the match. If Dalton's intent really was to restore integrity to the event, that controversial departure from the norm of the event would have to be reversed, along with the defender having anything to do with challenger affairs except the part it had to play in the protocol.

Embodying all the above elements, the new protocol would really facilitate a case of 'out with the old and in with the old', for the event was now headed back towards its roots: towards (not so) friendly competition between foreign countries in boats designed and built in the country of the yacht club challenging and on an 'ocean water course on the sea, or on an arm of the sea.'

Well ... headed back at least as far back as 2007, when Switzerland's Ernesto Bertarelli and his Alinghi syndicate successfully defended the Cup in Valencia in one of the most positive Cup regattas on record. That was, however, before Bertarelli and then Larry Ellison got sidetracked and turned their backs on what the Cup was supposed to be all about and changed the event so much that it bore little resemblance to the Cup of old.

Not everyone, however, would have liked what the RNZYS and Circolo della Vela Sicilia announced as their vision for the future. While those with traditional leanings would have applauded loudly, there were others who liked what Ellison's people delivered as the Cup in Bermuda – skittery catamarans on foils doing 45 and even 50 knots on Bermuda's Great Sound, sometimes never once dipping a hull into the water.

Britain's Sir Ben Ainslie, head of the Land Rover BAR team, for instance, in the *Daily Telegraph* of 27 June 2017, praised the Kiwi victory in Bermuda, saying: 'New Zealand absolutely deserved to win ... They were extremely aggressive with their boat design, taking big risks, and in the end they were rewarded for that. It was a ruthless display. Who dares wins.'

Ainslie admitted that, originally, he was not a fan of the switch to multihulls but now he applauded the vision of Ellison and Sir Russell Coutts. The 35th America's Cup, he said, was 'a wonderful advert for the sport and produced some incredible moments.'

Then, looking ahead, he added: 'There are a lot of rumours flying around that the Italians are keen on monohulls. I think going back now would be a mistake given where we have got to in these foiling multihulls.' He would, however, support the touted nationality quotas in crews.[2]

ACEA boss Coutts, in a 14 June 2017 interview with Sabine Colpart, of *Agence France-Presse*, commented: 'You know, no matter what the critics say about foiling, what I can tell you is that it's already having a dramatic impact in our industry. Of course, it's a more efficient way of sailing, and therefore that's going to translate in a fairly major way into a pleasure boat/leisure industry.'

Coutts said that other significant changes to the 2017 event included the shift from offshore to inshore racing, which, together with the shortening of the races themselves, had opened up the sport to a new fan base: 'In many ways we've seen a bit of a revolution in the America's Cup. We've developed a completely different television package, a different way of televising the event; the races are much shorter; there's more action and excitement.'[3]

On the other side of the debate were traditionalists, such as former America's Cup Hall of Fame president Halsey Herreshoff, the grandson of legendary Cup designer Captain Nathanael G Herreshoff. In interview for *Exposed* he said:

There are those who lament the direction the Cup is now taking – using smaller and smaller catamarans on so-called "stadium" courses close inshore. The early stated intention of Oracle to convey excitement and thus attention through television has been accomplished, though not to the degree intended.

Russell Coutts and others involved assert that being at the forefront of technology and athleticism fits the America's Cup tradition of excellence at the frontier. There is, of course, some truth to that opinion. But, the full virtues of a century and a half of America's Cup racing in large and great yachts include magnificent aspects missing from today's adventures on the race course. If you take the progress made in foiling from 2013 in San Francisco to 2017 in Bermuda, and extrapolate that to the future; the conclusion is that the contest will become one of foiling perfection rather than one of traditional sailing skills.

We are being asked to accept a version of the Cup that bears little resemblance to the genuine article – with the defender very much involved in the affairs of the challengers and even racing against them in lead-up events and in the challenger eliminations and qualifiers immediately prior to the match itself.

Prior to the 2017 event, Oracle persuaded four of the five challengers in 2017 to endorse two more matches in foiling cats. I would suggest a complete switch back to modern versions of J boat-size yachts, allowing appropriate design latitude to embrace the fact that the America's Cup has always been a contest of design as well as of sailing skill. Careful consideration would need to be given to how many boats and/or how much modern technology – like canting keels and/or foils – would be permitted, but arriving at the right decisions in those areas would be eminently manageable.

Opponents of this approach will probably scream "too much cost" but, look at the vast sums now being spent with inflated design research and fabrications. Also, modern construction techniques and materials have produced meaningful results in containing costs while building state of the art, brilliant monohulls.

The return to imposing large yachts, large crews, and real match racing tactics would restore the America's Cup to its rightful position, at the pinnacle of competition in the great sport of sailing and the same advanced methods of delivering and enhancing broadcast coverage would be just as applicable.'[4]

On 3 June 2017, with the prospect of a New Zealand victory gaining momentum, Coutts was quoted in *The Times* (London) saying that an old-style America's Cup in Auckland 'wouldn't work these days' and proceeded to make a case for his build-up regatta baby, labelled the AC World Series: 'It is hard to promote just a one-off event. The … America's Cup World Series created a tremendous amount of value for all of the stakeholders, teams, sponsors, venues and media partners.'[5]

Coutts and Ainslie had, of course, a vested interest in the Cup remaining on the same track as the regatta in Bermuda. They were, after all, prime movers of the ill-fated Framework Agreement that was now in the paper shredder in a variety of syndicate offices around the world. And Coutts was wrongfully confining the dramatic development of foils in sailing to multihulls only. Foils had every bit as much potential for dramatically increasing the performance of monohulls.

The Bermudan government was reported to have invested $US77 million in bringing the 2017 Cup to the British Overseas Territory. That sum did not, as some would have it, all go to ACEA. According to Mike Winfield, the chief executive of the America's Cup Bermuda Development Authority, in the *New York Times* on 23 June 2017, ACEA pocketed $US15 million for venue rights while Bermuda also underwrote a $US25 million-guarantee that would see it make good any shortfall in ACEA's sponsorship endeavours. The other $US37 million went towards capital works and operational expenditure.[6]

Initially, the Bermudans thought ACEA boss Coutts was using them as a stalking horse to extract better offers from American bid cities. However, he could not drum up the financial package he was seeking in the USA so he opted for the British Overseas Territory, which was prepared to stump up the dollar numbers he was seeking.

Was it all worth it?

The office of Bermuda's then Minister of Economic Development, Hon Dr E Grant Gibbons, on 7 July 2017, provided a first public report on the economic benefits and fan attendance at the 2017 event, which stated:

'Some information about AC35 is already available. I am pleased to note that through this prestigious sailing event, Bermuda received extraordinary visibility on the world stage as the Cup was broadcast to 162 countries with millions of people watching. This is only a snapshot. Over 100,000 people visited the Village over 22 days, there were 62,315 booked tickets on the special AC ferries alone, and some 2,000 boats registered as spectators of the event.

Bermuda hosted over 460 visiting boats, with over 80 of them being superyachts. We received extremely positive feedback from the owners and captains of these boats, some who had never been to Bermuda before. As *a result of this success, we have been developing a long-term superyacht policy and legislative framework. Another positive feature of AC35 has been the development of new marinas and marine services at the Hamilton waterfront, Hamilton Princess, Caroline Bay and the facilities at South Basin in Dockyard.*[7]

It appeared, however, that the general population of Bermuda was not as convinced that the $US77 million investment was such a good idea.

On 19 July 2017, Bermuda's *Royal Gazette* newspaper reported that the One Bermuda Alliance, the party that backed hosting the America's Cup, had lost control of the Bermudan parliament. The opposition Progressive Labour Party had won a snap general election with a large majority, winning 24 seats to the OBA's 12.

ETNZ and the Auld Mug, meanwhile, arrived back home to tumultuous welcomes in the country's four main population centres. Despite atrocious weather, an estimated 90,000 people lined the main street and Viaduct Harbour in Auckland to show their appreciation, and the exuberant throngs were repeated in Wellington, Christchurch and Dunedin where the crowds braved near- and sub-zero temperatures to show that pride in this latest crop of champion Kiwi sailors was not limited to just the City of Sails.

The television audience figures for the month of racing in Bermuda backed up the parade turn-outs. The number of Kiwi viewers for the 2017 Cup was up 8 per cent on 2013, to 33 per cent of the potential viewing audience. In the racing window, from 27 May to 26 June 2017, the broadcast rights holder, the pay-for-view broadcaster Sky TV, covered live the entire Louis Vuitton Cup challenger round robins, semi-finals and final, and then the Match itself, while its free-to-air affiliate Prime TV did the same with a two-hour delay. Between them, they produced 275 separate programmes – the live and delayed racing presentations, reviews, highlight shows and replays. The total audience for that coverage was 1,403,000 or 33 per cent of the 4.6 million population.

All coverage on the last day of racing attracted an audience of 800,000, which matched the daily viewer numbers for the Cup on NBC's nationwide network in the USA (population 326 million).

So, the America's Cup was Down Under again, starting a new chapter in its long and eventful history in a country that prided itself on its reverence of the trophy and everything it was supposed to represent.

For the first 40-odd years (1851–1895), competition for the Cup was the domain of the nouveau riche of the Industrial Revolution, on both sides of the Atlantic, of privileged memberships of the 'royal' yacht clubs of Britain and their closest American equivalent, the New York Yacht Club – luminaries such as John Cox Stevens, John Malcolm Forbes, James Lloyd Ashbury, William K Vanderbilt and the Earl of Dunraven.

In the near 40-year period of 1899–1937, it was the turn of Sir Thomas Lipton, John Pierpont Morgan, Cornelius Vanderbilt III, Harold S Vanderbilt and Sir TOM Sopwith, in some of the greatest yachts the world has even seen – before or since – including *Columbia, Reliance, Resolute, Enterprise, the Shamrocks, the Endeavours* and *Ranger*.

With the more austere economic circumstances post-World War II (1958–1987) came the new brigade of 12-Metre owners and sailors – Sir Frank Packer, Baron Marcel Bich, Alan Bond, Ted Turner, Dennis Conner and Michael Fay.

The 1988 Deed of Gift match between a catamaran and a monohull was a one-off that proved the catalyst for another era of stability with the introduction, in 1992, of the new International America's Cup Class (IACC), which was the boat used from 1992 to 2007 inclusive. The major players in this era were the now Sir Michael Fay, Bill Koch, Raul Gardini, Sir Peter Blake, Patrizio Bertelli, Ernesto Bertarelli and Larry Ellison.

Then, most recently (2010–2017), the Cup has been raced in multihulls with the major players being Ellison and Bertarelli again, Sir Russell Coutts, Grant Dalton and Sir Ben Ainslie.

It has been a sporting journey through continuously changing times, from the so-called 'gilded age' in New York, through two world wars to vastly different economic circumstances, and from amateurism to professionalism – leaving a wake of seemingly endless intrigue and controversy. But the Cup has survived it all to remain one of the most coveted trophies in sport and, backstopping it through thick and thin, has been that wonderful and historic document – the America's Cup 'Deed of Gift'.

Deed of Gift

This Deed of Gift, made the twenty-fourth day of October, one thousand eight hundred and eighty-seven, between George L. Schuyler as sole surviving owner of the Cup won by the yacht AMERICA at Cowes, England, on the twenty-second day of August, one thousand eight hundred and fifty-one, of the first part, and the New York Yacht Club, of the second part, as amended by orders of the Supreme Court of the State of New York dated December 17, 1956, and April 5, 1985.

Witnesseth

That the said party of the first part, for and in consideration of the premises and of the performance of the conditions and agreements hereinafter set forth by the party of the second part, has granted, bargained, sold, assigned, transferred, and set over, and by these presents does grant, bargain, sell, assign, transfer, and set over, unto said party of the second part, its successors and assigns, the Cup won by the schooner yacht AMERICA, at Cowes, England, upon the twenty-second day of August, 1851. To have and to hold the same to the said party of the second part, its successors and assigns, IN TRUST, NEVERTHELESS, for the following uses and purposes:

This Cup is donated upon the conditions that it shall be preserved as a perpetual Challenge Cup for friendly competition between foreign countries.

Any organized Yacht Club of a foreign country, incorporated, patented, or licensed by the legislature, admiralty, or other executive department, having for its annual regatta an ocean water course on the sea, or on an arm of the sea, or one which combines both, shall always be entitled to the right of sailing a match for this Cup, with a yacht or vessel propelled by sails only and constructed in the country to which the Challenging Club belongs, against any one yacht or vessel constructed in the country of the Club holding the Cup.

The competing yachts or vessels, if of one mast, shall be not less than forty-four feet nor more than ninety feet on the load water-line; if of more than one mast they shall be not less than eighty feet nor more than one hundred and fifteen feet on the load water-line.

The Challenging Club shall give ten months' notice, in writing, naming the days for the proposed races; but no race shall be sailed in the days intervening between November 1st and May 1st if the races are to be conducted in the Northern Hemisphere; and no race shall be sailed in the days intervening between May 1st and November 1st if the races are to be conducted in the Southern Hemisphere. Accompanying the ten months' notice of challenge there must be sent the name of the owner and a certificate of the name, rig and following dimensions of the challenging vessel, namely, length on load water-line; beam at load water-line and extreme beam; and draught of water; which dimensions shall not be exceeded; and a custom-house registry of the vessel must also be sent as soon as possible. Center-board or sliding keel vessels shall always be allowed to compete in any race for this Cup, and no restriction nor limitation whatever shall be placed upon the use of such center-board or sliding keel, nor shall the center-board or sliding keel be considered a part of the vessel for any purposes of measurement.

The Club challenging for the Cup and the Club holding the same may, by mutual consent, make any arrangement satisfactory to both as to the dates, courses, number of trials, rules and sailing regulations, and any and all other conditions of the match, in which case also the ten months' notice may be waived.

In case the parties cannot mutually agree upon the terms of a match, then three races shall be sailed, and the winner of two of such races shall be entitled to the Cup. All such races shall be on ocean courses, free from headlands, as follows: The first race, twenty nautical miles to windward and return; the second race an equilateral triangular race of thirty-nine nautical miles, the first side of which shall be a beat to windward; the third race (if necessary) twenty nautical miles to windward and return; and one week day shall intervene between the conclusion of one race and the starting of the next race. These ocean courses shall be practicable in all parts for vessels of twenty-two feet draught of water, and shall be selected by the Club holding the Cup; and these races shall be sailed subject to its rules and sailing regulations so far as the same do not conflict with the provisions of this Deed of Gift, but without any time allowances whatever. The challenged Club shall not be required to name its representative vessel until at a time agreed upon for the start, but the vessel when named must compete in all the races, and each of such races must be completed within seven hours.

Should the Club holding the Cup be for any cause dissolved, the Cup shall be transferred to some Club of the same nationality eligible to challenge under this Deed of Gift, in trust and subject to its provisions. In the event of the failure of such transfer within three months after such dissolution, such Cup shall revert to the preceding Club holding the same, and under the terms of this Deed of Gift. It is distinctly understood that the Cup is to be the property of the Club subject to the provisions of this deed, and not the property of the owner or owners of any vessel winning a match.

No vessel which has been defeated in a match for this Cup can be again selected by any Club as its representative until after a contest for it by some other vessel has intervened, or until after the expiration of two years from the time of such defeat. And when a challenge from a Club fulfilling all the conditions required by this instrument has been received, no other challenge can be considered until the pending event has been decided.

AND, the said party of the second part hereby accepts the said Cup subject to the said trust, terms, and conditions, and hereby covenants and agrees to and with said party of the first part that it will faithfully and will fully see that the foregoing conditions are fully observed and complied with by any contestant for the said Cup during the holding thereof by it; and that it will assign, transfer, and deliver the said Cup to the foreign Yacht Club whose representative yacht shall have won the same in accordance with the foregoing terms and conditions, provided the said foreign Club shall, by instrument in writing lawfully executed, enter with said party of the second part into the like covenants as are herein entered into by it, such instrument to contain a like provision for the successive assignees to enter into the same covenants with their respective assignors, and to be executed in duplicate, one to be retained by each Club, and a copy thereof to be forwarded to the said party of the second part.

IN WITNESS WHEREOF, the said party of the first part has hereunto set his hand and seal, and the said party of the second part has caused its corporate seal to be affixed to these presents and the same to be signed by its Commodore and attested by its Secretary, the day and year first above written.

In the presence of H. D. Hamilton.

George L. Schuyler [L S]   The New York Yacht Club
                                by Elbridge T Gerry,
                                Commodore.
                                John H Bird,
                                Secretary
                                [Seal of the NYYC]

WHO'S WHO OF THE AMERICA'S CUP
AMERICA'S CUP MATCHES

Year	Defender	Owner	From	Challenger	Country	Owner	Races	Winner	Score
1851	Britain	Fleet of 14	UK	America	USA	John Cox Stevens	1	America	1–0
1870	Magic	Franklin Osgood	USA	Cambria	UK	James Lloyd Ashbury	1	Magic	1–0
1871	Columbia	JB van Deusen	USA	Livonia	UK	James Lloyd Ashbury	Best of 7	Columbia	4–1
1876	Madeleine	JS Dikerson	USA	Countess of Dufferin	Canada	Charles Gifford	Best of 3	Madeleine	2–0
1881	Mischief	JR Busk	USA	Atalanta	Canada	Capt A Cuthbert	Best of 3	Mischief	2–0
1885	Puritan	J Malcolm Forbes	USA	Genesta	UK	Sir Richard Sutton	Best of 3	Puritan	2–0
1886	Mayflower	Charles J Paine	USA	Galatea	UK	Lt William Henn	Best of 3	Mayflower	2–0
1887	Volunteer	Charles J Paine	USA	Thistle	UK	James H Bell	Best of 3	Volunteer	2–0
1893	Vigilant	Charles O Iselin	USA	Valkyrie II	UK	Earl of Dunraven	Best of 5	Vigilant	3–0
1895	Defender	William K Vanderbilt	USA	Valkyrie III	UK	Earl of Dunraven	Best of 5	Defender	3–0
1899	Columbia	J Pierpont Morgan	USA	Shamrock	UK	Sir Thomas Lipton	Best of 5	Columbia	3–0
1901	Columbia	J Pierpont Morgan	USA	Shamrock II	UK	Sir Thomas Lipton	Best of 5	Columbia	3–0
1903	Reliance	Cornelius Vanderbilt III	USA	Shamrock III	UK	Sir Thomas Lipton	Best of 5	Reliance	3–0
1920	Resolute	Henry Walters	USA	Shamrock IV	UK	Sir Thomas Lipton	Best of 5	Resolute	3–2
1930	Enterprise	Harold S Vanderbilt	USA	Shamrock V	UK	Sir Thomas Lipton	Best of 5	Enterprise	4–0

Year	Defender			Challenger			Series	Winner	Score
1934	Rainbow	Harold S Vanderbilt	USA	Endeavour	UK	Sir Thomas Sopwith	Best of 7	Rainbow	4–2
1937	Ranger	Harold S Vanderbilt	USA	Endeavour II	UK	Sir Thomas Sopwith	Best of 7	Ranger	4–0
1958	Columbia	Henry Sears	USA	Sceptre	UK	Hugh Goodson	Best of 7	Columbia	4–0
1962	Weatherly	Henry D Mercer	USA	Gretel	Aust	Sir Frank Packer	Best of 7	Weatherly	4–1
1964	Constellation	Eric Ridder	USA	Sovereign	UK	Antony Boyden	Best of 7	Constellation	4–0
1967	Intrepid	William J Strawbridge	USA	Dame Pattie	Aust	Emile Christenson	Best of 7	Intrepid	4–0
1970	Intrepid	William J Strawbridge	USA	Gretel II	Aust	Sir Frank Packer	Best of 7	Intrepid	4–1
1974	Courageous	Robert W McCullough	USA	Southern Cross	Aust	Alan Bond	Best of 7	Courageous	4–0
1977	Courageous	Ted Turner	USA	Australia	Aust	Alan Bond	Best of 7	Courageous	4–0
1980	Freedom	Ed du Moulin	USA	Australia	Aust	Alan Bond	Best of 7	Freedom	4–1
1983	Liberty	Ed du Moulin	USA	Australia II	Aust	Alan Bond	Best of 7	Australia II	4–3
1987	Kookaburra III	Kevin Parry	Aust	Stars & Stripes	USA	Sail America	Best of 7	Stars & Stripes	4–0
1988	Stars & Stripes	Sail America	USA	New Zealand	NZ	Michael Fay	Best of 3	Stars & Stripes	2–0
1992	America³	Bill Koch	USA	Il Moro di Venezia	Italy	Raul Gardini	Best of 7	America³	4–1
1995	Young America	Team Dennis Conner	USA	NZL32 'Black Magic'	NZ	Team New Zealand	Best of 9	NZL32	0–5
2000	NZL60	Team New Zealand	NZ	Luna Rossa	Italy	Patrizio Bertelli	Best of 9	NZL60	5–0
2003	NZL82	Team New Zealand	NZ	Alinghi	Switz	Ernesto Bertarelli	Best of 9	Alinghi	0–5
2007	Alinghi	Ernesto Bertarelli	Switz	NZL92	NZ	Team New Zealand	Best of 9	Alinghi	5–2
2010	Alinghi	Ernesto Bertarelli	Switz	BMW Oracle	USA	Larry Ellison	Best of 3	BMW Oracle	0–2
2013	Oracle USA	Larry Ellison	USA	Aotearoa	NZ	Team New Zealand	Best of 17	Oracle USA	9–8
2017	Oracle USA	Larry Ellison	USA	Aotearoa	NZ	ETNZ	1st to 7	Aotearoa	7–1

America's Cup match winners (in 36 'matches', including the 1851 race Round the Isle of Wight)

USA	30
New Zealand	3
Switzerland	2
Australia	1

Nations to have been Challenger (in 36 matches):

UK	16 (14 times before WWII – ie, 14 of the first 16 challenges)
Australia	7 (all post WWII, four in succession by Alan Bond, including *Australia II*'s win in 1983)
New Zealand	5
USA	3
Canada	2
Italy	2
Switzerland	1

New York Yacht Club Record in Cup (1851 to 1983 inclusive)

America's Cup matches raced (including the 1851 Round IOW race)	26
NYYC won	25
Races contested	94
Races won	81
Races lost	13

Lost only one race in 32, in the first 13 matches (1851–1903 inclusive), winning 31.

Lost only four races in the four J-Class matches (1920–1937 inclusive), winning 15.

Lost only three races out of 35 in eight 12-Metre matches (1958–1980 inclusive), winning 32.

'WINNINGEST' SKIPPERS

Russell Coutts

1995: *NZL32* (for Team New Zealand and the Royal New Zealand Yacht Squadron)

2000: *NZL60* (for Team New Zealand and the Royal New Zealand Yacht Squadron)

2003: *Alinghi* (for Team Alinghi and the Société Nautique de Genève)

2010: *BMW Oracle* (for the Golden Gate Yacht Club and BMW Oracle – he was nominally skipper but James Spithill in fact fulfilled that role on board)

Charlie Barr

1899: *Columbia* (for the New York Yacht Club)

1901: *Columbia* (for the New York Yacht Club)

1903: *Reliance* (for the New York Yacht Club)

Harold S Vanderbilt

1930: *Enterprise* (for the New York Yacht Club)

1934: *Rainbow* (for the New York Yacht Club)

1937: *Ranger* (for the New York Yacht Club)

Dennis Conner

1980: *Freedom* (for the New York Yacht Club)

1987: *Stars & Stripes* (for the San Diego Yacht Club)

1988: *Stars & Stripes* (for the San Diego Yacht Club)

Henry C 'Hank' Haff

1887: *Volunteer* (for the New York Yacht Club)

1895: *Defender* (for the New York Yacht Club)

Emil 'Bus' Mosbacher

1962: *Weatherly* (for the New York Yacht Club)
1967: *Intrepid* (for the New York Yacht Club)

James Spithill

2010: *BMW Oracle* (for the Golden Gate Yacht Club)
2013: *Oracle* Team USA (for the Golden Gate Yacht Club)

'WINNINGEST' DESIGNERS
Olin J Stephens II

1937: *Ranger* (with W Starling Burgess)
1958: *Columbia*
1964: *Constellation*
1967: *Intrepid*
1970: *Intrepid* (modified with Britton Chance Jr)
1974: *Courageous* (with Dave Pedrick)
1977: *Courageous* (with Dave Pedrick)
1980: *Freedom*

Nathanael G Herreshoff

1893: *Vigilant*
1895: *Defender*
1899: *Columbia*
1901: *Columbia*
1903: *Reliance*
1920: *Resolute*

W Starling Burgess

1930: *Enterprise*
1934: *Rainbow*
1937: *Ranger* (with Olin Stephens)

Edward Burgess

1885: *Puritan*
1886: *Mayflower*
1887: *Volunteer*

POSTSCRIPT

CHAPTER 2

- Ben Lexcen, born on 19 March 1936, died from a heart attack on 1 May 1988, aged 52.
- Warren Jones, born on 24 September 1936, died after a massive stroke on 17 May 2002, aged 65.
- Alan Bond, born on 22 April 1938, died on 5 June 2015 as a consequence of complications during heart surgery. He was 77.

CHAPTER 4

- Lord Dunraven died in June 1926, aged 85, and is buried at St Nicholas' Church of Ireland in Adare, County Limerick.

CHAPTER 5

- On 13 May 1931, Lipton was finally made a member of the Royal Yacht Squadron, having previously been rejected as only a 'grocer' or a 'tea merchant'. Osridge, his London home of 50 years, he bequeathed as a retirement home for nurses. Lipton's 84-volume scrapbook of press cuttings and photographs recording his amazing life, his yachting trophies and the remains of his fortune – almost a million pounds – were donated to the sick and poor of Glasgow.

  Endeavour II was sold in 1947 for £7,000 and scrapped.
- Harold Stirling Vanderbilt was born in Oakdale, New York, on 6 July 1884 – the third child and second son of William Kissam Vanderbilt I and Alva Erskine Smith. To family and friends he was known as 'Mike'. As the great-grandson of

the shipping and railroad tycoon Cornelius Vanderbilt, he was born into great wealth and privilege, raised in the many Vanderbilt mansions and frequently travelling to Europe, and sailing the world on yachts owned by his father.

- Sopwith died on 27 January 1989, aged 101. His grave and that of his wife, Phyllis Brodie Sopwith, is in the grounds of the 11th-century All Saints Church at Little Somborne, near Winchester. Married twice, he was survived only by his son, Thomas, from his second marriage.

CHAPTER 6

- A check of records for the previous 13 years revealed that on only one other occasion had the 3pm wind speed off Fremantle exceeded 20 knots on three successive January afternoons. Statistically that should have happened on average only once every 36 years.
- In the short space of 10 months since her first race in Fremantle, *KZ7* posted a remarkable racing record. In the 1987 Louis Vuitton Cup, she was 37–1 to the good when she reached the challengers' final. After losing 1–4 to *Stars & Stripes*, she finished that regatta with a 38–5 score. She then won the 12-Metre World Championship in Sardinia, 7–5, to finish her 1987 campaigns with an overall win/ loss record of 45–10.

  KZ7 was later bought by Bill Koch, who would win the America's Cup, in *America*[3], in 1992. She remains an outstanding all-round performer in the active American 12-Metre fleet.

CHAPTER 8

- In 1994, Judge Ciparick was appointed to the Court of Appeals in Albany, New York, and, in 2009, was drawn to write the opinion in the only other Deed of Gift challenge dispute in the Cup's history.
- In June 1990, HM Queen Elizabeth II knighted Michael Fay for his services to New Zealand in merchant banking and yachting. Sir Michael Fay commented that the honour was the result of a partnership effort and that David Richwhite was really entitled to share it.
- After the 1992 America's Cup, Dennis Conner left his San Diego home and moved east to establish the USA Yacht Club, at the North Cove Marina in New York City, as a base for his future sailing operations, which were to include the 1993–1994 Whitbread Round the World Yacht Race.

The *Los Angeles Times* noted: 'San Diego won't like the implications. The USA Yacht Club is more of a promotional and marketing arm for Conner's business – understand, he is in the America's Cup business – than someplace for sailors to gather socially.'

- In November 1992, Sol Wachtler, the chief Judge of the New York Court of Appeals, who concurred in the decision in favour of the San Diego Yacht Club, was arrested by the FBI and charged with blackmail and extortion against his ex-mistress because she broke up their affair. The federal complaint also accused Wachtler of sending the woman's daughter a greeting card with an 'offensive sexual reference' and a condom, and quoted the judge in a telephone conversation with his former lover, as saying: 'Well, God damn, you better understand me. You're gonna get a letter from me, and you better listen to every word of it and do what it tells you to do or you're gonna be in serious trouble, and you're not gonna see your daughter again, you hear me? I'm a sick and desperate man. I need the money, and you'll be hearing from me.' A few days after his arrest, Chief Judge Wachtler resigned from the Court of Appeals. He, later, pleaded not guilty to the criminal charges by reason of insanity.

CHAPTER 9

- Somewhat ironically, the country that so passionately embraced the Cup, and everything it represented, suffered the international indignity of providing one of the Auld Mug's darkest chapters when the much-coveted trophy became the victim of its own celebrity.

    Following Team New Zealand's stunning 1995 Cup win in San Diego, and the huge welcome-home parades, the trophy entered a new phase in its colourful existence, in a specially built display case in the clubrooms of the Royal New Zealand Yacht Squadron on the waterfront of the City of Sails (Auckland).

    During specified hours, the general public were allowed in to view the glittering prize, which became something of a tourist attraction for local and overseas visitors alike. Until, that is, 14 March 1996, when Maori activist Benjamin Peri Nathan walked into the building, pulled a short-handled sledgehammer from his clothing, and smashed into the armoured-glass display case in order to severely damage the silver ewer that, arguably, represented the small nation's greatest sporting achievement. He would later claim he was protesting against white occupation of Maori land.

He was overpowered and arrested and subsequently charged with wilfully damaging the Cup. Found guilty, he was sentenced to two years and ten months in jail, the sentence to be served in addition to an 18-month term he was already serving for aggravated robbery. He later appealed and the term was reduced to 18 months.

The Cup was so badly damaged that there were doubts that it could be rebuilt, but the original manufacturer, Garrard of London, came to the rescue with a painstaking, intricate restoration that saw the Auld Mug fully restored.

NOTES

CHAPTER 1

1, 2   Sir Michael Fay in interview with Alan Sefton for *Exposed*

3   Bob Oatley quoted by the Australian Associated Press (AAP) on 19 July 2014

4   Matthew Sheahan, *Yachting World*, 2 April 2015

5–8   *Reuters*, 2 April 2015

9, 10   Bernie Wilson, Associated Press, 25 August 2016

11   www.americascup.com, 25 January 2017

12   James Spithill, www.americascup.com, 25 January 2017

13   Larry Ellison, www.americascup.com, 25 January 2017

14   www.americascup.com, 25 January 2017

15   Paul Lewis, *NZ Herald*, 26 March 2017

16   Bruno Troublé, *Seven Sharp*, TVNZ current affairs programme, 1 July 2017

17   Bruno Troublé, in interview with Larry Keating for *Exposed*

18, 19 Dennis Conner, *Newstalk ZB* radio network, 23 June 2017

20   Angus Phillips, the *Weekly Standard* magazine, 17 July 2017

CHAPTER 2

1, 2   Warren Jones in interview with Larry Keating for *Les Grands Duels du Sport*

3   Bill Trenkle in interview with Larry Keating for *Les Grands Duels du Sport*

4   Warren Jones in interview with Larry Keating for *Les Grands Duels du Sport*

5, 6   Peter van Oossanen in interview with Alan Sefton for *Exposed*

7   Warren Jones in interview with Larry Keating for *Les Grands Duels du Sport*

8   Gary Jobson in interview with Larry Keating for *Exposed*

9   John Longley in interview with Larry Keating for *Les Grands Duels du Sport*

10, 11 Vic Romagna in chapter 9 of *Upset: Australia Wins the America's Cup*, by Michael Levitt & Barbara Lloyd (Workman Pub Co, 1983)

12 James Michael in *Keelhauled: The History of Unsportsmanlike Conduct and the America's Cup*, by Doug Riggs (Simon & Schuster, 1986)

13 Warren Jones in interview with Larry Keating for *Les Grands Duels du Sport*

14 Dennis Conner in interview with Larry Keating for *Les Grands Duels du Sport*

15 Joop Slooff in interview with Barbara Lloyd

16 *Professional BoatBuilder Magazine* (October/November 2009)

17, 18 Rick Feneley in *Sydney Morning Herald*, 14 October 2009

19 John Longley in *Scuttlebutt*, 19 October 2009

20–23 Peter van Oossanen in interview with Alan Sefton for *Exposed*

24 Account of 1982 patent dispute involving Alan Bond, Joop Sloop, Ben Lexcen and Peter van Oossanen. Further reading: *Australia II and the America's Cup: The Untold, Inside Story of The Keel* by Joop Slooff, 2016

25 John Longley in *Scuttlebutt*, 19 October 2009

26 Rick Feneley in interview with Larry Keating for *Exposed*

27 Ben Lexcen, *Upset: Australia Wins the America's Cup*, by Michael Levitt and Barbara Lloyd (Workman Pub Co, 1983)

28, 29 Dennis Conner in interview with Larry Keating for *Les Grands Duels du Sport*

CHAPTER 3

1 *The New York Times*, 1 August 1890

2 All extracts quoting the late James Michael, in this and other chapters of *Exposed*, are reproduced with the permission of Sir Michael Fay, the holder of copyright to the Michael manuscript entitled 'Inside the America's Cup – the Kiwi Challenge, 1987–1990'

3 *The History of American Yachting* by Captain Roland F Coffin (October 1886)

CHAPTER 4

1,2 *America's Cup Book 1851–1983* by John Rousmaniere (WW Norton & Co Inc, 1983)

CHAPTER 5

1 *Leaves from the Lipton Logs* by Sir Thomas J Lipton (London, 1931)

CHAPTER 7

1 *San Diego Union*, 1988 (exact date unknown)

2 *International Herald Tribune*, 1988 (exact date unknown)

3   Walter Cronkite, *The New York Times*, 31 July 1988

4   Bill Schanen, *Sailing* magazine, December 1988

5–7   James Michael manuscript 'Inside the America's Cup – the Kiwi Challenge, 1987–1990'

8   Andrew Johns in interview with Alan Sefton for *Exposed*

9   Sir Michael Fay in interview with Alan Sefton for *Exposed*

10–12 James Michael manuscript 'Inside the America's Cup – the Kiwi Challenge, 1987–1990'

CHAPTER 8

1   James Michael manuscript 'Inside the America's Cup – the Kiwi Challenge, 1987–1990'

2   *San Diego Union*, 20 November 1987

3   *San Diego Union*, 2 December 1987

4   *San Diego Union*, 4 December 1987

5   Sir Michael Fay in interview with Alan Sefton for *Exposed*

6   *The Times*, 27 and 28 May 1988

7–14 James Michael manuscript 'Inside the America's Cup – the Kiwi Challenge, 1987–1990'

15   'America's Cup organising committee had nothing to do', *Canberra Times* (ACT, page 11, 2 April 1989) www.myheritage.com/research/record-10450-8915520/canberra-times-act

16–19 James Michael manuscript 'Inside the America's Cup – the Kiwi Challenge, 1987–1990'

20   John Rousmaniere, *Sailing World*, July 1990

21–23 James Michael manuscript 'Inside the America's Cup – the Kiwi Challenge, 1987–1990'

24, 25 George Tompkins in interview with Alan Sefton for *Exposed*

26   Andrew Johns in interview with Alan Sefton for *Exposed*

CHAPTER 9

1   Tim Jeffery, *Daily Telegraph*, 20 February 2003

2   The current America's Cup Deed of Gift

3, 4 *Arbitration in the America's Cup: The XXXI America's Cup Arbitration Panel & Its Decisions*, J Faire & H Peter, Kluwer Law International, 2003

5   *New Zealand Herald* Editorial, 1 February 2003 www.nzherald.co.nz/nz/news/article.cfm?c_id=1&objectid=3097886

6   Tim Jeffery, *Daily Telegraph*, 27 July 2004

7, 8   Patrick de Barros interview for *Exposed*
9, 10 Tim Jeffery, *Daily Telegraph*, 27 July 2004
11, 12 Tim Jeffery, *Daily Telegraph*, 28 July 2004
13   *New Zealand Herald*, 28 July 2004
14–16 *New Zealand Herald*, 8 September 2004
17   *Scuttlebutt*, 10 September 2004
18, 19 Alinghi Media Release, 24 March 2005

CHAPTER 10

1   America's Cup Media release, 6 July 2007
2   'Exhibit 2' letter, signed by seven would-be challengers, to the Club Náutico Español de Vela (CNEV) on 17 July 2007
3   Judge J Leland DeGrasse (of the Appellate Division of the New York Supreme Court) in his 29 July 2008 ruling on the eligibility of BMW Oracle's trimaran challenger
4   Court of Appeals Judge Carmen B Ciparick in interview for *Exposed*
5   Brad Butterworth to *Agence France-Presse*, 15 July 2009
6   Larry Ellison in post-match media conference
7   Harold Bennett in interview with Alan Sefton for *Exposed*
8   Patrick de Barros in interview with Alan Sefton for *Exposed*
9   George Schuyler letter to NYYC, July 1890

CHAPTER 11

1   Regatta Director Iain Murray in notice to competitors
2, 3   ETNZ response to Regatta Director's notice
4   Max Sirena in interview with the Italian daily newspaper *La Repubblica*
5   Regatta Director Iain Murray in *Scuttlebutt Europe*
6   Paul Cayard in the *San Francisco Chronicle*, 22 June, 2013
7   Iain Murray, *Sail World*, 4 July 2013
8, 9   International Jury's 3 September 2013 findings on alleged cheating
10   Mike Drummond in interview for *Exposed*

CHAPTER 12

1–4   Grant Dalton on *Newstalk ZB Breakfast* show, 8 June 2017
5   Sir Ben Ainslie, to Suzanne McFadden on the *New Zealand Newsroom* news and current affairs site, 9 June 2017

6, 7   Matteo de Nora, in interview with Jane Phare for the *New Zealand Herald*, 8 July 2017

8   Groupama Team France in the online newsletter *Scuttlebutt*, 11 July 2017

9–11   Grant Dalton in interview with Alan Sefton

12   Matteo de Nora, in interview with Jane Phare for the *New Zealand Herald*, 8 July 2017

13–16   Suzanne McFadden in a feature on Peter Burling for Newsroom, 16 June 2017

17, 18 Tom Slingsby, in interview for the 2 April 2015 edition of *Yachting World*

19, 20 *New Zealand Herald*, 11 June 2017

21   Craig Leweck, *Scuttlebutt*, 14 June 2017

22   James Spithill, post-match press conference, 26 June 2017

CHAPTER 13

1   Grant Dalton on *Newstalk ZB Breakfast* show, 26 June 2017

2   Sir Ben Ainslie in the *Daily Telegraph*, 27 June 2017

3   Sir Russell Coutts to Sabine Colpart, of *Agence France-Presse*, 14 June 2017

4   Halsey Herreshoff in interview with Larry Keating for *Exposed,* May 2017

5   Russell Coutts, *The Times* (London), 3 June 2017

6   Mike Winfield, *New York Times*, 23 June 2017

7   Report by the Office of Bermuda's Minister of Economic Development, 7 July 2017

ACKNOWLEDGEMENTS

For their contributions and permissions to use materials:

Paulo Barata
Patrick de Barros
Harold Bennett
Judge Carmen B. Ciparick
Dennis Conner
Shayne Currie (*NZ Herald*)
Mike Drummond
Sir Michael Fay
Rick Feneley
Bob Fisher
Richard Gladwell
Hamish Hooper
Halsey Herreshoff
Gary Jobson
Andrew Johns
Judge Bentley Kassal
Peter Lester
Craig Leweck (*Scuttlebutt*)
Barbara Lloyd
John "Chink" Longley
David McCreary (*Scuttlebutt Europe*)
Dan Nerney
New York Yacht Club
Barry Pickthall
John Rousmaniere
William Schanen III

George Tompkins
Bill Trenkle
Bruno Troublé
Peter van Oossanen

And, for their unstinting patience and support, Janet Murphy and her team at Bloomsbury Publishing in England (notably Clara Jump and Lucy Doncaster) without whose 'above and beyond' attitude the bringing of this book to publication would not have been possible.

INDEX